Faith
that hurts
Faith
that heals

Faith *that* hurts
Faith *that* heals

STEPHEN ARTERBURN
& JACK FELTON

Foreword by Michael Doucette, M.D.

OLIVER
NELSON

Thomas Nelson Publishers
Nashville

Published in Nashville, Tennessee, by Oliver-Nelson Books, a division of Thomas Nelson, Inc., Publishers, and distributed in Canada by Lawson Falle, Ltd., Cambridge, Ontario. Originally titled *Toxic Faith*.

The Bible version used in this publication is THE NEW KING JAMES VERSION. Copyright © 1979, 1980, 1982, Thomas Nelson, Inc., Publishers.

Some names and circumstances have been fictionalized for protection of privacy.

Library of Congress Cataloging-in-Publication Data

Arterburn, Stephen, 1953–
   [Toxic Faith]
   Faith that hurts, faith that heals / Stephen Arterburn & Jack Felton.
     p.   cm.
   Originally published under title: Toxic faith.
   ISBN 0-8407-9657-9 (pbk.)
   1. Religious addiction. 2. Compulsive behavior—Religious aspects. I. Felton, Jack, 1953– . II. Title.
BL53.A75   1993
248.2—dc20   92–27754
                                               CIP

Printed in the United States of America.
1 2 3 4 5 6 — 97 96 95 94 93 92

To Madeline Victoria Arterburn,
a wonderful gift from God.
May we raise you to
come to know God as He is.

Contents

Foreword

I have always been interested in the spiritual pursuits of the people I help in my psychiatric practice. How does true faith become a part of an individual's return to mental health and wholeness? Why does faith often seem to be distorted by many in need of psychiatric care? These have not been easy questions to answer, especially working as a Christian in a field where many consider religion a form of avoiding reality.

In my practice I have seen people burdened beyond their ability to cope, with guilt placed on them by their church or an unbalanced minister. I have seen them become compulsive in their church work and attendance. They have attempted to work their way toward perfection and favor with God—sometimes leading themselves into psychosis (a delusional world which often requires psychiatric care in order to return to reality) because of such an ill-defined faith.

The disintegration of real faith into a harmful belief system and even religious addiction is born out of several motivations. For some it is the need to avoid the tough reality of our high stress society. For others, it is a retreat into this delusive world of false beliefs to prevent dealing with the reality of a painful childhood or the loss of a spouse, child, or loved one. Unwilling to process the pain, they have hidden behind the walls of denial built with stones of work, activity, trying harder, shame, and perfectionism. These hurting people are greatly in need of care, yet often believe they are doing God's work while the rest of the world is out of step. Breaking through their denial becomes extremely difficult as they invest more of their identity into their poisonous ideas.

These past few years I have seen a growing number of people face their compulsive behavior, their harmful belief, and seek a real faith in a living God. Perhaps many are waking up because they have seen their religious leaders fall. No longer trusting in them, they turn to find a real faith in a real God. Others look at their obsession-compulsive, religious workaholistic existence and find despair rather than God's blessings. They wake up to declare in desperation, "There must be a better way."

There is another reason people are turning away from their harmful faith. Although there seems to be an increasing number who have rejected God and matters of faith in the past, more and more are now ready to embrace faith in God. This could be due to some of the incredible changes globally. What the military or political systems could not do, faith has achieved. As swelling numbers of faithful believers prayed for peace and reconciliation, walls came down and governments changed. Agnostics and atheists saw real faith in action. The world changed. I think this has inspired many to give up their old ideas about a dead God and come face to face with the Creator.

Egos, desire for power, searching for a quick fix for pain and the need to manipulate have produced a generation of faithful followers with harmful faith. We all need to examine our beliefs and rid them of the dangerous lies that cause us to develop a harmful faith. The following pages will provide you with insight on how to develop a helpful faith, a real faith in a real God. If you have wondered what is good about religion and what is damaging, you will find those answers here. If you want to help someone who has been victimized by a leader or religion, you will find a way to help here. If you are living with someone whose faith has been derailed, someone living in an unreal world of false hope, there is hope for you and that person here. If you are a compulsive religious addict, you will find a way out by putting the principles learned here into practice.

I am privileged to have watched sick and hurting people throw away their harmful distortions of God and find a loving God who cares for each person. The authors of these pages have communicated well why people turn from God and how they come full circle to a new awareness of the Creator. The concepts and principles in this book are part of our work at New Life Treatment Centers. They have been tried and proven effective in bringing people back to a balanced faith. If your faith has been battered by a tragedy, an unscrupulous minister, or a society that would prefer to deny God, I hope you find relief within these pages. I hope you find a way back to real faith.

MICHAEL DOUCETTE, M.D.
Anaheim, California

Acknowledgments

A special thank you to a few people who were instrumental in the creation of this book: to Victor Oliver, who had the idea and talked me into writing it; to Lila Empson, a most able editor who can take ordinary words and make them sing; to Jack Felton, who spent many hours developing material and hammering out his thoughts on paper; to Katie Temple, my assistant who sacrificed many weekends and opportunities to insure we made the deadline—I am forever grateful for her dedication, talent, and writing abilities; and to Margaret Snyder and Jim Burns, who reviewed the manuscript and kept us all on track with pure faith.

Introduction

My grandmother died last year. If there was ever a person of strong faith and conviction, it was Nany. She raised her three children, including my mother, alone after the suicide of my grandfather. She never gave up, she never stopped believing, she never lost faith. For her, death was just a step over into a better place. She didn't fear it. Her faith kept her at peace, motivated her to care, and provided hope. She was always active doing her part while she trusted God to do His. God's love seeped through every pore of that marvelous woman who cheered up just about everyone she was with. I think much of my own faith came from watching her and hearing her talk about a loving God who loves His children.

At her funeral, the minister told of one of the frustrations my grandmother had to endure. She was audited by the Internal Revenue Service. The IRS went to a lot of trouble to make sure that someone who made every bit of eight thousand dollars a year paid her fair share of income taxes. While others were keeping millions of dollars from the federal government, special agents were at work on the case of Pearl Russell. They were working to insure the country would not be shorted a few hundred dollars by a sweet old lady in Athens, Texas.

The issue in the case between the United States of America and Pearl Russell was her large deduction for charitable contributions. They could not believe that a person making so little could give 35, and some years 40, percent to the church and still have enough money left over to pay her bills. The IRS was finally satisfied when she dug out of the attic all the cancelled checks to TV ministers, radio preachers, and her local church. They did not understand it, but they were convinced that she had given every penny she deducted.

She not only gave away almost half her income, she paid off her car loans early, paid off her mortgage, and still had enough money left over to bake her special pies for people who were hurting. My grandmother was an amazing woman of faith, and it seemed that no matter how much she gave away, she still was provided with enough to live comfortably. What little she could do for God she did. She did it because of a real faith in God, not a faith motivated by the idea that if she gave she would get rich. She knew she would never have a lot of money. Neither did she give because she was buying her way to heaven. She had taken care of her place in eternity years ago. She gave because she wanted to give back to God a portion of all He had given her. Her motives were pure, and she set a great example for all who were privileged to be around her. There was nothing harmful about her faith. She never gave to a particular minister, it was to the ministry, such as to a children's home or to a project to feed the homeless. When she gave a dollar she knew how that minister was going to spend it. At least, she thought she did.

Some of the people she gave her money to were not so admirable. Their hurtful faith robbed my grandmother of the great blessing of knowing her money had been used to further the kingdom of God. They took her money and spent it on themselves and their big plans that had nothing to do with my grandmother's desire to tell the world about God's love or feed and clothe orphans. Some of those ministers that she so faithfully supported wound up in jail, divorced their wives, were arrested for indecent exposure, or who knows what else. They proclaimed a faith on television or over the radio, but they lived something else. They had no difficulty in asking my grandmother and others like her to sacrifice part of what she used to buy food just so they could help pay the jet fuel bill to fly to Palm Springs for the weekend. What they did was dishonest. It was unfair. It was very human. They proclaimed a faith on television or over the radio, but they lived something else.

These unfaithful human beings who spent Nany's money had more faith in themselves than they did God. They relied more on their manipulations than on God's providence. They were more concerned about their own comforts than the people that gave them money or the people the money was intended to help. They built big empires for themselves while my grandmother turned off her heater at night to save money in order to give more. Their faith was toxic. It poisoned many who trusted them, and it distorted the view of God held by many who watched as these media ministers fell from grace. As a result, there are those who believe all ministers are charlatans and out to fleece the flock. They have derived a harmful, unhealthy view of faith from the hurtful examples they saw in the media.

Media ministers are not the only ones who poison faith. Faith is tainted from many other sources. Perhaps it is the loss of a child that causes a mother to no longer trust in a God she thought would protect her child from the evils of the world. It could be the early loss of a parent that left someone feeling abandoned and searching for care and nurturing they believe was robbed from them by an uncaring God. A business failure, a broken relationship, and the death of a wonderful friend are all common events that change the way some view God. The roots of bitterness and unresolved anger are allowed to poison their faith. Some turn away from God and never come back.

Rather than turn from God or live with a distorted view of God, others manifest their harmful faith in more obvious ways. Feeling unloved by God, maybe due to an early incident of child abuse, they want to earn God's love. They believe that if they work hard enough and put in enough effort for everyone to notice their dedication, they might win favor with God. Of course it is not a conscious effort to win God's favor. They believe they are doing what any godly person would do. When the church doors are open, they are there, not because they want to, but because they are driven and feel extreme guilt if they don't sacrifice family, friends, and themselves in service of the church. Their faith is harmful, poisoned by an unfortunate trauma or a desire to work their way to heaven. What should be a source of strength and hope becomes an addiction, trapping the misled believer in painful obsessions and compulsions.

There are still others whose harmful faith provides a way to avoid the realities of life. They expect God to work miracles at their beck and call, as if He were a genie. They seek a personal magician, not the Creator of the universe. Rather than face up to a child that is ill and in need of extensive and expensive medical care, they pray for healing and allow the child to die. Others pray for hours for a weakening marriage rather than seek counseling to repair broken communication and mend wounds. They expect God to do for them what perhaps God is waiting for them to do for themselves. They are not really looking for God, they are searching for relief and a means to avoid the pain they need to face. They are addicted to a harmful religion that lets them live in a fantasy world of quick fixes and easy solutions. Rather than growing deep in their faith, they are growing weak in their ability to cope. Looking for the religious high, these wounded faithful are not far from functioning like heroine addicts searching frantically for the next fix.

Those who have a harmful faith have stepped across the line from a balanced perspective of God to an unbalanced faith in a weak, powerless or uncaring God. They seek a God to fix every mess, prevent every hurt, and mend every conflict. The following questions beg to be answered:

- Where is the balance between an ungodly independence that leaves the person overwhelmed from the need to be self-sufficient and an ungodly passivity that leaves them doing nothing unless "God has spoken" with personal direction?
- Where is the line between conviction to help people out of a love of God and addiction to compulsive work and striving to please God?
- What is the difference in giving money to honor God and in giving to buy God's favor?
- When does growing in faith become a futile attempt to be perfect?
- When does dependence on God become a cop-out, a way to avoid dealing with tough life situations?
- At what point does faith turn into something ugly, void of a loving God, harmful to the believer, and harmful to those who are near?
- How can a person determine when it is right to follow a leader and when it is dangerous?
- Having developed a harmful faith, how does one recover and grow in the grace and knowledge of God?

GOOD AND BAD SPIRITUALITY

"If I were asked for a yardstick to discern good from bad spirituality, I would suggest three criteria to be detached from: material gain, self-importance and the urge to dominate others. Unfortunately, much of what is labeled spirituality in America today moves in the opposite direction. It means using the names of God and Christ to promote one's own importance, material gain and right to oppress others," says Rosemary Radford Ruether, professor of theology at Garrett-Evangelical Theological Seminary in Evanston, Illinois.

—Rosemary Radford Ruether, "Don't Fall for Every Spirit
Lurking Under the Name of Spirituality," National Catholic
Reporter, October 14, 1988, p. 15.

These are the issues we will examine. Most likely, you have dealt with at least one of these issues in your search for truth about life and the God who created it. You may have not done too well in your search and now claim that there is no God. Your faith may have become so poisonous you felt you had to get away from it altogether just to survive. You may be left wondering if God exists, what would real faith in a real God be like? It is my desire that you will find answers here. I want you to find hope for a return to faith that can add meaning to your life. I especially hope that you will find the reality of true faith and be able to separate that from those who model only a caricature of faith. I want to help you throw out that harmful faith and bring you back to the real thing.

My grandmother had the real thing. I'm grateful for her example of trust in God through the tough times and the good times. Not just when it was convenient, but when she did anything, she exemplified God's love. When she died, Pearl Russell was able to walk through the pearly gates because of a faith that would not be distorted by events, circumstances, pain, or false teaching. She made it to a place where harmful faith does not exist. I pray that you will be able to sift through your pain, your circumstances, and our cruel world and find the God who meant so much to my grandmother, and now to me.

Colossians 2:8   *Beware lest anyone cheat you through philosophy and empty deceit, according to the tradition of men, according to the basic principles of the world, and not according to Christ.*

18   *Let no one cheat you of your reward . . .*

20   *. . . why, as though living in the world, do you subject yourselves to regulations—*

21   *"Do not touch, do not taste, do not handle,"*

22   *which all concern things which perish with the using—according to the commandments and doctrines of men?*

23   *These things indeed have an appearance of wisdom in self-imposed religion, false humility, and neglect of the body, but are of no value against the indulgence of the flesh.*

Colossians 3:2   *Set your mind on things above, not on things on the earth.*

CHAPTER 1

The Extremes
of Faith that Hurts

Rebecca Grant had lived a hard life in the hot desert town of Barstow, California. Her father had died when she was very young, and her mother struggled to keep her and her sister in clothes. They rented a small house, and her mom worked two jobs. During the day, her mother sold tickets at the Greyhound Bus depot, and at night she sold tickets at the theater. On her days off she cleaned the house and did chores. It wasn't a wonderful existence, but her persevering spirit kept her going.

Rebecca loved her mother and knew how hard she worked to provide the family with the basics of food and clothing. Some of her friends made fun of the fact that she didn't have a dad and that her mother had to work so much. Their comments bothered Rebecca, but they made her respect her mother more.

At fourteen, Rebecca began to work. All the money she earned went into a bowl along with her mother's money. They took out only what they needed for the essentials. Rebecca's mother put the rest in a passbook account at the savings and loan for the days when Rebecca and her sister would need assistance with college fees.

Rebecca's mother was a woman of faith, a Christian who believed that God had a plan for her life. If she was faithful, she believed she would see that plan, and God would bless her faithfulness. She didn't waver from her beliefs. In the toughest of times she didn't doubt God's love for her. She trusted Him to take care of her and her two daughters. She would do all she could do to provide for her family, and she would leave the rest up to God. She never worked on Sunday and always took the girls to church where they prayed and sang together.

Rebecca was close to her mother, but she wasn't close to her mother's God. She enjoyed going to church because of the people there. It was something out of the ordinary routine of the week. She liked it, but she didn't become a Christian. She doubted that there was a God, and if He did exist, she felt distant from Him. He had never spoken to her or shown Himself to her, and He certainly hadn't made life easy for her. She wanted to believe, but she rejected what she heard in the church.

What Rebecca heard was a gospel that many preachers preach. It is a distortion of truth and sometimes manipulative. She heard that if a person becomes a Christian, life will become easy. God will take care of everything. Miracles will occur, and there will be no more problems. She was told that true believers in Christ are protected from the evil of the world. Faith in Christ was presented as an insurance policy against any pain in the present. Rebecca's question was one that many others have hung themselves and their faith on. She wondered, *If God is so loving, why does He allow my life to be so hard, and why does He force my mother to struggle so much? If there really was a God, He would help us.*

The expectation of a problem-free life because of a faith in God caused harmful faith to take over Rebecca's life. Her distorted view of what God should and should not do, acquired through her experiences at church, caused her to abandon the search for truth and latch onto anything that would bring relief from her misery and pain. She turned to alcohol first. Then it was drugs. Finally, she became so promiscuous that she contracted genital herpes that could not be cured. Her resulting maladies were only more proof to her that a God, a real God, either did not exist or was not interested. Her behavior became increasingly self-destructive because her faith was harmful.

The Promise of Problem-Free Living

Rebecca's faith experience is a common one. There are more agnostics and atheists due to an expectation of an easy life from God than from any other false belief. Not finding a faithful life free of pain and discomfort, people turn from what they thought was to be easy living. The preachers who preach it cause many to fall away because they haven't fully explained the whole experience of a life of faith. If they were on target with their theology, they would convey that with faith in God your perspective changes so much, and you trust Him so much, that the pains of existence have less impact. Each time a negative event occurs, God can use it to bring greater faith and deeper peace from trusting that He is in control. But what people hear is entirely different. They hear that acceptance of Christ or belief in God will cause all problems to vanish; they learn that the present problems will go away once you have turned your life over to God.

It just isn't so. Like many others, when I turned my life over to God, problems that I never knew existed seemed to cling to me like leeches. If my motivation had been for the easy life, I had made a serious error. If I didn't believe God had a standard for my life, I could have given in to every temptation without guilt or shame. But believing in God, I had a strong desire to fight each opportunity to sin and stray from the will of God. At times it seemed that some new temptations had been developed just to taunt me. It didn't take me long to discover that the life of faith is not sugarcoated or pain free.

Rebecca was no different from all the others who have heard of an easy life of faith and seen one full of the same tragedies and mistakes experienced by believers and nonbelievers. The misconception leads to a harmful faith or the extermination of faith entirely. The problem can be summed up as false expectations of God.

Naive Faith

My mother grew up with one version of harmful faith. She believed that dedicating her sons to God would spare them the heartache that other children had to endure. She felt that somehow her prayers and faith vaccinated us from evil and that temptations would not be likely to come our way, but if they did, we would not succumb. When her father committed suicide, it devastated her. It hit her much harder than it would most people because she thought she and her family of believers were protected. However, she didn't give up her belief in a God who would prevent the natural course of nature or evil from harming her family.

There are more agnostics and atheists due to an expectation of an easy life from God than from any other false belief.

PICK-AND-CHOOSE CHRISTIANITY

A three-year study of Minnesota Christians, "Faith and Ferment" gives some interesting results on Americans and their church identity or lack thereof: "Instead, says church historian Martin E. Marty in his analysis of the data, they have developed a '"pick-and-choose" Christianity' in which individuals take what they want from church tradition and pass over what does not fit their own spiritual goals. Two-thirds of the 1,017 respondents saw no harm in rejecting some of their church's doctrines; as one woman put it, 'I feel that in religious training, as in any other thing, you are taught the basics. From those basics, you sort out what you want or pick it apart as you see fit.'" Does this mean that there is no absolute truth?

—Kenneth L. Woodward, "Pick-and-Choose Christianity,"
Newsweek, September 19, 1983, p. 82.

When my brother contracted AIDS and eventually died,[1] my mother was confronted in a most painful way with the fact that her faith, the faith of her family, was not a supernatural vaccination to safeguard us from terrible events. She struggled with his illness, and she struggled with her faith. Her depression was deep, and at times I didn't know if she would return to being the wonderful lady she had been all her life.

Fortunately, she did return to that person. She made it out of her depression and back to reality because she dealt with her confusing ideas about faith and God. She yelled at God. She told Him it wasn't fair. She admitted she had come to her faith as a way of making life easier. As she shared her anger and frustration with a God who did not do things in accordance with her fondest wishes and expectations, she recovered from the death of my brother. She also recovered her faith in the process. It is no longer hurtful; it is whole. It has brought her into a new understanding of who God is and how He works. She is more deeply committed and better equipped to help others looking for someone who understands.

As she shared her anger and frustration with a God who did not do things in accordance with her fondest wishes and expectations, she recovered from the death of my brother.

Harmful Faith Headlines

Many variations of harmful faith are prevalent in our fast-paced, push-button society. People traveling on the narcissistic roller coaster, looking for the next thrill or quick fix, are interested in a God who can make things easier or less painful. A God who would allow pain is not a God members of this generation are willing to cling to. Unable to get the quick fix, they don't walk in faith long enough to discover that God actually lightens the burden and eases the pain. The decrease in discomfort doesn't come overnight; it comes as a relationship with God grows stronger. As a person studies the attributes of God and understands how He really works, what once would have devastated the individual now becomes an opportunity for growth in a richer faith. Character grows out of the inconveniences.

Unfortunately, there are manifestations of harmful faith more bizarre than the concept of a God who makes life easy. Many vulnerable and well-meaning people become victims of lies and hurtful beliefs. Stories about these people, which reflect the state of belief in our country, appear in newspapers and magazines almost every day. They are true-life examples of harmful faith that has become a deadly religious addiction. Look at some instances where harmful faith has destroyed lives, fortunes, and families.

HEADLINE: Faith-healing parents guilty in son's death.

A jury in Boston found a Christian Science couple guilty of involuntary manslaughter. The couple did not seek medical help for their son in 1986 when he developed a bowel obstruction. The parents sought help from a church practitioner but not a doctor. After five days, the little boy was dead. Christian Science teaches that all illness can be cured by prayer.

In a similar case in 1989, a couple in California were acquitted of murder but charged with child endangerment when their fifteen-month-old daughter died of meningitis. In Florida that same year, a couple were found guilty of third-degree murder for letting their

Unable to get the quick fix, they don't walk in faith long enough to discover that God actually lightens the burden and eases the pain.

seven-year-old diabetic daughter die without receiving medical attention.

In this recent case, church officials claimed that a parent's right to only pray for a child's health was on trial. The prosecutors claimed that what was being established was the required conduct of parents, whatever their beliefs. During the trial, the father testified that now if his other two children became seriously ill, he would probably seek medical care.[2]

HEADLINE: **Despondent mother kills her three children and herself—Reseda woman who killed her three children and herself had cloaked her remarks in religious references. Apparently no one took her seriously.**

Roxanne Jones shot her three children to death and then killed herself. She had talked about it for two months prior to the tragedy. No one took her statements about death seriously because they were misinterpreted as part of her new religious beliefs.

Two weeks before the deaths, her seven-year-old son Jerimiah told his first-grade teacher that his mother was taking him to "a good place, where God is and there are no worries." The teacher thought the boy was talking about a religious retreat.

A suicide note left by Jones asked for God's forgiveness and outlined the family and financial problems that had burdened her. Detectives said religious sayings had been written in black ink on walls throughout the house. Her husband said his wife had been consumed by a desire to be "someplace better" and turned to religion for solace and guidance. He stated, "She was into nature and wanted to go to God, where the trees and grass were nice."

Mr. Jones said his wife was religious but "didn't quite interpret the Bible the way it should have been. She comprehends things her way and no way else. Whatever she thinks is right is right." She had sought counseling from her pastor one week earlier, but he was not alarmed at what he heard. Two weeks earlier Jerimiah had told his teacher that the family was going to the "house of David."

A fifteen-year friend of the family described the latest changes in Roxanne as "getting pretty heavy into God." He added, "She would start reading Scriptures to everyone when we were around." Another family friend said that she heard her say often that if she died and went to heaven, she would take her children with her. She wanted to go to heaven very badly, and she wanted the kids to be with her.[3]

HEADLINE: **"Wealth, religion were used to lure investors," clients say.**

A man in Oregon has agreed to plead guilty to mail and bank fraud charges in a scheme that took $12 million from over two hundred people. The investors were promised annual returns on their money between 12 and 30 percent. The money was to be used for real estate investments. The man lured investors into the scheme with seminars and cassette tapes in which he described his rags-to-riches rise and his being born again to traditional Christian beliefs. Because he said he was a Christian, the people trusted him and put their faith in him to make them wealthy. They took out second mortgages on their homes to invest with him. What he sold them was either worthless or nonexistent real estate. Misplaced faith became the financial ruin of these people, who believed that they could get rich quick because a man claiming to be a Christian promised financial gain.[4]

HEADLINE: **The curse of the black lords—What demons drove so many members of a Dallas New Age cult to kill themselves and leave their money to their guru?**

Dallas was shocked at the double murder or murder-suicide or double suicide of a Southern Methodist University business professor and his wife, who was the daughter of a North Dallas physician. Their deaths were the end of a spiritual journey they had hoped would bring them enlightenment. In their New Age search they discovered, according to their teachers, that they had originally been incarnated as Adam and Eve, one of the 800,000 lifetimes they had lived. Their names were changed to Jupiter and Venus, the Roman god and goddess.

Their journey toward enlightenment ended up traumatizing them. They spent their last days trying to protect themselves from dangers and what they believed to be karmic poisons. In a letter she never sent to her son, the dead woman wrote, "I am extremely depressed right now—and would love to have the nerve to kill myself." Records revealed that for several weeks their lives had been directed in every detail by a self-appointed Dallas spiritual guru who had led them through suicide practice sessions by pointing guns at each other's heads. Before the deaths of the young pair, they had given more than $110,000 to their spiritual guide.

They were not the first to have tragedy befall them after linking up with this guru. Among the followers in Dallas, eight lives have come to a premature end. Five of the deaths were suicides. Of these five suicides, two were husbands of the spiritual guru. Three others, including a fourteen-year-old, died in sudden accidents. Several had been through tremendous pain and mental anguish. In every instance of death and torment, the spiritual guru was made the beneficiary of their wealth, whether they lived or died.

The writer of the article on this subject noted,

> The framework of this dogma fit easily within—indeed, borrowed heavily from—writings that inspired the widely popular New Age movement during the eighties. *The leader of this small cultic band was tapping the angst of a restless generation dissatisfied with traditional religion and its inability to provide clear answers to impossible questions* [emphasis added]. Dallas proved fertile territory for her teachings. Divorce, materialism, and pursuit of personal pleasure were rampant. Her doctrines offered forgiveness of sin, reinforcement of pleasure. She told followers what they wanted to hear: They would become comfortable with wealth; they would find bliss in every sexual encounter.

A fifty-two-year-old woman who looked like someone's grandma was able to gain control of every detail of the lives of hundreds of followers, followers who attributed to her supernatural powers equal to a god's. They were affluent and well educated, but they all fell under her evil plans to destroy their lives and take their money. Her

---

THREE ALTAR BOYS MOLESTED

"In 1989, the archdiocese agreed to an out-of-court settlement of $358,000 to parents of three altar boys molested by a priest at a suburban Atlanta parish. The Rev. Anton Mowat pleaded guilty to four counts of child molestation and was sentenced to 15 years in prison."

—*Mark Mayfield, "Atlanta Bishop Resigns," USA Today, July 11, 1990.*

unwholesome faith was passed on to them, and it poisoned their lives, killing some.[5]

HEADLINE: Psychiatric hospital weans youth away from satanism.

In Chicago a young boy painted his room black, decorated it with black candles, an altar, and satanic symbols all over the walls. His behavior became erratic and rebellious, including drinking, smoking marijuana, and threatening his parents. His parents sent him to a treatment center to help him sort out his problems. When he entered the program, he believed satanism could provide the answers he sought. Through the practice of that religion, he believed he could control all things. Since his treatment ended, he has not returned to any of the satanic rituals, and there have been no other crises.[6]

HEADLINE: Lawyer—Man who killed family had love in heart.

The defense attorney for a man who killed his family eighteen years ago says that he did it with love in his heart. The TV show "America's Most Wanted" broke the case and led a neighbor to turn in the man. He wrote that he shot his family because of financial problems and his *fear that they were straying from their religion.* When he had completed their executions, he knelt and said prayers for them.

The man, now claiming to be mentally ill at the time, says he left himself in the hands of God's justice and mercy. He wrote that God could have helped him in his time of distress but chose not to do so. He went on to say that many would look at the additional years his family could have lived, "but if they were no longer Christians, what would be gained?"[7]

HEADLINE: A test of faith.

A legal battle continues between a mother, her daughter, and the Hare Krishnas. There are charges of brainwashing, mind control, kidnapping, libel, and intentional infliction of emotional stress. Seven years ago the mother and daughter were awarded $32.5 million in actual and punitive damages from the international Hare Krishnas orga-

IS PAIN REAL?

"Pain is a perception, not a reality" says Shirley MacLaine at a gathering where each of the 1,200 faithful paid $300. This session was part of a fifteen-city national tour (estimated earnings: $1.5 million).

—*Otto Friedrich, "New Age Harmonies,"* Time, *December 7, 1987, pp. 63–64.*

So after all the money has been made, and the tour is complete, I wonder what happens to those left in its wake, those who, like the rest of us, have some degree of pain in their lives that they now are supposed to brush off as unreal.

nization. It was the first time that anyone had won a case against them for brainwashing and false imprisonment. The jury agreed with the plaintiffs that the young girl's father had died of a stroke as a result of a nationwide hunt for her. Now, the amount of money has been reduced, but the ruling still stands.

At age fourteen, the girl visited the temple in Laguna Beach, California, because she was curious. At first she participated in only Sunday activities but then became increasingly interested in the beliefs of the group. Her mother said her daughter quickly became a vegetarian and erected an altar in her room where she chanted the Hare Krishna mantra daily. Two months into her freshman year she joined the temple in Laguna where they told her to become totally committed or be reincarnated as a worm. The girl states that they said her parents were demons that would hamper her spiritual progress. She does not know when she crossed over the line from doubting the Krishnas to believing in them.

The girl is quoted as saying, "I was so convinced I was right that no sacrifice was too great. Even my parents." When police found the girl five months later in a New Orleans temple, she had lost twenty pounds, was filthy, had yellow teeth, and possessed a blank stare. It took her five years of counseling before she was back to normal.

The girl's father died ten months after she returned home. His dying wish was that the suit continue against the Krishnas, even if it

Faith becomes harmful when individuals use God or religion for profit, power, pleasure, and/or prestige.

meant giving up everything. He said, "We've got to sue the Krishnas, because people need to know about these cults."[8]

The examples cited here are the extremes. They are the exceptions of how most people experience and practice faith. That is why they made headlines. It is the very nature of reporting to find the exceptions and the extremes. Naive critics of faith in God accept these bizarre exceptions as the norm, pushing people away from God. In the study of the faith experience, these extremes provide a perspective on the more subtle forms of harmful faith. In each experience, whether extreme or closer to the norm, faith becomes harmful when individuals use God or religion for profit, power, pleasure, and/or prestige. These four goals of much of our population are the foundation of any addiction. They must be segregated from faith. Each time faith is distorted or minimized because of them, people are hurt, some are killed, and many are left to suffer alone after families, friends, and fortunes have been lost.

The headlines shock us with the reality of the people next door who become involved in strange addictive practices of faith. One would think these aberrant manifestations could be easily identified by rational people. It seems impossible for someone to be led away from a powerful God into a faulty ideology of life. But the gradual drift into an unreal world of false belief results in bizarre consequences. The subtle changes go unnoticed until the victim of harmful faith is completely blinded to the true God and true faith.

Within us all are poisonous beliefs that need to be neutralized. Our faith cannot help being soiled in a drug-filled, self-obsessed world such as ours. We may never turn our backs on God, join a cult, or

"BOY, 6, STABBED 10 TIMES; DAD SETS HIMSELF ABLAZE"

So read the top story on the front page of the *San Antonio Express News* on July 11, 1990. A frightening headline indeed. But what is perhaps more frightening is the fact that upon arriving at the scene, investigators "were told by the man: 'God told me to do it.'" This is a man who neighbors said was a nice man, one who never yelled at his children. And yet, something was dangerously amiss.

—Jeff Davis, "Boy, 6, Stabbed 10 Times; Dad sets Himself Ablaze," San Antonio Express News, *July 11, 1990.*

BEWARE OF RATTLE

"Every state except West Virginia has made snake handling illegal. But the ritual is still practiced in isolated communities in southern Appalachia and parts of Ohio, Michigan and Indiana—with occasionally deadly results. In West Virginia alone there have been 11 documented deaths of supplicants from snakebite since 1945." Dewey Chafin, a church leader of the Church of the Lord Jesus in Jolo, West Virginia, has been bitten 106 times. And he is lucky: his sister, Columbia, was killed by a snakebite in 1961. His mother who is 72 has survived a mere 17 bites. Says Chafin regarding the thought of dying of a snakebite, "I don't think there could be a better way to go."

—David Grogan and Chris Phillips, "Courting Death, Appalachia's Old-Time Religionists Praise the Lord and Pass the Snakes," People, May 1, 1989, pp. 81, 84.

handle a snake, but we all are victims of poisonous ideas that distort the image of God and negate our faith. Though we tell ourselves we would certainly be able to escape such misled perspectives of faith, we would do well to remember that the headlines are often about people just like us who thought they were in touch with reality but ended up with a compulsive addiction to an unreal religion.

——— N o t e s ———

1. Jerry and Steve Arterburn, *How Will I Tell My Mother?* (Nashville: Oliver-Nelson Books, 1988).

2. Kathleen Lavey, "Faith-Healing Parents Guilty in Son's Death," *USA Today,* July 5, 1990, April 16, 1990, p. 3A.

3. Michael Connelly and Aaron Curtiss, "Despondent Mother Kills Her Three Children and Herself," *Los Angeles Times,* March 22, 23, 1990.

4. John Polich, "Wealth, Religion Were Used to Lure Investors, Clients Say," *Orange County Register,* June 24, 1990.

5. Peter Elkind, "The Curse of the Black Lords," *Texas Monthly,* May 1990, pp. 95–179.

6. "Psychiatric Hospital Weans Youth Away from Satanism," *Lake Charles American Press,* March 24, 1990.

7. "Lawyer—Man Who Killed Family Had Love in Heart," *USA Today,* April 3, 1990, and *Orange County Register,* March 29, 1990.

8. C. B. Harris, "A Test of Faith," *Orange County Magazine,* April 1990, pp. 83–95.

CHAPTER 2

What Is Faith that Hurts and Religious Addiction?

Faith that hurts is a destructive, dangerous relationship with a religion that allows the religion, not the relationship with God, to control a person's life. People broken by various experiences, people from dysfunctional families, people with unrealistic expectations, and people out for their own gain or comfort seem especially prone to it. It is a defective faith with an incomplete or tainted view of God. It is abusive and manipulative and can become addictive. It becomes so central to the person's life that family and friends become insignificant compared to the need to uphold the false beliefs. Those with hurtful faith use it to avoid reality and responsibility. It often results in a perfectionist existence; people are driven to perform and work in an attempt to earn their way to heaven or at least to gain favor with God. Like other addictions, its persistent use to alter moods produces adverse consequences, but the addicted continue to pursue the addiction.

Harmful faith has nothing to do with God, but everything to do with men and women who want to concoct a god or faith that serves

Faith that hurts is a destructive and dangerous relationship with a religion that allows the religion, not the relationship with God, to control a person's life.

self rather than honors God. In short, hurtful faith is an excuse. It is an excuse for an abusive husband to mistreat his wife because he believes God would want her to submit to him as if he were God. It is an excuse to put off dealing with the pain in life. It is an excuse to wait for God to do what He wants you to do. It provides a distraction through compulsive "churchaholism" or religious ritual.

Harmful faith is also a counterfeit for the spiritual growth that can occur through a genuine relationship with God. The misled faithful find a replacement for God. How they look becomes more important than who God is. Acts of religion replace steps of growth. A facade is substituted for a heart longing to know God. The facade forms a barrier between the believer and God, leaving the believer to survive with a destructive addiction to religion.

Characteristics of Religious Addicts

Plenty of people are susceptible to religious addiction. Their brokenness, misery, and conflict leave them open to becoming hooked on working hard to win God's favor and believing anything that will make life easier. They develop harmful faith practices that become as addictive as heroin. Out of a desire to delay or deny pain, they come up with their own distorted beliefs. There are many variations of religious addicts.

COMMON CHARACTERISTICS OF RELIGIOUS ADDICTS

- Rigid parents
- Experience of disappointment
- Low self-worth
- Victims of abuse

Rigid Parents

As strange as it may seem, the child who had a rigid parent (or parents) enters adulthood clinging to someone serving up any form of rigidity. One would think that having gotten free from the rigidity, the adult child would avoid it. Instead the individual is drawn to it, which makes the person likely to get caught up in an addictive religious system or to follow a harmful faith leader. One explanation for this tendency is that human beings are creatures of habit, we are comfortable with what we know.

Perhaps people are drawn toward a rigid system because they have a hidden desire to fix it, to loosen themselves up and free themselves to enjoy life. This is something they were unable to go through with their parents. The tight restraints of the parents' beliefs feel so much like the manipulation, they become faithful followers.

One boy was brought up in a very rigid family where it was difficult for him to express who he was or what he wanted. His father would communicate with directives, offering no reasons for his demands, just expecting compliance. The boy rebelled severely. He became a heavy drug user and at age eighteen quit school and went to live with several other drug addicts. Eventually his addiction put him out of work, and he found himself at the bottom with no hope.

When a cult follower befriended him, he responded. He felt love and support and a genuine offer for help. Inside the cult he was confronted with a controlling leader who dictated every decision of the group. He had found home. He had come full circle back to a variation of his original situation. He was a faithful follower, unwilling to question the validity of the group, its rules, or the demands it placed on him.

Experience of Disappointment

A deep wound from a major disappointment is in the background of most religious addicts. It might have been the early loss of a parent or a parental divorce. It could have been their own divorce or abandonment in later life. The loss and the disappointment cause a tremendous fear of yet another abandonment. Addicts become attracted to and attached to any group that promises acceptance without risk.

THE YOUNGER GENERATION

"Young people don't trust politicians, they don't trust their church leaders, they don't even trust their parents anymore. But at the same time they're very gullible in regard to the more exotic types of claims."
—Ingrid Groller, "Do You Believe in the Supernatural?"
Parents, October 1989, p. 32.

Often the group promises instant relief or gratification. Feeling the pain from their disappointment, religious addicts want relief, especially if it does not require effort on their part.

I worked with a vulnerable woman who was devastated by the loss of her parents and her own nasty divorce. Somehow she felt she could have done something different to prevent the tragedies. Seeking relief, she began a dating spree that included frequent sexual intercourse. In addition to her grief over the loss of her parents and her divorce, she began to believe God was going to punish her for having sex outside marriage. She was filled with guilt. She knew God didn't want her to have sex with anyone she dated, but she succumbed frequently. She was convinced that God was going to punish her by giving her the AIDS virus.

She became obsessed with God's wrath and the idea of His swooping down on her to wipe her out. Each month she would have another AIDS test, but she didn't change her behavior or use precautions in her sexual relationships. She went on trying to say no, giving in, and then waiting for God to provide the death sentence. Her disappointments with death and divorce led her to abandon God for quick sexual relief from her pain. However, her source of relief only increased her pain.

Low Self-Worth

The power of peer pressure has a well-established role in the destruction of many young people. But we seem to forget it is just as powerful among adults, and it leads many adults down the wrong path. If people do not value themselves or have their own beliefs, they will fall victim to the pressures to conform. Like the girl involved with the Hare Krishnas, they cross over a line from rational to irrational belief. Not believing in their ability to discern truth from manipulation, they go along with the group consensus, even if it invalidates everything they have been taught.

Persons with low self-worth feel alienated and isolated. They want to belong and be accepted. Harmful faith leaders know this. They can pick out wounded followers who are looking for someone to make them feel important. Under the guise of ministry they cater to people's

If people do not value themselves or have their own beliefs, they will fall victim to the pressures to conform.

weaknesses until those people believe they are receiving genuine caring. Thus, the religious group gets new members, potentially forever.

This care con game is similar to one of the oldest money tricks among scam artists. They ask you to trust them with a little money. When you do, the return is large. They tell you to give them one dollar, and in a few days or weeks they give you ten dollars back. Convinced with the evidence of a real return on your money, you increase your investment to one hundred dollars, and the thieves are never heard from again.

Harmful faith practitioners find those with low self-worth and minimal boundaries. They ask them to trust just a little. With that first step of trust, the persons are flooded with affirmation and love. Every need is met. Childhood trauma is forgotten because of the euphoria of so much affection. The ones being manipulated then place greater trust, sometimes selling all possessions to belong. Making this radical decision, they reinforce it with justifications for their behavior.

The new followers don't turn astray, even when they see the exploitation, because they continue to reinforce their own decisions. They feel bad about themselves already, and admitting they had been

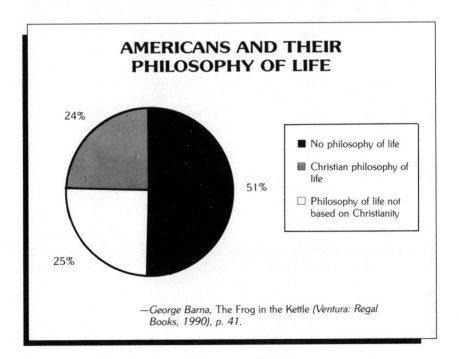

AMERICANS AND THEIR PHILOSOPHY OF LIFE

24%

25%

51%

■ No philosophy of life

▨ Christian philosophy of life

☐ Philosophy of life not based on Christianity

—*George Barna*, The Frog in the Kettle *(Ventura: Regal Books, 1990), p. 41.*

duped into submission would be devastating. Their minds block out the reality of the harmful beliefs, and they become faithful followers under an exploitive leader. If their self-worth had been present in the beginning, they would have discerned the unhealthiness of the group and refused to be part of it. Their addiction moves them to believe the unbelievable if it will provide at least a moment of relief. They don't see the exploitation because their low self-worth has allowed them to be exploited all their lives, so it seems almost normal.

Victims of Abuse

Whether sexual, physical, or emotional, childhood abuse often leads to further victimization in adulthood. The abused feel detached and unloved. They function with a feeling of loss. Often they will go to great extremes to fill that void left by abusive parents. Their faith is almost always poisoned by these early incidents. Some forsake God, blaming Him for the abuse. Others believe but consider God to be detached and uncaring about individuals in pain. Still others replace God with a human being.

Attention from an adult friend, especially a father replacement, can set off a craving for more attention and a vulnerability to be victimized again. Seeking a savior, the adult child of abuse repeats being the victim. When the "savior" turns out to be yet another victimizer, the act is so horrifying and degrading that there is often a complete break with reality. The victim blindly complies with the victimizer as the poisonous faith continues to grow.

Susceptible people have something in common with those who are not susceptible: they are hurting. We are all hurting people; we all

---

AFRAID OF BIG ANIMALS

Jo Ann Karl charges $15 a customer for channeling. "'The lesson I learned in one of my past lives was about taking risks,' says Karl. 'I was married to St. Peter. We traveled widely with Jesus, teaching with him. After he was crucified, we continued to teach and travel for several more years, until we were caught by the Romans. Peter was crucified, and I was thrown to the lions, after being raped and pilloried. Now I understand why I've always been afraid of big animals.'"

—*Otto Friedrich, "New Age Harmonies," Time, December 7, 1987, p. 66.*

struggle with pain and disappointment. However, religious addicts believe they are the only ones who hurt. They think no one else cares or has to endure their kind of pain. When a practitioner of harmful faith arrives with what appears to be a heart of gold and a simple plan for an easy life, the followers are quick to join in.

Forms and Variations of Faith that Hurts

Hurtful faith is not professed by cookie-cutter religious addicts. It has many variations—some Christian, some atheistic, and some affiliated with other world religions. The following are the most common ways it is manifested.

> ### FORMS AND VARIATIONS OF TOXIC FAITH
>
> - Compulsive religious activity
> - Laziness
> - Giving to get
> - Self-obsession
> - Extreme intolerance
> - Addiction to a religious high

Compulsive Religious Activity

Compulsive religious addicts are driven by guilt and a desire to earn favor from God. They work hard in hopes of a day when God will look down on their efforts and change reality for them. They hope He will see their hard work and decide to relieve their pain or make life magically more easy for them than for others. They have an "earn as you go" mentality that places their future in the hands of their ability to achieve, accomplish, and sacrifice.

They have an "earn as you go" mentality that places their future in the hands of their ability to achieve, accomplish, and sacrifice.

My wife and I were in Thailand a few months ago where we observed Buddhists practicing their faith. There were hundreds of temples and thousands of worshipers. I was overwhelmed by their dedication to their gods, those they said were alive and those who had died. I watched as they bought gold filament and pressed it into a Buddha statue to the point of experiencing pain in their own bodies. They sought relief through purchasing gold and then applying it with faith.

We were often confronted with requests to do something for Buddha. They wanted us to buy a bird and set it free. They asked us to give money to restore the temples. We were also invited to buy lotus blossoms. According to them, all of those things would bring us "good luck." They constantly suggested new ways for us to please Buddha and obtain favor from him. A person just couldn't do enough in that land where faith was replaced by hard work.

It is not much different here in the U.S. There are those who feel compelled to serve on every church committee or represent the church on every possible community council. The family is placed second to the flurry of activity surrounding the church. There is the underlying belief that work will gain favor. But there is another dynamic as well. Like every other addiction, it involves running from pain. If these people can stay busy enough, they will not have to resolve their pain. They work hard and run fast to stay one step ahead of the hurt they feel will incapacitate them. But the pain has already incapacitated them. It has driven them to work and drive and try harder to please God.

Laziness

Some people with hurtful faith are lazy. Their laziness is their most common form of self-defeating behavior. Their faith actually dumps responsibility on God. For example, rather than work to heal a marriage, they want God to fix it instantly. Rather than make an appointment with a counselor, they pray for a miracle, asking God to do for

They work hard and run fast to stay one step ahead of the hurt they feel will incapacitate them. But the pain has already incapacitated them. It has driven them to work and drive and try harder to please God.

JESUS CHRIST

What do you believe about Jesus Christ—do you think Jesus Christ was God or Son of God, another religious leader like Mohammed or Buddha, or do you think Jesus Christ never lived?

- 84% God or Son of God
- 9% Another Leader
- 1% Never Actually Lived
- 2% Other
- 4% No Opinion

—George Gallup, Jr., and Sarah Jones, 100 Questions and Answers: Religion in America *(Princeton, N.J.: Princeton Religion Research Center, 1989), p. 6.*

them what God probably wants them to do for themselves. It is inconvenient to go to a marriage counselor. It is expensive, too. So rather than do the responsible thing, the lazy believe that if they just pray, God will take care of their marriage. Marriage counseling is a painful growth process. And yet, God may want the lazy believers to go through it.

One of the first illustrations I heard about the balance between realistic and unrealistic faith involved two girls on their way to school. The moment for the bell to ring grew closer and closer. They had been late several times before, and there would be grave consequences if they repeated the offense. One girl suggested they crawl down in the nearest ditch to pray to God that they would not be late. The other little girl made the more realistic suggestion: they should pray and run.

Thousands of religious addicts have crawled down in ditches of unreality. They have retreated into a lazy world where they want everything worked out for them in a magical, mysterious way. I think God might be watching, hoping they will crawl out of the ditches and continue to grow through facing their difficulties one at a time. Instead they are lazy. They want a servant god; they don't want to serve God. They want a god drug that will wipe out consequences and quickly

They want a god drug that will wipe out consequences and quickly ease all hurts.

THE "WHYS" BEHIND RELIGION

"Why are people religious? Because they cannot tolerate a completely random and plotless existence. Because someone they trust beckons them to believe. Because they hear the call of God. Or it may be that they need suprahuman instruments to cope with human tragedy: Cancer, earthquake, auto accident, terrorism. And, just as likely, people respond to the transcendent as they celebrate joys undeserved: Births and marriages, boons and blessings. Still others are religious as they find belonging and purpose by congregating in sanctuaries. . . . The questions faith signals and the tentative answers it implies are too urgent to go unheeded."

—Martin E. Marty, "What People Seek—and Find—in Belief," U.S. News & World Report, *December 29, 1986/January 5, 1987, p. 43.*

ease all hurts. That view of God is harmful and addictive. It is irresponsible and leaves believers stagnant, full of false hope and unrealistic expectations.

Giving to Get

I believe my grandmother gave her money because she thought it was a way to give back to God some of what He had given to her. Others do not possess those same motives. They give out of a belief that the more they give, the more they will get in return. It is more like a materialistic investment than a spiritual act of worship and sacrifice. They believe that their affluence will increase as they give more to a ministry. God promises to bless His people for faithful stewardship, but that blessing is not necessarily in the form of cold hard cash.

I don't know of many people who give 35 percent to 40 percent of their money like my grandmother did. So, if anyone would be rewarded materially, she would be a likely candidate. However, though she never had to struggle, she was no wealthier after ten years of sacrificial giving. The promise of wealth was never her motive, and wealth was not her reward.

God cannot be bribed or bought, but the actions of many people appear to be attempts to do just that.

I have heard some fund raisers ask people to claim their material blessings. They are told to claim the Rolls Royce they want, trust God to provide it, give money to secure it, and it will come. Some charlatans arrange for the unsuspecting to acquire the automobile they claimed. They go out and buy a car, deliver it, and then write up the miracle in a newsletter that is dispensed to all the other faithful whose automobiles have not arrived. They are told that if they have more faith and give more money, they will have the material possessions they want. With this proof before them, they shell out more money, hoping God will give them what they believe they deserve.

God cannot be bribed or bought, but the actions of many people appear to be attempts to do just that. Their money might be better spent in Las Vegas where luck, not God, is the rewarder of money. This form of religious addict has more in common with a compulsive gambler than with a faithful follower of God.

Self-Obsession

This comprehensive problem leads to the practice of hurtful faith, religious addiction, and all other addictions. Poisoned by their constant focus on their own needs, hurts, and desire for relief, the self-obsessed have little room left for worshiping God or meeting the needs of others. For people living in this selfish state, it is no wonder that their expectations of God are so high. Christ was quoted as telling Peter to show his love by feeding His sheep (i.e., meeting the needs of others). The self-obsessed are not interested in feeding anyone else's sheep or helping others in any way. They concentrate on how others can meet their needs, especially how God can relieve them of their burdens.

God does relieve burdens. He does bless. He meets needs in miraculous ways. He brings babies to infertile couples. He will at times heal or reverse a terminal disease. There are many evidences of divine intervention. They are called miracles. The reason they are called miracles is that they rarely happen. To have faith in God because He will perform miracles is to have faith in miracles more than in God. True

---

There are many evidences of divine intervention. They are called miracles. The reason they are called miracles is that they rarely happen.

faith in God is not focused on only what God can miraculously do or provide; it is focused on what the individual can do for God. Additionally, the individual must make an effort to care for those God loves, His sheep, one's neighbors.

I was discussing with a psychiatrist friend how faith has become so self-serving. He described another friend's habits, which are the qualities of a person after God's heart. He said the man's motivation for everything he did was to please God and serve Him. He worked with people not to make money but to serve God. He was dedicated to the needs of others and derived joy from meeting those needs. This self-less man had a faith that went beyond his own needs and self-obsession. It is a rare faith. More often today people proclaim faith in God as long as that faith will increase the bottom line and make life better. There is no greater sin than self-obsession, no greater poison of faith.

Extreme Intolerance

Religious addicts are extremely intolerant of varying opinions or expressions of faith. Either walk their way or be out of step. Their rigidity rejects other believers rather than accepts them. They routinely judge others and find the negative in everyone else's life. From a position of superiority, they put down others for what they believe and how they manifest their faith. They want to control the lives of others, especially their beliefs.

One gentleman, a member of a conservative group, was fearful that his sons would veer into a more liberal faith or that they would end up with no faith at all. He believed that one of the most beautiful pictures to God was of a family going to church together. He took his family to church twice every Sunday and also on Wednesday nights. If the church doors were open, he walked through them with his family.

His oldest son had some friends who attended another church on the edge of town. He developed other friends there and liked it much better than his father's church. He asked to leave his parents' church to attend the one on the edge of town. It was no strange religion or cult; it was part of the same denomination. But the father couldn't handle it. He told his son he had to stop going to the other church. He

They will sacrifice relationships with family and friends to uphold a standard or ideal of their own faith.

wanted the entire family to attend church together, and nothing would stand in the way of achieving that goal. He was intolerant of his son's expressions of faith and of the other church and its members. His demands caused a severe split between him and his son. It was not their first problem, but it was the biggest. Tremendous bitterness and resentment grew from it and destroyed their ability to relate to each other.

This kind of intolerance is common among those with harmful faith. They will sacrifice relationships with family and friends to up-hold a standard or ideal of their own faith. As long as they believe they are doing what God would have them do, they won't hesitate to push their ideas on others and judge them as less faithful and less in touch with the way things should be done. Certain they are upholding God's standards, they control others by demeaning their beliefs and the practice of faith. They create a fake faith and a legalistic caricature of what faith is. Their children, resisting this intolerance, flee from their parents' faith and often never seek a relationship with God.

Addiction to a Religious High

The practice of faith can produce tremendous relief from the pain and frustrations of life. Trusting in God, a person no longer feels bur-dened with problems or overwhelmed from believing all problems must be resolved alone. This is a natural result of placing faith in a God who promises His burden is light.

But there is another kind of relief, an emotional frenzy that becomes an addiction and robs the individual of real faith. I was on a Christian talk show and afterward had the pleasure of going to lunch with the staff. They related stories of the variations of faith and the strange incidents that develop when faith becomes unbalanced.

One story was of particular interest to me. The program had spon-sored a tour to Israel, and about five hundred people signed up to visit the Holy Land. A woman traveling with them had felt led to become a nun. Unable to find an order to accept her, she established her own order of one and wore the attire of a traditional nun. Each time she visited a site, she would work herself into a frenzy, chant loudly, then

---

But there is another kind of relief, an emotional frenzy that becomes an addiction and robs the individual of real faith.

pass out, claiming to be slain in the Spirit. Although most people on the tour were charismatic Christians, they were not impressed with the performance. Each time they approached a monument, they stood back and waited for the show to begin.

The development of her order of one nun was the woman's first major leap from reality. Her repeated frenzies were further steps of escape. She was addicted to the self-manufactured highs supposed to be religious experiences. There are many other gradations of this extreme form of religious intoxication. Often the misled faithful become so enthralled with the religious experience that they reduce God to secondary importance.

Anyone who has ever been to a church camp knows what it is like to have a religious high, commonly called a mountaintop experience. When the kids leave camp, they are warned that the wonderful emotions they feel will go away. An eventual "downer" experience will come when the emotions of the mountaintop wear away. The kids must learn to adjust to reality where everyone is not as supportive and loving as the kids and staff at camp.

Yet some people cannot or will not handle the downs after a marvelous spiritual experience. Rather than deal with reality, they manufacture a pseudoreligious experience or a spiritual frenzy. The adrenaline rush actually energizes and stimulates them, alters the mood, and provides relief from real pain. The hysteria is repeated any time they need to escape or feel differently. These "instant religious experience" practitioners might as well take a drink, swallow a pill, or inject a drug. The intent of their actions is not to worship God but to alter their perception of reality. They are religious junkies, obsessed with mood alteration and a quick fix to face life.

The variations of hurtful faith and religious addiction never bring people closer to God. They form barriers between individuals and God, which allows the affected persons to stay busy and active in every way except for a true worship experience. With the barriers to God and others in place, the misled faithful are left with many more painful feelings to compound the original pain that was the nucleus of their harmful faith.

The intent of their actions is not to worship God but to alter their perception of reality. They are religious junkies, obsessed with mood alteration and a quick fix to face life.

Faith has been eroded, and as persons place distance between themselves and God, the chasm formed is filled with compulsion, activity, addiction, manipulation, control, and extreme effort.

Every addiction has as its end the destruction of intimacy with family, friends, and God. The addicted have an aversion to placing themselves in a position of vulnerable trust with another. Hurtful faith is no different. Those with harmful faith cannot or will not trust God. Faith has been eroded, and as persons place distance between themselves and God, the chasm formed is filled with compulsion, activity, addiction, manipulation, control, and extreme effort. The work is never done, and the heart is never at rest because the faith has become so distorted.

A Paradox of Harmful Faith

A paradox of harmful faith sets it apart from any other compulsion or addiction. It is the issue of moderation. In alcohol consumption, the goal is abstinence or moderation. When a person moves beyond moderation, evidence of addiction mounts as the level of consumption increases. Eating works the same way. Compulsive overeaters must learn to eat less and find fulfillment in less consumption. Faith is not this way. True faith, real and pure faith, is not practiced in moderation. One cannot trust God too much or seek God too much. Persons whose faith has grown to encompass every aspect of life are spiritual faith giants to be modeled. A little faith, a faith that knows only a bit about God, is a form of hurtful faith. It pays a small tribute to God instead of developing a strong relationship with God. As poisonous as these varieties of faith are, they are minimal compared to the most destructive faith: no faith at all.

True faith, real and pure faith, is not practiced in moderation. One cannot trust God too much or seek God too much.

Once faith is poisoned, it is a complex process to detoxify the person and restore a pure faith. Identifying the toxic elements one by one is the beginning of hope. Seeing harmful beliefs and practices can allow someone who walked on the fringe of faith to plunge deeply into it to know and serve God.

Herein lies the most formidable challenge: to look within oneself and find the harmful elements of faith and remove them. Some people are so self-obsessed, so sold on their faith in themselves, that it is difficult for them to break through denial and see what is sick at their core and how that sickness has damaged their relationships, including the one with God.

Yet it is not impossible to break through the denial and clean up faith. Individuals willing to take a second look at God and faith and why they mess up the relationship so badly are in for a painful experience. Be assured, the pain is less than that experienced in continuing to use God rather than relate to God. It is less painful than realizing they are afraid and continuing to live with that knowledge. By making the effort to detoxify faith they will go through some difficult times to find what God designed for a relationship with Him. But a relationship based on pure faith leads to complete contentment and joy.

Herein lies the most formidable challenge: to look within oneself and find the harmful elements of faith and remove them.

CHAPTER 3

Twenty-One Harmful Beliefs of a Faith that Hurts

Faith is slowly poisoned as lies and false beliefs are integrated into a person's beliefs about God. For some, this occurs after a major disappointment in adult life. Others are distorted from early years, watching parents practice a faith with little truth and hope. Harmful beliefs are tough to counter. At first glance they make such good sense. And plenty of people support the distorted beliefs that have been around for thousands of years.

Once persons are deceived, they vigorously resist changing their beliefs. Since they are so self-obsessed, they want to believe that they are right and are incapable of being wrong. Additionally, these people invest much time, money, and energy in harmful beliefs, which they hold more sacred than God. Whether handed down, learned later in life, supported by others, or reinforced by denial, harmful beliefs take root and spoil the relationship with God. These beliefs must be countered and replaced with truth.

For example, years of pain grew from a set of harmful beliefs that took root when Melody was a child. At one point in her growing-up

---

Whether handed down, learned later in life, supported by others, or reinforced by denial, harmful beliefs take root and spoil the relationship with God.

years, her minister father became obsessed by her beauty and form. He fought the temptation to touch her for two years. Finally, on an overnight outing, he went to her sleeping bag, and while she slept, he molested her. He unbuttoned her shirt to see her breasts. When she awoke, he was sitting beside her, staring at her.

She was horrified, but she didn't scream. He took that as an invitation to come closer, and he lay down beside her and fondled her. She cried silently the whole time. When he was finished, he buttoned her shirt and returned to his sleeping bag.

Melody didn't sleep the rest of the night. As she lay awake, the nucleus of a lifetime of harmful beliefs began to form. She wondered why God had allowed this. She felt that she must be bad or this bad thing wouldn't have happened. She felt this must be some kind of punishment for something she had done. Her faith was shattered. Since her father was a fake, all believers must be fakes, also.

Melody kept the secret. And although her father never touched her again, his relationship with her changed dramatically after that incident. There was no more sexual abuse, but the emotional abuse was just as destructive. He became negative with her and very critical. It was as if he blamed her for what had happened. She never again felt an ounce of love from her father.

Over the course of the next year, Melody became a drug and alcohol abuser and a compulsive eater. Hoping to resolve the pain, she de-

WHICH OF THE FOLLOWING TELEVISION EVANGELISTS DO YOU HOLD IN HIGH REGARD?

According to a 1987 poll conducted by *U.S. News & World Report:*

	High Regard	Not High	Don't Know
Billy Graham	51%	37%	12%
Robert Schuller	21%	45%	34%
Jimmy Swaggart	19%	61%	20%
Jerry Falwell	18%	62%	20%
Pat Robertson	17%	56%	27%
Oral Roberts	14%	76%	10%
Rex Humbard	12%	53%	35%
Jim Bakker	6%	73%	21%

—"TV Preachers and Public Trust," U.S. News & World Report, *April 13, 1987, p. 15.*

cided to tell her mother what had happened. Melody's mother could not believe it. She accused Melody of lying. It destroyed her relationship with her mother. She felt isolated and abandoned by her father, her mother, and her God. In a deep depression, she slit her wrists and hoped to die. However, her mother found her in time and saved her life.

The suicide attempt forced Melody's mother to find treatment for her, and she found it with us at New Life Treatment Centers. Through the program and staff, the molestation was verified, and the father was arrested after the authorities were notified. There were no legal consequences from the incident, but he lost his church and his family.

Melody was bitter and angry. She felt guilty about the molestation, guilty that she had not told her mother sooner, and guilty that her father had lost his job. She took all the burdens of the molestation on herself. Yet she also contrived to blame God for deserting her when she needed Him. She had no place for a God who could not be counted on or who must be punishing her for some long-forgotten sin.

Treatment did not restore Melody's faith immediately, but it did restore her to spiritual and emotional health. Through hard hours of therapy, Bible study, and prayer, she worked through her self-deprecating feelings and emerged with a new sense of self-worth. She had tremendous support from the staff and other patients to see herself in a new way. As each day passed, she grew more and more in her quest for peace.

Before leaving treatment, she began to work on an aftercare plan. One question concerned church attendance. Melody stated that she had no plans to attend church, that she needed more time to heal before facing another male minister in a church setting. Her plan was very realistic. She did need more time. She might have been devastated to return to a church that would possibly stir up much of what was not yet manageable for her. The counselor expressed her approval of Melody's plan. She asked Melody to describe her feelings about

IS THE CHURCH TODAY RELEVANT?

(Unchurched people respond)

☐ Yes   38%

☐ No   64%

—*George Barna*, The Frog in the Kettle *(Ventura: Regal Books, 1990), p. 138.*

God. Melody slowly responded, "I believe He is there. I believe He is real. But I believe He is tougher than I could have ever imagined."

Melody had come a long way in her short stay. Changing a belief from an uncaring God to a God who is interested in each life is a long journey. By saying He is real and He is there, she was on the verge of reaching the realization that He cares about her and loves her. Destroying the roots of harmful faith is a process that takes time and effort. It requires vulnerability and the admission that life can be viewed incorrectly. God can be viewed incorrectly. The first step is to identify the incorrect beliefs. Once identified, they can be changed and a real faith in God restored.

Melody's molestation was the core of the harmful beliefs she developed. Her faith changed as she struggled alone to figure out who she was and who God was in light of the molestation. Through treatment, she identified some of those harmful beliefs: she felt that she must have been bad and that God was punishing her; she believed if she had been better, it would not have happened; she believed her behavior determined how much God would love her; she thought God should have protected her from a terrible incident; and she found her father was a fake, so she came to believe all Christians were fake. She could see how one incident affected her whole concept of God, life, and her future. Those harmful beliefs are not unique to Melody. They are shared by millions. The following are the most common beliefs of a faith that hurts.

1. Conditional Love

GOD'S LOVE AND FAVOR DEPEND ON MY BEHAVIOR

God is love is the central theme of the Bible. But persons plagued with harmful faith neglect that fact. They see God as a critical Parent, waiting to say, "It's not good enough. Try harder. You could do better." Their faith is so wounded that they turn to a faith in self rather than a faith in God. They depend on their performance, not God's wondrous love.

A young man came to me who had heard of my problems in the

Destroying the roots of harmful faith is a process that takes time and effort.

past. He had paid for a girlfriend's abortion and felt extreme guilt because of it. Before that happened, he believed he had a great future. His faith in God's willingness to use him was strong. However, after the abortion, he doubted God had a place for him. He felt like a complete reject, and he began to focus on his behavior rather than on God's love. He worked and worked to resume his place of favor. No matter how hard he tried, it was not good enough. He kept coming up short. He asked me, "Will I ever know God's love and acceptance again?"

His knowledge of God's love totally depended on his willingness to put himself aside and focus on a loving God. If he would not, he had no chance of knowing and feeling God's love. In his desire to redeem himself he had become a religious workaholic, addicted to the job of making himself feel good about what he had done. He was driven by a deep hurt and lack of self-worth. The sad thing is that the work he was doing might not make God love him more, but he might get to see God sooner. His self-induced pressure might have caused a heart attack or a stroke. It certainly made him miserable, feeling there was no hope for restoration.

Restoration cannot come from more work or more focus on fixing your own attributes. All you get is a miserable life of perfectionism where nothing is ever good enough. This attempt at restoration produces further destruction of faith and relationships. The difficulty with turning away from a belief of harmful faith is that most of the world acts as if it is true and many are convinced it is true. They operate under the belief that God is looking for a "few good people."

Some of my friends teach their children that if they are good, God will be good back to them. That is probably the most common theology in existence. People are out there trying to earn God's love. What is so ludicrous is how they go about trying to earn His love. They make $100,000 a year and give $5,000 away, expecting God to be appreciative. Or if they give a substantial amount, they place their names on a plaque for public display. Too few know that is not the way of God.

Restoration comes from worshiping God for who He is and trusting

If, like my friend who was burdened with guilt, your need is for forgiveness, God has gone to a lot of trouble to provide that for you. You cannot earn God's love. His love does not depend on your behavior.

The future for the person professing to have instant peace will be troubled. It will be full of pain greater than the original loss and disappointment.

Him to provide for your needs. If, like my friend who was burdened with guilt, your need is for forgiveness, God has gone to a lot of trouble to provide that for you. You cannot earn God's love. His love does not depend on your behavior. Knowing that should be a very big relief.

2. Instant Peace

WHEN TRAGEDY STRIKES, TRUE BELIEVERS SHOULD HAVE A REAL PEACE ABOUT IT

This infectious problem leads to denial, unresolved emotions, and a complete split from reality. I have heard people who have lost children, spouses, fortunes, and dreams say they have this wonderful peace about it just moments later. What they have is shock! Shock is the natural reaction to protect ourselves, to deny the reality and depth of our pain and other feelings. The stages of grief begin with denial, and this conjured peace is a form of that denial. The future for the person professing to have instant peace will be troubled. It will be full of pain greater than the original loss and disappointment.

If this personal harmful faith isn't bad enough, it is inflicted on others who deal realistically with the heart's condition. Persons who express their anger and disappointment are often countered with a challenge to be stronger, trust more, and find peace. The true believer will find peace, but it will be on the other side of resolving the rage that comes with almost every lost expectation. I have heard these "spiritual giants" tell people in pain to have more joy. But they cannot even spell joy while trying to grasp a life with the pain of divorce or the void of a lost child who was dearly loved. People need time to resolve emotions. Instant peace delays and prolongs the time it takes to adjust and move on to a new life.

People need time to resolve emotions.

Acceptance precedes gratitude.

Scripture tells us to be thankful in everything. True faith will lead a person to gratitude for adversity, but it is not instant. Alcoholics who go through years of misery finally reach a point of gratitude if their recovery is real. They relate that if alcoholism had not developed, they would not have recovered, and they would have possibly missed the most meaningful dimensions of life. This gratitude comes after alcoholics completely accept all aspects of the condition and how it will alter their future. Acceptance precedes gratitude. Scripture does not demand that we be grateful immediately. It takes time, lots of time. Those who experience instant peace are not showing instant gratitude to God; they are denying how God made them as physical, spiritual, and emotional beings.

Having said all that, I must add that there are some supernatural exceptions. There are times that God intervenes in a miraculous way to provide peace to persons experiencing extreme pain and adverse circumstances. For example, one mother had done everything to help her child and had to leave the rest to God. Her son's kidneys had failed, and physicians told her that he would die. She described an experience that was not denial; it was an instant awareness that her son would not die. God had decided to intervene at that moment. She said she felt a calm overwhelm her. She remained silent, in awe of the experience. He would be healed, and she knew it. She prayed that God's will would be done. Even though she felt he would be healed, she told God that she would accept whatever the outcome. That night her son was miraculously healed. Her peace was the reality of a supernatural intervention from God.

After I put down my pen, having finished the previous paragraph, I went to a dinner for authors, which is usually a boring time of hearing all about potential best-sellers. However, that night was different. I met Becky Smith Greer, an author from South Carolina who had just completed her first book. It is the story of the sudden loss of both her husband and a twelve-year-old son in a plane crash. With this harmful

There are times that God intervenes in a miraculous way to provide peace to persons who are experiencing extreme pain and adverse circumstances.

People in pain do not need sermons on peace. They need love and care and assistance through the healing process.

faith concept on my mind, I asked her if she had an immediate peace about those deaths. Her response was strong and insightful. She said that there was no peace. Instead, she had tremendous anger that took three years to resolve. But the resolution did come, and her faith in God was restored. She had needed more time than an instant to heal her relationship with God.

Tragedies bring various responses. God does not seem to deal with them or the people affected by them in a predictable manner. For some, there seems to be a gift of peace that prevents a total collapse in the midst of a crisis. For others, that peace does not surface for months or even years. Whatever the reaction, those who experience peace early are no better or worse, no stronger or weaker. The experience of one should not be transposed on the unique circumstances of another. Lack of peace does not mean lack of conviction of faith. People in pain do not need sermons on peace. They need love and care and assistance through the healing process. Remember, faith in God will produce a peace that will go beyond all understanding. It probably won't be an instant peace, but it will be a *real* peace.

3. Guaranteed Healing

IF YOU HAVE REAL FAITH, GOD WILL HEAL YOU OR SOMEONE FOR WHOM YOU ARE PRAYING

My brother died from AIDS. (He and I wrote the story of his struggles in *How Will I Tell My Mother?*) He died because God chose not to intervene in the natural course of events to cure my brother's disease. However, before he died, there was tremendous hope that this type of intervention would happen. Many churches, my parents, my brother, and I prayed for him to be healed. We were not asking for a spectacular event. Utilization of modern medicine would have been fine with us. But it didn't happen. Jerry died, but not because of a lack of faith; there was plenty of that.

Jerry spent his last days on his knees praying and reading Scripture. He would meditate on memorized Scripture and pray fervently.

MOST-MARRIED MAN CUTS KNOT

"Glynn 'Scotty' Wolfe, 81, Blythe, Calif., who holds the Guinness record as the 'World's Most Married Man,' says he'll divorce 27th wife, Daisy, 19, and marry her fifteen-year-old sister. The ordained Baptist minister wants to pay for his bride-to-be's trip from the Philippines by having Daisy pose nude for 'Playboy', but 'they didn't seem too interested.'"

—*Jeanette Hyduke, "Most-Married Man Cuts Knot," USA Today, July 11, 1990.*

It is amazing that one man could be married twenty-seven times in his lifetime; it is astonishing that this man could be an ordained Baptist minister.

His faith was rich and deep, and he had grown close to the God he was prepared to meet face-to-face.

My father's faith has always been strong. It grew stronger through Jerry's ordeal. Dad wanted Jerry to have hope, and he wanted hope for himself. On numerous occasions he asked me to believe with him that Jerry would be healed and survive.

Jerry didn't wait at home for the healing to come. He went looking for it. He attended many healing services in several states. Each time he went he had a strong faith that on that night God would intervene in his history and change the probable outcome. But the change didn't occur. Each time Jerry left a healing service, he felt worse about himself and his faith. He started to believe that if only he had more faith, he could direct the hand of God. So, his guilt continued to grow each day because God's hand could not be moved through faith.

Thousands of mothers of babies with handicapping conditions or serious illnesses pray with angelic faith for those babies to be remade and infused with a supernatural change. Each day that drags by with no change can bring on great guilt and even anger. Faith can become poisoned from the belief that "if only I were better, if only I were stronger, if only I had more faith, my baby would be healed." I empathize with those mothers. Some of them feel like second-class citizens

Faith will help us adapt to His will, understand it better and grow from and through it.

in God's kingdom, and they often believe they are being punished for being bad and the baby is paying the price.

God doesn't work that way. That He chooses to allow a child to remain sick is His will. Faith will help us adapt to His will, understand it better, and grow from and through it. But God is God. He heals whom He chooses. We may not like that one bit. We want to be God or partly God, able to change events to meet *our* pleasures. When we find this to be impossible, because a healing does not occur, our guilt and anger come between us and God.

Just because God didn't heal my faithful brother doesn't mean that He doesn't heal other faithful believers. It also doesn't mean He doesn't heal unbelievers. It is quite the contrary. While preparing to write this book, I was discussing its content with a dear friend. We were talking about how God chooses to heal some and not to heal others. He relayed a story about his secretary that is a miraculous example of God's supernatural interventions.

His secretary had not been a believer, but she had always paid close attention whenever someone mentioned God and faith. While watching television one day she flipped through the channels and stopped to see Pat Robertson on the "700 Club." He was praying for people to be healed of various ailments. This nonbelieving skeptic was startled to hear him say that he believed someone with a deformed bone structure in the hand would be miraculously healed. The surprise came because her hand was deformed, a bone protruding in an unsightly way. At the instant she looked at her deformed hand, a sensation overcame her. It was a peaceful calm she had never felt. She looked up to see something that was bright, like a large beam. A finger of light came from the ceiling and ended at her hand. In an instant, the bone deformity was gone. Her hand was completely and instantly different. The impact of God's intervention was profound. She became a believer and has grown in her faith ever since.

STUMBLING BLOCK

"The No. 1 stumbling block to the unbeliever about the Christian faith is not the Cross or the Second Coming or the Virgin Birth. It is the money angle," says Presbyterian Minister Ben Haden of Chattanooga, Tenn., a pastor and radio-TV speaker.

—*Richard N. Ostling, "TV's Unholy Row," Time, April 6, 1987, p. 67.*

FAITH DEATHS

"Of all the things that can be said about Wesley Parker's death at age 11, the saddest is this: His parents let it happen. Burning with religious fervor, Larry and Lucky Parker watched the eldest of their four children succumb to diabetic shock while they clutched Bibles and withheld insulin. . . . In the past 15 years at least 126 children in the U.S. have died because their parents . . . withheld medical treatment out of doctrinal conviction that prayer is the only allowable treatment for illness." Said Larry after the fact, "Many times we've prayed, 'Lord, why couldn't we have learned another way that this kind of faith is wrong, that it's not really faith at all, but presumption?'"

—Jack Kelly, "How Could Parents Let a Child Die? TV's Promised A Miracle Explores a Tragic Case of Misguided Faith," People, May 16, 1988, pp. 136–38.

Some key elements of this story can teach us real faith versus harmful faith concepts. Her faith was not the reason for the supernatural event. She didn't have any faith, yet God decided to deal with her and show His love to her. This should provide relief for those who have tried to earn God's attention and hope for those who feel that God is not healing them or their children because they lack faith. This secretary is not the only nonbeliever God has changed. Look at Saul (who became the apostle Paul) smitten on the road to Damascus. The degree of faith does not direct the divine will of God. He knows the needs of persons and has a mysterious plan to meet those needs.

The second thing to remember is that God does not deal with everyone this way. You may have the most incredible, powerful, mature faith in the world, but if God has a different plan, you will not be healed. You can't "faith it" into a divine intervention that God knows might lead you away from Him rather than toward Him.

The third element from the secretary's story is more mysterious than the healing. The show she was watching was not live. It was a rebroadcast of an old show. A powerful God can work any way He chooses. Just because He doesn't choose to intervene in your problem

You may have the most incredible, powerful, mature faith in the world, but if God has a different plan, you will not be healed.

in a miraculous way doesn't mean He doesn't love you. Lack of healing is not an indication of lack of faith. It is simply an indicator that the all-powerful God cannot be controlled or predicted. If He could be directed at our beck and call, He would cease to be God. He is God and does or does not do what He chooses. As frustrating as it may be, we can't control Him with our prayers.

4. Irreproachable Clergy

ALL MINISTERS ARE MEN AND WOMEN OF GOD AND CAN BE TRUSTED

I was discussing the elements of harmful faith with a group of people one evening. I asked if anyone had ever had a negative experience with a minister that affected his or her life. A woman in the group told a story that was not shocking, like those that have made headlines, but it was very significant to her. When she was in high school, she won the honor of attending Girls State. (Girls State is an educational program that sends kids to the state capital for a week-long lesson in state government.) She was thrilled with the opportunity, and she was excited to receive the honor. Then her pastor heard of her plans.

The pastor was a very controlling, manipulative individual. He told her that if she went to Girls State, it would be the beginning of many problems. He explained to her that Satan would use the experience to damage her faith. He demanded that her parents not allow her to go.

As a former Boys Stater, I can tell you that nothing happens there to hurt a person's faith. It was one of the best experiences of my life. I learned more about being a responsible citizen in that week than in years of civics and political science classes. The pastor was terribly misinformed. His influence led to the parents' decision not to let her go. It hurt her deeply, and she never forgot it. Her chance to shine was stolen from her.

Compared to the Baker-Swaggart scandals, this incident seems insignificant. But more people have been the victims of mistrust in small ways than have been hurt by major media figures. Ministers,

He is God and does or does not do what He chooses. As frustrating as it may be, we can not control Him with our prayers.

BLIND BECAUSE OF HER SINS?

"Valerie Moreno of Tucson, Ariz., a Roman Catholic convert to Pentecostalism, finally left [the church] because she refused to believe that the ministers' repeated failures to heal her blindness were due to her own sins. 'I had more demons cast out of me than McDonald's has french fries.'"

—*Kenneth L. Woodward, "Is Fundamentalism Addictive?"*
Newsweek, August 5, 1985, p. 63.

whether in a church speaking to fifty or on television reaching out to millions, are real people with real problems. They are not superhuman, and they are not immune to all the temptations of the rest of us. Even those ministers who remain faithful must be seen as imperfect and flawed. No matter how full of integrity, they cannot be the ultimate authority on every area of life.

Authority figures can provide tremendous relief to persons needing counsel and advice. A single person living alone may feel secure in trusting a pastor. Looking to that person for authority is okay as long as there remains a high degree of discernment about what that person demands or how he or she directs.

While I was living in Texas, I developed a close relationship with a pastor. Because of some problems, I needed strong counsel and guidance. I met with this man for several weeks and grew to respect his judgment and counsel. As the relationship progressed, he learned that I was paid a base salary along with quarterly bonuses. I trusted that he had integrity and was not afraid to share anything with him.

Two sessions after I told him I had been paid the bonus, he asked me for a sizable loan. Blindly believing in him, thinking his purposes were noble, I lent him the money at no interest. Eventually, I discovered he had no intention of repaying the loan. With extreme difficulty I got the money back. I felt victimized, and my faith was shaken. Fortunately, I realized I had placed more faith in him than in God.

When a defective pastor crops up occasionally, those who have placed their faith in him or her rather than in God come to believe that God is defective. They attribute all the negative of that one individual

But more people have been the victims of mistrust in small ways than have been hurt by major media figures.

Because a particular individual doesn't have pure faith doesn't mean that the object of faith is also impure.

to all people of faith. This reasoning is irrational and causes many people to turn away from God. Because a particular individual doesn't have pure faith doesn't mean that the object of faith is also impure.

God needs ministers who face life's problems and grow from them. He will not remove temptation from them so that more people can have faith in them, seeing their perfect behavior. Each time ego, greed, power, or lust turns a minister away from the faith, it should strengthen our faith in God by taking our eyes off other people. I am always saddened to hear people say they have turned away from God due to a disappointing experience with one person. Those pastors who molest or cheat are always the exception and show us how vulnerable we all are and how much we need to grow in the faith. For every one who falters in the faith, there are thousands who remain faithful and true. We must not allow human failure to hamper the development of a godly relationship of faith and trust.

5. Monetary Rewards

MATERIAL BLESSINGS ARE A SIGN OF SPIRITUAL STRENGTH

This harmful belief is a reflection of our materialistic society that measures people by the amount of money they make. Those who have much want to believe it is a direct result of God's blessing them for their faith. A physician stated that he believed his house and cars and booming practice were results of God's rewarding him for his faithfulness. This wonderful Christian had been tainted by his own materialistic existence. Those who get puffed up over all they own should reevaluate the lives of the truly faithful who have been living in poverty and inconvenience so they can serve others. Wealth is not a reward for faithfulness or spiritual strength.

Those who get puffed up over all they own should reevaluate the lives of the truly faithful who have been living in poverty and inconvenience so they can serve others.

Before Sandy and I were married, we took a missionary trip to India. There we met the most Christlike person either of us has known on this earth. He was a physician practicing out of the Baptist Hospital in Bangalore, India. Seeing the need for emotional care of so many mentally ill people, he went back to school after his children had been raised and left home, and he obtained a degree in psychiatry. He then started a counseling center next to a Methodist church where he would see people free if they had no money.

While psychiatrists around the world drove expensive sports cars or had chauffeured limousines, he drove a car that had to be pushed to start. The only thing that worked consistently through the streets of Bangalore was the horn. On Sundays he would go to a small church in the slums just outside town and hold a service for faithful believers. We went with him to participate in the service.

The church was a small lean-to shack made of scrap boards and raw lumber. As the hot sun beat down on the roof, it became a sultry oven with extreme humidity; the open sewers outside pumped billows of odors through the church walls. The faithful walked, limped, and dragged themselves to that mat-covered room to worship.

No one made more than one hundred dollars a month; most made nothing. It was poverty at its most extreme. The people listened to the sermon, sang, prayed, and had communion. Then they did an astonishing thing. They gave their money. Having almost nothing, they gave very little, but the percentage of their earnings that went to God was extraordinarily high. Although they were barely able to feed their families, their donations were signs of great spiritual strength.

If God blessed people materially for their faithfulness, that slum area would have miraculously turned into a row of mansions or at least a subdivision of tract houses. But it did not because faith does not work that way.

HEALING AVAILABLE FOR ALL?

Kenneth Hagin and others like him "consider divine healing and perfect health both preferable and attainable. But critics accuse faith teachers of unbiblical dogmatism and a lack of compassion for the sick. Author and artist Joni Eareckson Tada, a quadriplegic, cited in a recent fund-raising letter for her ministry 'the insensitive nature of health-wealth theology,' which leaves disabled persons 'nearly shipwrecked.'"

—Bruce Barron, "Faith Healers: Moving Toward the
Mainstream?" Christianity Today, July 10, 1987, p. 50.

Our doctor friend did whatever he could to serve people in need. While others sit through retirement, he and his wife became a wonderful ministry team. His wisdom and insight are unparalleled by anyone I know. Yet he lived in a small house that did not even have hot running water. The material blessings have not come his way, but I have a hard time thinking of what he could do to have more faith. Many have more money, but few are closer to God.

If, in your harmful faith, you believe that the more faithful you are, the more material gain you will get, you can look forward to great disappointment. Many live a life of faith, and in the back of their minds they have this strange hope that the reward will be more money. In my experience, greater faith has often brought an end to financial wealth. For some reason, God has tempered a faithful follower in the fires of loss and financial poverty. They seem to prove that when all you have left is God, you get as much of God as you possibly can. The comforts of wealth often rob people of dependency on God. It is hard to believe God would bless someone with something that would mar that relationship. Although wealth is not bad, and can be a great blessing, it is no indicator of spiritual strength.

6. Investment Tithing

*THE MORE MONEY YOU GIVE TO GOD, THE MORE
MONEY HE WILL GIVE TO YOU*

It just is not so. You hear this all the time from fund raisers who need to manipulate you for their gain and the establishment of their empires. If you give your money to churches and other ministries so you can get more money back, save your money; you are wasting it. God is not a financial investment opportunity. He isn't "a good bet" to place your money on. What kind of faith would guarantee a return on money invested? That would not be faith; that would be a bank account.

Giving a portion of what you make is an act of faith going back to the days when the Jews would sacrifice the very best lamb and give

*Although wealth is not bad, and can be a great blessing,
it is no indicator of spiritual strength.*

They sacrificed to God because they wanted to show Him their love and dedication.

one-tenth of their earnings to the temple. This form of giving has always been an act of worship and an act of faith. They sacrificed to God because they wanted to show Him their love and dedication.

It was not a scheme for wealth accumulation. Today the element of sacrifice is not there. Too few understand time-honored principles of giving. Rather than sacrifice, they essentially give God a little tip, but they tip God far less than they would a waiter. The key in giving is motive. Do you give to honor God, or do you give to get?

An interesting phenomenon occurs when people give with godly motives. I have heard many people say that the money they have left over after giving to God seems to go further than when they kept all the money. They did not become wealthy, but they were much more satisfied with what they had. The worry factor was also greatly reduced. Once they gave the first portion of what they earned to God, they were better able to relax about how the rest would be spent. Putting their money where their faith was allowed them to have a stronger belief in a God who would provide all their needs.

I never had strong faith in God until I trusted Him with my money. Once my faith was strong enough to let go of the money, I was able to grow spiritually as never before. I believe this to be a common experi-

WHAT DOES IT MEAN TO LEAD A VERY CHRISTIAN LIFE?

"One-fourth of U.S. adults who state their religious preference as Christian claim to lead a 'very Christian' life. . . . The top categories in terms of descriptions of 'person who lives a very Christian life' are: a good person (22%), someone who helps other people (19%), one who seeks God (16%), an honest and trustworthy person (11%), happy and contented (10%), charitable, giving or kind (10%). 'A person who lives a very unChristian life' is most often described as self-centered (16%), a person who does not follow the will of God (14%), unconcerned or uncaring (14%), indulges in immoral conduct (11%), unhappy or sad (10%), lost, without direction (9%)."

—*Princeton Research Center,* PRRC Emerging Trends, *vol. 4, no. 3, March 1982, p. 1.*

ence with others who finally learn to write out the first check to the church. Giving to God first is a real test of motives. It is an act of faith that strengthens commitment at every other level.

Giving is often the first step in moving out of merely believing into taking action. When people do not commit their money in this way but use it as a ransom for future blessings, they might as well toss their coins in a wishing well. Giving money to get more money always ends up with their getting less God. If the motivation is for money, faithless givers have chosen a master: money. No one has ever been able to serve two masters at once. Money will master the heart and rob the greedy of any relationship with God.

7. Salvation by Works

I CAN WORK MY WAY TO HEAVEN

Just as there are those who think they can get God's love by being good, or those who think they can overcome some bad event in the past by working hard, there are those who believe heaven can be earned. They spend their lives in a working frenzy, trying to do more and more so God will look down, observe their fine works, and decide they will be fit to enter heaven. It seems that most people working so hard have never resolved some tremendously debilitating issues from the past. If they could deal with those issues, perhaps they wouldn't need to punish themselves through all of the work they hope will be the key to eternal life.

A man in a small town had kept a secret from his wife that very few people knew. But those who did know his secret never told his wife. They were all willing participants in his personal cover-up. The man had been married before for only a short while, and then he divorced his wife. When he met the woman he wanted to be his second wife, he discovered she would never marry a previously married man. He loved her, so he decided not to tell her about the first marriage. After a month of dating it seemed less appropriate to tell her than it did in the first week. Months of courtship made his love grow deeper and the truth more difficult to reveal. He just never got around to telling her.

The key in giving is motive. Do you give to honor God or do you give to get?

In this cover-up mode where the inside is dirty, they try to clean up the outside so it looks spotless.

Ten years into the marriage, there was no way he was going to blow the whistle on himself.

His dilemma created one of the most driven businessmen and church workers I have known. He would do anything to help someone. It went well beyond servanthood; it was an illness. His marriage could not have been worse from the revealed secret than it was from his religiosity and perfectionism. He died at forty-five. I think he discovered then that most of his work had been in vain. If only he could have revealed the secret, it would have saved him and his family a lot of misery.

Many others live like this due to some event of the past, some terrible secret they fear would cause rejection if they revealed it to others. In this cover-up mode where the inside is dirty, they try to clean up the outside so it looks spotless. When you see them, you think they are perfect, incapable of any wrong. They succeed in fooling most of the people because it is hard to see through the mask of perfectionism to the pain and other problems on the inside. Their drive to be and look good is deceptive as they try to earn enough points to be accepted into heaven.

I'm glad I don't have to function under a system like this. I have messed up so many times, there is no way I could ever be good enough to make it to heaven. I know I could never make up for my messes by church work, church attendance, or bribes to God. I have to trust that He has forgiven me for my sins, just as He said He would. I must believe in Christ and what He did to wipe out the consequences of sin. Believing that behavior gains one entrance into heaven is a no-win situation.

Good behavior as a ticket to heaven is a much-taught theology. I was having dinner with one of my friends and his family. He and his two girls were discussing heaven. One asked him what a person needed to do to get to heaven. He told his kids that if you were a good person, you would make it. He said that God honors good work and lets those who measure up be with Him forever.

Believing it is behavior that gains entrance into heaven is a no-win situation that can drive a person crazy.

I thought of how sad that must be for a young girl to hear. She will think of that every day she messes up, gets punished, or just can't seem to live up to the standards that the other family members have set for childhood behavior. It must be very depressing for a child to believe the one thing that you have to do to get to heaven is the one thing you cannot do.

Heaven is a gift. It cannot be earned. Those who are trying to work their way to heaven possess a harmful faith that will drive them into a useless frenzy of activity, exhaustion, and depression. Those who live around these people will also find it very difficult to live comfortably as the driven workers impose their standards on the rest of the family. What a relief it must be to discover that you cannot earn a place in heaven!

8. Spiteful God

PROBLEMS IN YOUR LIFE RESULT FROM SOME PARTICULAR SIN

A parent hoping and praying for a normal child but ending up with a defective one is in pain beyond comprehension. My wife and I have some friends who have been through this devastation with two girls. Both have been born with severe birth defects. One will never outgrow the defect; the other has a good chance of developing normally. The parents' great pain was not lessened by the remarks of some Christian friends who told them that there must be some hidden sin in their lives for which God was disciplining them. Their grief was only compounded by the insensitive remarks.

It is amazing to me how many people believe God is too busy to be involved with people, and yet in bad times they seem to think He has plenty of time for destruction. In other words, He is not there to help, but He still may hurt. Although many are living in this self-inflicted misery, it is a sad way to live. All problems are not results of sin; they are results of reality.

Those who are trying to work their way to heaven possess a harmful faith that will drive them into a useless frenzy of activity, exhaustion, and depression.

Pain is often a result of sin but not necessarily a punishment for it.

Life is imperfect. No matter how hard we try to change that, it will not change. Believers or not, we are going to experience tragedy and failure as long as we live in this difficult world. God has given us the freedom to make choices. Some choices will be better than others. The worst ones will cause us discomfort and pain, but the pain will not always be the result of God's punishment for sin. When people play with fire, often they feel the heat, and some get burned. The pain is from the fire, not the punishment of God. Sin is like that. Pain is often a result of sin but not necessarily a punishment for it.

In the Bible is a story of Jesus and a blind man. The disciples asked Him who had sinned to cause the man's blindness. Was it the father or the mother or the man? Jesus replied that none of them had sinned. Plain and simple. He told them to forget about the sins-of-the-fathers idea because it did not apply. This belief was poisoning faith thousands of years ago. Christ told them that the blindness was not a result of some particular sin. (See John 9:1–7.)

Problems result from poor decisions, negative circumstances, and the fact that we live in an imperfect world. God does not choose to remove the imperfections, and until He does, we must deal with those problems. To inflict further difficulty on ourselves by believing for every problem there is a sin behind it serves only to drive us further from true faith in God. Rather than focus on a past sin that does not exist, it is better for us to focus on how God can use the problem to build our faith and the faith of others.

LONG-TERM BELIEFS

Gordon Melton, author of *Encyclopedic Handbook of Cults in America,* said, "What we call the cult experience is a one-generation phenomenon. It is the experience of a first generation of intense converts. You know it's not so much opposition to cults that makes them change. It's time." This is very different from true Christianity. Over time the faith has spread and endured much opposition.

> —Jay Kinney and Kevin Kelly, "Why Cults Flourish, Interview with Gordon Melton," Whole Earth Review, Spring 1987, p. 51.

*Problems result from poor decisions, negative circum-
stances, and the fact that we live in an imperfect world.*

We cannot rule out that some problems directly result from certain
sins: intravenous drug users can get AIDS; theft can land you in jail;
arrogance and selfish greed can lead to the pain of loneliness. God
does not "zap" us each time we choose to sin, but if we partake in
sinful behavior, we may in effect be zapping ourselves.

9. Slavery of the Faithful

I MUST NOT STOP MEETING OTHERS' NEEDS

An old joke, though not a very funny one, is full of insight. It is
about a mother who worked all her life meeting every need of every
family member. After her children were raised and out of the house,
she was ready for a wonderful life. She had lived for everyone else, and
just when she was ready to take time for herself, she died. On her
tombstone they wrote, "Now maybe I can get some rest!"

A lot of great moms out there have worked themselves to death
meeting everyone else's needs, taking no time for themselves. They
see themselves more as slaves to God and family than as free persons
equal to others. For them, life is one miserable sacrifice after another.
I am sure God will honor that dedication, but I think He would be a
lot happier if they would take some time for themselves. After all, He
created them and loves them just as much as the people they so inces-
santly serve.

Women in the nineties have a lot of pressure on them. Their children leave home later, marrying in their late twenties. Their parents
live longer and often need intensive care. Just when a mother finally
scoots her children out the door, she often stands there welcoming her
mother or father or in-laws into the home because there is no other
alternative. She spends the next ten years playing mother to elderly
people, and before it is all done, she has spent 90 percent of her adult
life as a caregiver. This role frequently produces anger, depression,
and resentment of God and family. A late nervous breakdown is a
likely outcome.

It does not have to be this way, and thousands are starting to find
out that there are alternatives to modern slavery. The whole codepen-

dency movement is opening the eyes of many who thought they were helping out of love when they were actually helping because they knew of no other way to exist. They become so wrapped up in everyone else that they lose who they are and what they want to accomplish. One woman described it this way: she was so codependent, so caught up in others' lives and meeting their needs, she said that if she had a near-death experience, someone else's life would probably flash before her eyes.

It is healthy for all of us to recognize that we have some basic needs that must be met. The codependency movement has done that for us. However, it has been carried to such an extreme that some people question whether or not every nice, loving, or serving deed is a codependent act. There must be a balance. It is a wonderful life when it is spent serving others. Putting other people first seems to be a theme in every religion. The Christian faith is one of self-sacrifice, but carried to an extreme, it can become a compulsive act rather than an act of compassion.

After all, what good does it do to meet needs of others if that produces so much anger in you that you cannot relate to them in a loving manner? Why should a person work hard for others if the end result is exhaustion and depression, disabling the person and causing a break with reality? Each helping heart must self-assess needs and determine if some have been neglected that could cause major problems later on. God does not just love the rest of the world and expect you to serve those He loves. He loves you, too, and He knows you have needs and wants those met.

An analogy of hunger helps explain the concept. You cannot feed the poor if you do not eat. Sacrificing your need to eat will kill you, and then you won't be around to feed anyone else. The same applies to the emotional and spiritual dimensions of life. When they are not met, those areas shut down. The longer they go unmet, the greater the problems that arise.

Christ came to serve people, and yet He took time to maintain His health so He could meet others' needs. There was balance in His life. Christ took time to eat. He took time to rest. He took time to pray. He

---

After all, what good does it do to meet needs of others if that produces so much anger in you that you cannot relate to them in a loving manner?

could not go on until His own needs were met. He spent time alone, getting away from the crowds.

Likewise, Christ calls those who choose to follow Him to serve others as He did. Similarly, I think He would desire for all of us a place of rest and a time to regain perspective. If you do not have that time because you are driven to meet the needs of everyone else, take a second look at where you are. If you are angry, exhausted, and depressed, take the time to back away and find the rest that God wants for you.

10. Irrational Submission

I MUST ALWAYS SUBMIT TO AUTHORITY

Growing up in Texas, I witnessed some strange marriages and beliefs about marriage. The issue of submission was always a big controversy. Some people believed the ultimate act of faith was to submit to an authority that was abusive. My parents helped one woman who lived with an alcoholic husband. He would get drunk and beat her; then she would hide in her home for a couple of weeks after each incident so no one would see the bruises. He was a very angry man, and the alcohol would bring out the worst in him. The abuse grew more intense until finally he broke her jaw. Yet she stayed with the man.

My father became involved in the situation and helped the woman talk about the abuse and why she continued to live that way. She revealed that a pastor had told her she must stay even if it meant that she would be killed from the abuse. He told her that she could have no greater act of faith than to die while submitting to her husband. He promised her that God would honor her decision to be loyal and faithful to authority.

In working with people in need of psychiatric care, I have seen some very depressed mothers who let their children be abused because they didn't think they could counter the head of the house. It was too late and their children had been badly hurt before they realized that was not what God wanted. The realization that they could

---

Christ came to serve people, and yet He took time to maintain His health so He could meet others' needs.

have done something to stop the abuse produced severe depression and emotional turmoil. Their desire to be submissive was poisonous to themselves and to their families. Their faith was also destroyed because they questioned how God could allow those things to happen.

The submission issue is not just for abused wives. It applies also to employees of unethical managers. Certain things are not right, and God wants you to move out of those circumstances or make the deadly secrets known. The God I know would not want a wife to stay in a home where there is the risk of death or bodily damage. God would not want a check to be written out by a submissive accountant as a bribe because the accountant was submitting to a boss involved in wrongdoing. And when governments have become oppressive and abusive, the protests of faithful believers who felt they must stand up to unfaithful laws have produced needed changes over the years.

I was aware of an organization in Texas that had a misguided leader. He was pursuing all sorts of wrong activities, one of which was an affair. A secretary there was the only one willing to see that the leader was flawed, at least he was when he was with a certain woman. The secretary sacrificed her comfortable position to challenge the authority of the organization and her boss. No one believed her.

Although she lost her job, I believe she did the right thing. Fortunately for her, she was vindicated later when it was found that the same man had a part in other wrongful activities. Many people would not consider an affair a problem that a secretary should be concerned with. They would say a secretary should not question her boss's personal life and a boss should not question his secretary's personal life. But it was a Christian organization. The affair affected his job performance, and it harmed his integrity in a job where integrity matters. As a result of his actions, the integrity of the organization was in jeopardy. The secretary did what most would not do. She placed the principle of integrity above the principle of submission.

When authority is well placed, it respects the individuals it has authority over. When it is not well placed, it is our responsibility to expose the abuse and be part of the solution. Christ challenged the authorities who had turned their faith away from God and into a practice of following rules developed by men. The oppressive rules were

---

Silent submission in the face of violence, dishonesty, and abuse will only allow or enable that abuse to be passed to new generations.

taught as God's rules but were merely the tenets of men. The teaching of man's rules as God's way always produces problems for the followers.

Christ stood up to those people and told them they were wrong. He tried to produce change by what He said to them and the life He lived. If we are to follow His example, we must intervene when submitting is part of abuse. We must have the courage to follow Christ's example and overturn the system, be it a marriage or an organization, if that system is wrong. Silent submission in the face of violence, dishonesty, and abuse will only allow or enable that abuse to be passed to new generations. Developing a transitional generation out of abuse requires declaring that the abuse must end—even if it means risking financial security. Faith in God allows us to move into uncomfortable zones for the sake of honoring Him and proving our faith is real.

Submission to authority is a powerful principle that is protective and liberating. When we submit to God, when we act according to His parameters, we are freed, not bound. When children submit to their parents, they are protected. The experience of a husband and a wife submitting to each other is liberating rather than confining. The relationship is strengthened and better defined as each person finds the areas that need and demand submission. Submission is part of God's plan, and it is a biblical principle. Submitting to a husband, to a boss, or to a parent is a model for our relationship with God and helps us grow closer to Him. Rebelling, confronting, and not submitting are to be done only in cases that merit that type of behavior. When God's work is compromised or when a person's life or well-being is at stake, blind submission must be replaced with responsible actions.

11. Christian Inequality

GOD USES ONLY SPIRITUAL GIANTS

This generation has seen many so-called spiritual giants fall. The myth that if you are in the ministry, you are always a wonderful and dedicated human being has been shattered. Yet some people still do

---

When God's work is compromised or when a person's life or well-being is at stake, blind submission must be replaced with responsible actions.

> *God often uses those who have major flaws or who have been through a great deal of pain to accomplish many vital tasks for His kingdom.*

not believe we are all on equal footing. They believe God has called some into service, the ministers, and the rest must assume second-class status to the "great called ones." Rather than minister to others' needs, many prefer to pass that on to those who have a special calling to do so. Plus, they feel that because they are such terrible sinners, God could not use them anyway. Many fail to receive the blessings that come from ministering to others because of the belief that God uses only the perfect, the near perfect, or those He called into a special ministry.

A preacher in the twentieth century can talk to millions of people with one broadcast on television. Because one person's reach can be so broad, others start to think of their contribution as meaningless. They become lazy in their service and are not motivated to find a way to further the kingdom of God. They neglect the gifts God has given them because they are not as great as others'. They view themselves as inferior believers.

In my life as well as in Scripture, I have seen nothing but the opposite to be true. God often uses those who have major flaws or who have been through a great deal of pain to accomplish many vital tasks for His kingdom. Look at Moses the stutterer, Paul with his thorn in the flesh, and David the adulterer. It seems that God uses the "spiritual giants" despite their flaws.

No one is too messed up for God to use, and no task is too unimportant to matter to God. On the sidelines and in the lower levels of the organizations where the very visible ministers work, hundreds of faithful invisible believers do the valuable, powerful work of prayer, the foundation for greatness in organizations as well as in people. When people pray, miracles occur, people change, countries develop new political systems, and God unleashes His power.

Everyone has some gift granted by God that can be exercised in a mighty way. Through stories about people who developed their tal-

> *Out of a pure faith we must act first; then we will be amazed at just how much God can do with so little.*

Sometimes we wait for God to do what God is waiting for us to do.

ents and others who neglected their talents, Jesus communicated our need to cultivate our talents. When we do that, we will accomplish greater things than we ever imagined. When we do not develop our gifts, chances are, we will never be satisfied or fulfilled. Some could never speak in front of over fifty people, but they have felt comfortable for years teaching a Sunday school class of five. Year after year they teach, not knowing the long-term impact they have on people's lives. Although they may belittle their contribution, God is using them to lay a foundation for years of future service.

When I was in the third grade, my public school teacher was a great woman of faith. She wanted her kids to know the Bible when they left her nine months later. Each day after we returned from lunch, my teacher would read from a huge Bible story book. The stories started with Adam and Eve, and before the year was over, we had parted the Red Sea, gone with Moses through the wilderness, and moved into the Promised Land.

Those stories increased my faith greatly. I believed them. And I believed that if God could watch over the Israelites for forty years in the wilderness, He could watch over me. I learned a lot from those stories. They taught me of God's power and His forgiveness. When I messed up later in life, I remembered how His chosen people messed up, and He always found a way back for them.

There have always been people who have had an impact on the world in small but powerful ways. They take what God gives them and use it the best they can. They don't stop to compare their gifts with others'; they just trust God to use them. We must not allow sins of the past or limited gifts to stand in the way of working for God and being used by God. A simple prayer to God, telling Him to take what we have and use it as He sees fit, can open up a whole world of opportunity. God is big enough to take the simplest contribution and make it as significant as anything the greatest of the "giants" could do. He wants us to trust Him to do wonderful things with our skills. Out of a

Too often in the name of waiting on God, people fail to take responsibility or action.

pure faith we must act first; then we will be amazed at just how much God can do with so little.

12. Passivity

HAVING TRUE FAITH MEANS WAITING FOR GOD TO HELP ME AND DOING NOTHING UNTIL HE DOES

This harmful belief is the foundation for laziness and disaster. I have seen many people hurt as they waited around for God to do something God expected them to do. Let me repeat that just so you don't miss one of the biggest problems facing dedicated believers. Sometimes we wait for God to do what God is waiting for us to do. Wives of alcoholics allow drinking to continue when taking the steps to intervene would reverse the course of the problem. Church leaders allow a minister to crash and burn under the influence of sex, silver, or self-obsession. They pray God will change him when they need to exercise the tough side of love and confront the person with the character defects that need attention. Parents allow a child to grow up spoiled and immature because they pray God will protect him rather than force the child to take responsibility for himself.

Too often in the name of waiting on God, people fail to take responsibility or action. They wait for God to perform a miracle while God waits for them to act. Remember, they call them miracles because they rarely happen. It is often easier to wait on a miracle than to do the difficult thing and take action. Tomorrow, the pain will still be there or the person will still be involved with the destructive behavior unless they take action today.

God wants an active faith. As that faith is developed, the relationship with God is stretched during uncomfortable times when we must act beyond our comfort zones. These painful times make us more reliant on God. We seek His comfort as we strive to accomplish those things that would be easier to delay. The risk we take in accomplishing each one brings us closer to God and builds up our faith.

I met a couple who loved their son very much, even though he had disgraced them repeatedly with his drinking and drug taking. There seemed to be no end to the agony they went through for him. Instead of making him face his responsibilities, they paid his way and made life "safe" for him. They prayed that God would heal him of his affliction. They felt it was their job to support him while God worked on the addiction. One night in a drunken stupor, he walked off a balcony and was killed. Those parents had to live with the guilt of knowing they never did anything to help. They only enabled his negative behavior as they waited for God to perform a miracle. Out of a harmful faith in God they loved their son to death.

I am aware of a wife who let her husband's unfaithfulness go unchecked. She knew he was running around, but she fervently prayed that God would change her husband. When she developed genital warts, she wondered how it could have happened. When she came down with herpes, she knew the cause. Her husband left her with a gift that cannot be cured. If she had taken action, she could have spared herself a lifetime disease and perhaps saved her marriage.

The Bible makes many references, especially in the Psalms, to waiting on the Lord. Some people have misinterpreted waiting on the Lord as a call to roll over and play dead. Waiting on the Lord does not mean turning off the brain. Waiting on the Lord is waiting on God's timing and power. If we are unemployed, we should not use waiting on the Lord as an excuse to just sit and idly wait for a job to magically appear. God wants us to look for a job and go through interviews, all the while remembering that God is still God and we must wait on Him.

Waiting on God for help does not mean we should not use the mind He gave us or the will we have to accomplish things. We must take action and do those things within our power and trust God to do those things not in our power. The balance of this approach will accomplish much without producing a driven need to do it all alone. God gave us all many strengths. He expects us to use those strengths while we depend on His strength to assist us.

13. Biblical Exclusivity

IF IT'S NOT IN THE BIBLE, IT ISN'T RELEVANT

The battle between religion and psychology has been waged on this harmful belief for years. Many have nothing to do with anything relating to emotions unless it is in Scripture. Their train of thought goes

Waiting on the Lord is waiting on God's timing and power.

like this: *If there is not a Scripture to back the idea, it must be harmful.* This is close to the truth but not quite on the mark. True faith means that a person should not do anything that goes against something from God's Word. It doesn't mean that *every* behavior or insight into life is going to be found there.

The Bible is not a manual for brain surgery. It does not tell us not to smoke crack cocaine. There is no Scripture on what music is bad or what is good. How to operate a computer has been left out. We must figure out some things for ourselves; when we do, we should base our figuring on the foundations of Scripture. If that is a priority, what we think and feel about things will continue to line up with biblical truth. If we don't start with that foundation, we are victims of the crowd and the mood of current thought. When we have no foundation, we get into trouble and poison our faith with half-truths. But just because something is not in Scripture doesn't mean it is evil or a half-truth.

One woman who came into New Life Treatment Centers had been dealing with depression for years. She had been sent to a psychiatrist who diagnosed her problem as a manic-depressive condition needing medication. Without medication, she would never be able to maintain a stable life, keep a job, or relate to her family. She was fine with her medication, and her life improved dramatically. For the first time in years she was happy and able to accomplish things without breaking down.

Then she made the mistake of attending a church that frowned on anything other than the Bible to help a person cope with life. The members found out she was on medication and confronted her with her "lack of faith." They told her she was a new creature; old things were behind her, and everything was new. That included her problem with depression. She was instructed to stop taking the medication and have faith that God would meet her needs and help her stay in control if she had enough faith.

Our patient blindly trusted the minister and stopped the medication. For a couple of weeks it was difficult, but she managed to ride a religious high until her body could no longer respond to her. Then in a fit of depression she slit her wrists, called the people in the church office to tell them, and hung up. They called an ambulance as the men on staff rushed over to help the woman. When they arrived ahead of

But just because something is not in Scripture doesn't mean it is evil or a half-truth.

the ambulance, they found her lying unconscious in a pool of blood. They tried to stop the bleeding as they waited for the paramedics. Fortunately, they made it in time to save the woman.

This event had a dynamic impact on the staff of the church. It changed the way they thought about medication and the need for some people to have help beyond what the church can provide. The church had a counseling ministry that, before this incident, instructed people to fast, pray, and read Scripture to handle any problem. The woman now goes to the same church where there is no longer any problem with her need to take medication. The members realize that the medication does not stand in the way of people's obtaining help or growing closer to God. It is the one thing that allows many to continue to develop a relationship with God. The medication is a gift from God to help some individuals function in the real world. Of course it can be abused, but that does not mean it is evil when used as prescribed.

Why do some ministers function out of the belief that the only truth is found in Scripture? Why do they resist assistance from counselors outside the church? Why do they reject the idea that many faithful believers who have degrees in mental health are following God's calling for their lives? I think many ministers are threatened by anything outside their field. They want to play physician, counselor, and parent to the flock. They want nothing of anything that might challenge their authority over their people. They often will lead people down a path of misery rather than suggest the individuals get help from a specialist.

At one time few counselors could be trusted to build rather than destroy faith. Now there are thousands who can integrate counseling and faith to help a person. Ministers need to feel comfortable in suggesting help beyond what the church can provide. If a minister ever needed brain surgery, I doubt he or she would have the same feelings. At that point I think he or she would seek out someone who knew more about brain surgery than was revealed in Scripture.

The balance between real and misled faith lies at the root of one's

SATANISM INQUIRIES GROWING

"The number of inquiries about Satanism received by the Chicago-based Cult Awareness Network has increased from 5 to 100 per month."

—Terry C. Muck, "Salt Substitutes—Grassroots gullibility for spiritual counterfeits demonstrates a great hunger for things of the spirit," Christianity Today, February 3, 1989, p. 14.

beliefs. Is your faith based on godly truth, or is it based on a make-it-up-as-you-go philosophy? Those who make it up lead very insecure lives. Those who base life on God's truth and have faith in Him develop a security found no other place. But to believe that every fact needed to survive is contained in Scripture is naive or the result of manipulation. Once a misled believer wakes up to this reality, he or she finds a new world that does not need to be feared.

14. Heavenly Matchmaking

GOD WILL FIND ME A PERFECT MATE

Lisa was raised in a conservative Christian home in a small town in Texas. She came to Baylor University as a naive and beautiful young woman. The boys lined up to ask her out. I'm afraid I wasn't eligible for the line. She was too pretty and too good. Lisa loved to date and to get the attention. She stayed true to her belief of waiting until marriage to have a sexual relationship. She was determined to marry as a virgin.

Lisa's senior year was a good one. She dated a senior from a respected fraternity. They became very serious, and following the traditional meeting of the parents, they decided to marry after graduation. Lisa had been taught that through prayer and faith, God would provide her with the perfect mate. Her system said that someone out there was perfect for her in every way and God would deliver him to her. Her senior-year romance was what she had been looking for. She loved Jim and was excited to marry him.

They were married, and shortly afterward, Lisa began having terrible headaches. The doctor discovered a tumor that required brain surgery. She needed the perfect mate God had provided. He stood by her through the ordeal. He was supportive in every way. She recovered fully after a year of bed rest and chemotherapy. At the end of that year, when she was ready to resume her life, Jim left her and eventually married another.

Coming off the surgery and chemotherapy, Lisa was devastated by the divorce. It pushed her into a very heavy depression. She had been

Hurtful faith always has an element of quick fix and once-and-for-all thinking.

deserted by Jim, but she focused most of her anger on God. How could He have let her down? How could He have taken away the perfect mate she had longed for and saved herself for? It was an extremely difficult time for her. Her faith was shaken. A new reality about God crashed in on her. Eventually, she accepted her new awareness about God and life, but it was not easy.

The perfect mate belief has caused tremendous heartache for many people. They search for the one person God is to provide, and when they think they have found him or her, they expect marriage to be instant bliss. When nirvana does not occur, the naive believers will move from a faith in a God who provides perfect marriage partners to a belief in an impersonal God who probably does not care about them. Going from one extreme to the other, they lose faith in God, and they lose hope for a wonderful future.

After Sandy and I married, we had a very rocky first six months. We were convinced we had married the wrong partners. Whoever God had picked for each of us was lost forever. We would argue, turn around, and quietly shake our heads and murmur, "Well I've married the wrong person." Sandy sometimes slept in her clothes just in case she wanted to leave in the middle of the night. If we had not been totally committed to each other and to marriage, we would not have made it through the first year. The change came when we stopped focusing on the imperfections of God's perfect mate and started working on the relationship. We went from faith in a onetime event that would fix our problems for life to a life of work that helped us grow toward each other and a faith in God.

The perfect mate belief is a nice idea, but it has some major problems. I would hate to think that there was one perfect person for me and I could never be happy with anyone else. What if that one was killed in a plane crash before I met her? Would I be stuck with number two all my life? What if the perfect mate made a mistake and picked someone else? Would I be forced to live with next best because of another person's mistake? If I marry God's perfect mate and she dies, am I destined to be married to a number seven or fifteen?

I don't like that system, and I haven't found much evidence that it is the way God works. God has a will for each of us, and that will could involve any one of several people. There is a will for marriage, work, and every other area of life. But in addition to this direction from God, He gave us free will. We are not robots programmed to make the "right" choices. God's way is bigger than that. He can work in our lives, no matter what foolish or wise decisions we make.

You could probably choose from several people to find someone to be happily married to. Some choices would be better for you than others; some would be a disaster. God wants you to use your faith and your ability to reason in attempting to find a person who will be wonderful as a spouse. The more you use your mind, the more likely you are to discover aspects that could be problems later. Courtship is no time to overlook the obvious because of a belief that God has sent a person your way.

Hurtful faith always has an element of quick fix and once-and-for-all thinking, and if you apply it to mate selection, one of the most important decisions in life can produce a disastrous situation for you and your future kids. You need to make informed decisions and not rely on blind faith. Six sessions of premarital counseling go a long way in building a good start for a marriage. Opinions of friends and family can also help.

Once the marriage begins, nothing will take the place of realistic thinking and hard work. No matter how perfect the person was before marriage, flaws will continue to be revealed after the ceremony. If you aren't expecting them, they can be horrifying. If you realize that all marriages require effort, you are more likely to get busy, go to work, and create a great marriage. Marriages are never made in heaven; they are developed on earth by two committed partners.

15. Pollyanna Perspective

EVERYTHING THAT HAPPENS TO ME IS GOOD

A preacher on the radio described the plight of a woman who married a man, lived with him ten years, and watched him die of cancer. A woman in her church insisted she be happy about it: "God has done a good thing. Everything He does is good." Two years later, the woman was married again, and after one year of marriage, her husband died. Again, the lady from church demanded she claim this as a great and good victory provided by God. The woman recovered from her loss, and the preacher went on to say, the woman married for a third time and shortly afterward discovered her third husband had cancer.

They deny how they really feel and delay dealing with the pain and agony they feel due to death or loss.

Some people in the church believe everything is an immediate blessing. To them, only a real Christian is able to say, "Praise the Lord!" as the house burns down, the car is totaled, a child is hurt, or the cow dies. I believe if you told these people they were going to be fried in oil, they would grin and say, "Praise the Lord anyway!"

Is this real? Can a person in touch with reality be grateful in times of crises? Is it a real test of faith to be able to greet each new piece of bad news with a big grin and a trite expression? I don't think so. I think it is evidence of unreal people manufacturing an unreal response. They try to rationalize that everything is good, even though it looks bad, feels bad, and is bad. They grow up believing that a positive attitude must be used to face every crisis. They deny how they really feel and delay dealing with the pain and agony they feel due to death or loss.

The woman who lost two husbands and was about to lose another was not grateful nor did she believe the events were good. She was quite angry until she resolved her hurt over the losses. Years later she looked back and said that none of the problems was good but that God used each one for her good. He took the crisis and made it a faith-building experience.

The widow's perspective is much more accurate than the lady who demanded each new loss be viewed as a good thing. They were not good; they were terrible losses. But God takes such losses and over time makes them into something good. God will work everything together for our good if we will allow Him. Bad things provide God a stage to produce something good on.

I have worked with many alcoholics who go from acceptance of their problem to gratitude. They mourn the loss of being able to drink, and then finally they see their lives as more meaningful because of recovery. The admission of alcoholism is a starting point for maturing and concentrating on life's deeper meaning. It is not instant and the problems caused from drinking were not good, but allowing God to work through the problems produced many good things.

People in pain have enough problems without some well-meaning folks trying to short-circuit the grief process by declaring everything as a good event sent from God. I think God *allows* bad things, He does not *cause* them. The toxic thinking that all things are good makes peo-

---

He took the crisis and made it a faith-building experience.

ple question whether or not God is a cruel God. It forces them to see God as a cruel joker who inflicts pain and expects His followers to be happy about it. This perspective is a means of avoiding reality. It is an addictive habit, producing quick relief, blocking reality with poisonous faith. A loving God wants the best for us and is grieved when the best is missed. True faith in Him allows these bad things to be woven together in a protective covering that grows stronger in fiber and softer to the touch.

16. Bullet-Proof Faith

A STRONG FAITH WILL PROTECT ME FROM PROBLEMS AND PAIN

On the celebration of the one hundredth birthday of Rose Kennedy (mother of John, Bobby, and Ted Kennedy), NBC aired a tribute to the matriarch of the United States' most famous family. I was surprised to hear of the depth of her faith. A daughter died in a plane crash, a son died in World War II, and two sons, John and Bobby, were killed by assassins' bullets. She had reason to be angry with God. Her faith had not protected her children. And yet, she was not angry. She said that she often would think of how Mary felt as she watched her Son die by crucifixion. Rose expected no less or more for herself. She shared in the sufferings of others who had great faith.

For many, a belief in God and the practice of faith are just fine until tragedy strikes. Then there is the realization that the practice of faith does not add up brownie points of protection. It does not bring God's intervention. Bad things do happen to good people, and it has nothing to do with degrees of faith. We live in a world where big animals eat little animals. Decay, rot, and death are realities. Faith provides perspective, endurance, and purpose through the tough times, but it will not protect anyone from them.

This harmful belief isn't just conjured up by unknowing believers. It is preached from many pulpits across the land. It is used manipula-

Faith provides perspective, endurance, and purpose through the tough times, but it will not protect anyone from them.

tively to bring people to Christ. Rather than seek Christ, they seek relief. Then when evidence of lack of protection confronts them in the form of a death or other loss, sufferers become nonbelievers. They were never true believers to begin with, however. True believers know that those who walked with Christ were beset by pain, poverty, tragedy, poor health, beatings, and other problems that stretched their faith, but the problems were faith builders. They drew believers closer to God because their faith was real *before* the difficulties started. Those who believe because they want protection have picked the wrong faith; in believing, we often invite problems that were not there beforehand. Those who preach this poisonous faith have ruined many lives; the individuals turned away when they learned the hard truth about life.

If you're disillusioned because you were sold a form of faith that didn't pan out, you're not alone. Your pain is shared by many others who had to deal with tragedy and at the same time resolve many harmful issues with their beliefs. Their disappointments in God increase their pain, just as they may have increased yours. Let the Great Teacher use your pain to bring you closer to Him. It does not have to be a barrier to God. It can be a bridge.

17. Vindictive God

GOD HATES SINNERS, IS ANGRY WITH ME, AND WANTS TO PUNISH ME

The view of God as an angry, vindictive old man ready to hurl lightning at those who get out of step is pervasive. Some people do not accept a real God because they fear Him too much. They write Him off as a myth because they are so afraid of what He might do if He was real. And yet, He is real, and He loves those He created.

A loving God is an incongruity for many people because they were raised in a family where an angry father inflicted his wrath on every member. Because a concept of God is frequently shaped by the relationship with one's father, having unresolved feelings about a father can poison a relationship with God. Individuals come to believe God is

People live their whole lives in constant fear of a God out of control who might make them the next target.

angry, just as their fathers were angry. They may even associate all love with anger. Until the father issues are resolved, the God issues will remain to cloud faith.

Ever since God wiped out Sodom and Gomorrah, there has been a rumor that He is very angry with all of us here on earth. We envision a God not just angry with the world but angry with specific individuals, ready to send down His wrath. People live their whole lives in constant fear of a God out of control who might make them the next target. This view of God prevents a personal relationship with Him and produces tremendous fear and anxiety.

The confusion arises over the just nature of God and the balance of His character. Does He get angry? Look at the people of Sodom and Gomorrah. They were living ungodly lives of self-obsession, lust, and pleasure. Their wayward lifestyle resulted in fire and brimstone from an angry God. God finally had to inflict the punishment that was deserved for such self-indulgence. He loved those people, but in the face of total disregard for Him, He destroyed them. In God's economy, sin must be paid for.

Fortunately, the coming of Christ was designed to change all of that. What animal sacrifices did before Christ's coming, His atoning death was to do forever. His life was offered in place of ours. His sacrifice enables us to flee the justice that should be involved. Christ paid the necessary price that wipes away our sin and wrongdoing so that we can enter into a relationship with a holy and perfect God.

Sin may produce dire consequences that should not be mistaken for God's anger. An unwed teenager who gets pregnant should not look at her circumstance as punishment from God; it is the natural result of an action she chose to take part in. God has created an ordered world where there is a direct relationship between cause and effect. If we do *A*, then the result is most likely going to be *B*. It would be God's punishment, but it is most likely the consequences of our negative choices. We do so many things with undesirable results that in essence, we punish ourselves; God chose to punish us, but we are so busy punishing ourselves, He often does not have to.

When the AIDS epidemic hit the scene, many ministers said God was angry with homosexuals and was sending a plague to wipe them out. At a time when men and women of faith should have been reach-

We do so many things with undesirable results that in essence, we punish ourselves.

HOW TO EASE DEPRESSION

To ease feelings of depression, we do these things:

	Total	Men	Women
Telephone a friend	44%	29%	58%
Get together with friends	36%	33%	39%
Watch TV	34%	35%	32%
Listen to music	29%	27%	31%
Read	24%	21%	27%
Try to figure it out	24%	23%	25%
Pray	24%	18%	30%
Eat	22%	16%	26%
Sleep	20%	19%	20%
Clean house	20%	7%	31%
Never get depressed	4%	5%	3%

—Source: The Roper Organization, Inc., New York City, 1988, as reported in "American Voices," American Demographics, September 1989, p. 16.

ing out to those who were dying, many were standing back and yelling, "I told you so!" The angry-God belief was used as an excuse to condemn not acts of homosexuality but the homosexuals themselves. Many dying from AIDS have sought to restore their relationship with God, but the anger of so many preaching the plague theory has caused them to search for God as far away from a church as possible.

The plague scenario doesn't make sense and I think many ministers have figured that out. If God was sending plagues to wipe people out, He would have wiped out millions of unfaithful spouses. Adultery is rampant, as are greed, lying, cheating, and thousands of other sins. The AIDS epidemic is not a plague from God. It is an opportunity for many believers to reach out to a group of people who have been alienated from God.

God does not wipe us all out because He loves us. He knew us before we were born, and He knew all the trouble we would get into. Even knowing all that, He paid the price for our sins because we could not do it ourselves. If He hated us and wanted to punish us, He could. His loving nature and Christ are our assurances that He will guide us back to Him if we are willing to follow. If we are unwilling, the consequences are of our own doing.

One of Christ's greatest messages was that of forgiveness. When asked how often a person should forgive someone else, He said sev-

God does not wipe us all out because He loves us.

---

enty times seven. His answer indicated the need to never stop forgiving. (See Matt. 18:22–35.) Confronted with an adulterous woman, Jesus didn't want her stoned for her evil acts. Instead, He took the occasion to challenge the accusers to look at themselves. Because they all realized they were equally guilty, they threw nothing at her. Christ didn't take the opportunity to lecture the woman, make her feel bad, or try to convince her of the seriousness of her sin. His compassion for her was the convicting element. He encouraged her to go and sin no more, refusing to condemn her even after she invited His condemnation. (See John 8:2–11.)

When people talk of the wrath of God, I refer them to the story of the woman caught in adultery. The case made for a God who punishes people is countered by this wonderful story of love. We should do no less. We should communicate love and compassion. That does not mean we have to compromise what we believe. Our standards don't have to change. All that needs changing is our attitude toward people who are hurting and confused and in need of encouragement. We must hate not the sinner but the sin. We must not confuse the two. God is very clear at confronting us with His love for us in sending His Son, but He is just as clear in His opinion of sin. Wanting a relationship with those He loved so much, He provided a way to cover the payment necessary for sin. It is obvious that God does not hate the sinner; He hates the sin.

One day I was visiting with some patients at New Life Treatment Centers. They were discussing various childhood tragedies. Many felt that God had singled them out from birth and was angry and vengeful, bringing terrible abuses into their lives. One man had never moved beyond childhood to adulthood. He had been badly abused while young and was opening up for the first time. His view of God had been distorted by his sexually abusive father. Our program stresses forgiveness and the loving nature of God. He said to me, "Coming here and finding that God loves me is the greatest experience of my life."

I wish everyone could see the love of God rather than a distorted

---

Wanting a relationship with those He loved so much, He provided a way to cover the payment necessary for sin.

image of His anger. Many people use this hurtful faith as an excuse. They mess themselves up because they are irresponsible and then blame a vindictive God who is supposedly evoking wrath. They behave just like those who continue to walk around with guilt for something they did years ago, and their guilt becomes an excuse to stay stuck in pain and disappointment and not move on.

An angry God is used as an excuse for too many behaviors and mistakes. God loves us. He wants the best for us. God doesn't want to punish us. He wants us to be free from the past. He doesn't want us to spend the rest of our lives trying to hide the skeletons in our closets. He went to a lot of trouble so we would not have to be punished and feel guilty. His system is an incredible world where we can start over. He is there for all of us, encouraging us to go and sin no more. No lightning, no plagues, no earthquakes—just love with the expectation that we will respond to that love.

God's love, grace, and expectations are balanced with justice. He is not vindictive, but He disciplines those He loves as a father or mother would discipline a child. This is not out of anger; it is out of a love that is tough enough to stop the progression of irresponsibility. The discipline is always for our own good, provides opportunity for growth, and stems from God's love. It is hard to differentiate between problems we cause and problems that come as God's discipline. Perhaps God simply uses the consequences of our own poor decisions to discipline us.

No one seems to have the authoritative word on consequences and discipline. The key to understanding both is God's love and desire to help us grow toward Him in faith. He will never give us more problems than we can handle, and He will assist us through the problems if we will trust Him for help. His loving discipline comes when we veer away from His will and He moves to bring us back.

18. Mortal Christ

CHRIST WAS MERELY A GREAT TEACHER

Moses, Muhammad, Buddha, and Christ are often placed in the same category. They are viewed as great teachers and philosophers.

God loves us. He wants the best for us. God doesn't want to punish us. He wants us to be free from the past.

Many people say they believe in Christ but they really mean that they believe He existed as an historical reality. There is plenty of evidence to document His existence. Believing that He lived and was one of many great teachers is different from accepting Him as the Savior of the world. From what He said, He was the Savior, or He was a liar, or He was crazy.

Christ made some fairly exclusive statements about Himself. He said that He was the way to God and to heaven. He stated that except through Him, there was no way for a person to come to God. Was He a liar, or do you believe there is only one way to God—through Christ? He also went so far as to call God His Father. That is a very heady statement for a normal but wonderful teacher to make. He claimed He was the truth and the light. Either He was truth and light, or He was a psychotic with delusions of grandeur.

To see Christ as just a great teacher is to dismiss what He taught. He did not just tell people to be good and go to heaven. He told those around Him that He came to save the world. No sane great teacher would make that claim. Christ was either who He said He was or He was a fraud, an egomaniac, a manipulator, and a deceptive leader. Those around Him were following either the Savior of the world or a man who masterminded one of the all-time great hoaxes of history. He came to save us, or He deceived us and went down in history as the most significant person ever to live.

Many of the disciples laid low after the Crucifixion, thinking their leader had come to a tragic end. They were hurt and confused until they saw an empty tomb and met Him face-to-face as the risen Christ. Scripture and historians record major changes overtaking each disciple after the Crucifixion. They became stronger in their beliefs with more determination than ever to spread the message He left them. I doubt a mere good, *mortal* teacher could have developed this kind of posthumous following.

Jesus certainly was a great teacher. He was also the Savior He claimed to be. I know this to be true. I suffered tremendous guilt and depression until I finally accepted that Christ died for my sin. Because of His sacrifice, I didn't have to experience the punishment I deserved for the problems I caused. I had tried every other way to live. Nothing

---

Believing that He lived and was one of many great teachers is different from accepting Him as the Savior of the world.

worked until I asked Christ to be who He said He was, the Savior of the world and the Savior of *my* world.

19. Impersonal God

GOD IS TOO BIG TO CARE ABOUT ME

People who do not believe in a personal God, One who cares for individuals as well as groups of people, are missing out on a personal relationship with God that can make life bearable in the bad times and incredible in the good ones. I believe God cares for people individually, and He will reveal Himself to each of us if we will allow Him to do so.

One of the first people to enter New Life Treatment Centers was a confirmed atheist. One night he was in a suicidal rage and out of desperation went to the phone book to find the number of a psychiatrist. At 3:00 A.M. few psychiatrists are available by phone, but ours answered her own phone. She instructed the desperate man to come into our center that night. He woke up the next morning and said that if there was a God, then He had played a terrible trick on him by landing him in a Christian treatment center. It was tough for him to stay, but he struggled and managed to make it to the fourth day.

On the evening of the fourth day a remarkable event happened. The man was an alcoholic and went with the other alcoholic patients to an Alcoholics Anonymous meeting. At the end of the meeting a young boy stood up and asked for help from the group. He told them he was suicidal. He said that he was visualizing in color putting a gun to his head and pulling the trigger. The atheist could relate to him since he had been in the same frame of mind four days earlier.

When the boy sat down, the room was silent. Suddenly, the back door of the room opened, and a man walked in wearing what looked like a turban and a robe. He said his wife and kids were in the car, but he felt that God wanted him to come in the room and say something. He had not heard the boy but relayed the following: "If anyone here is thinking of killing yourself, I want to encourage you to reconsider.

I believe God cares for people individually, and He will reveal Himself to each of us if we will allow Him to do so.

God loves you and wants you to live. This turban on my head is a bandage from where I put a gun to my head and pulled the trigger. Fortunately, I survived so I could come here and tell you not to do it. God loves you."

Our atheist patient was no longer an atheist. He believed God had sent that man especially to talk to that boy. The other patients believed God had sent the boy and the man to show the atheist that He is a real God. I believe God interrupted the natural course of events to build the faith of all those in that room and potentially all who read this story.

This is one of millions of stories about people who have met a personal God who is not too big to care about each individual. That He knows the number of hairs on our heads is not too difficult to believe when we understand how powerful He is. Over the years people can refer either to many coincidences or to numerous times when God has moved to intervene personally. I believe in a thousand ways, through good times and bad, that God has tried to make Himself known through meeting personal needs. Everyone could point to instances where God's divine intervention makes more sense than a coincidence. Our agnostic society encourages us to explain events in any way except that God stepped in. We search the universe for God, but all the time He is with us. I believe He is in love with each of us and cares for us individually.

Faith in God has declined with the decline of the family. As divorced and working parents have spent less time with kids, the concept of a personal God has faded. Our ideas of God are wrapped in our experiences with our parents. An absent father is almost a guarantee for a belief in an absent God, too busy to care about individuals. If your parents were not individually devoted to spending time with you,

THE YEAR 2000

"Groups outside evangelical and mainline Christianity will continue to expand rapidly. The Mormon church will reach 10 million members by 2000, largely due to their emphasis on relationships between members. Eastern faiths, especially Buddhism and Islam, will more than double in the number of adherents. The New Age religions will prosper, although many of the groups that will be prolific by 2000 are not yet in existence."

—George Barna, The Frog in the Kettle (Ventura: Regal Books, 1990), p. 141.

you have begun life feeling overwhelmed from a lack of support. If you carried that experience over to God, your sense of being overwhelmed may have grown to an unmanageable point. You may have broken down because you felt there was too much difficulty in life with too little support from a distant God.

20. Divinely Ordained Happiness

*MORE THAN ANYTHING ELSE, GOD WANTS
ME TO BE HAPPY*

Every day a career is ruined, a marriage is destroyed, and a sexual relationship is started in pursuit of happiness. People want to be happy. In our society, everything is acceptable as long as it makes a person happy. An entire belief system is based on the search for happiness, and someone is always around to utter the twentieth-century bromide, "Well, as long as you're happy."

When people are asked why they do certain things, they reply,

"I was never really happy in my marriage. I have found it in my new eighteen-year-old wife of three weeks."

"I don't think God would object to my finding what makes me the most happy. I moved in with him, and I've never been happier."

"We divorced because of the kids. If we didn't do what would make us the happiest, we knew our kids would never be happy."

Wrong!

Wrong!

Wrong!

God's primary goal is not for us to be happy. Although He grieves with us when we are in pain and would prefer that no one experience problems, He sees the bigger picture and knows that the pain is only temporary. He wants more than just happiness for us. Trusting in God will allow the pain to be transformed into joy, which is a deeper, richer experience than happiness.

Although He grieves with us when we are in pain and would prefer that no one experience problems, He sees the bigger picture and knows that the pain is only temporary.

Pain can be a great motivator to draw closer to God.

You cannot justify going against His teachings for the sake of happiness. A female who is abused may need to leave a marriage for the sake of survival, but to leave just to be happy would be the wrong motive. The search for happiness always ends in ruin. When you search for something more meaningful, happiness develops as a by-product.

If God wanted us happy, the world would be one big Disneyland with no lines, no admission fee, and continuous rides. That is not the world I live in. That might be a modern-day description of what God intended for us when He created us in the Garden of Eden. But because of Adam and Eve and our fallen humanity, we live in a fallen world. Laws govern our created world: for example, a knife always cuts, whether in slicing a piece of bread or in committing murder. God does not magically make it not cut because it is doing an evil deed. And so there is pain, not because God intends it but because we live in a fallen world.

Pain can be a great motivator to draw closer to God. I have been closest to God when I allowed Him to produce a deep satisfaction and joy, even in the midst of the worst sacrifices or pain and hardships. Exhausting all my resources to find joy, I finally turned to God and drew closer to Him.

God's primary goal for us is not happiness. Happiness is a temporary good feeling based on our circumstances. It is a meaningless pursuit. It is the counterfeit of what God wants for each of us. The heroin addict who shoots up is instantly happy. The word joy cannot be associated with the quick fix. Joy is a deeper satisfaction—regardless of circumstances. It comes only from faith in God and His involvement with a person who trusts Him totally. Happiness can be obtained alone; joy requires teamwork with God. Happiness is always fleeting; joy can grow over time.

Joy and satisfaction are results of faith in God and living in that faith. With God, circumstances are much less important than perspective. Perspective allows you to accept that each painful moment matures you to handle greater pain and develop wisdom from the experience. Growing closer to God through adverse circumstances pro-

With God, circumstances are much less important than perspective.

duces joy. Going against His teachings may result in a quick thrill and a fleeting bit of happiness, but it will diffuse joy and satisfaction.

God wants us to be mature, wise, and full of satisfaction. He paid a big price for those things to occur. Once we begin to mature and develop wisdom, we want more of it. As we grow in wisdom that produces a lasting joy, we are less satisfied to return to those childlike behaviors that provided cheap thrills and instant relief. We can no longer act out the opposite of God's standards and rationalize that we are doing what God would have us do to find happiness. God wants us to find lasting joy, and the cheap counterfeit of lasting joy is fleeting happiness. In the twentieth century, the search for happiness has destroyed our joy and left us empty, looking for another fix. When we stop seeking happiness and start seeking God, joy—lasting joy—comforts and sustains us.

21. Possibility of Becoming God

YOU CAN BECOME GOD

This is perhaps the most depressing of all the harmful beliefs. Many ungodly people believe they can become God. They say if you just focus on all that you are, you will discover that you are God and in control of your fate. This all becomes overwhelming and confusing.

I was listening to a lecture by a woman who said that each individual knows everything. She said inside everyone is an unconscious knowledge. According to her, you know it all, but you don't know that you know it. Now it seems to me if you knew everything, you would know that you know it. If you didn't know you know something, you wouldn't know everything. It is a crazy process when you try to become God and have absolutely no ability to do so. There are many rationalizations and mental games to go through to come up with a divine nature when you know you are not God.

Many men and women devote their lives to trying to achieve the

---

In the twentieth century, the search for happiness has destroyed our joy and left us empty, looking for another fix. When we stop seeking happiness and start seeking God, joy—lasting joy—comforts and sustains us.

power that only God has. They pick up trinkets along the way and attribute special powers to those trinkets. The latest power-trinket fad involves crystals. For many, crystals have become the source of healing and power, the cure-all to life's frustrations. Playing God becomes easier if you have the right crystals with the right powers. The message comes through: "There is nothing you can't do."

I have been amazed that those who reject the traditional values and teachings of the Jewish faith or those who refuse to believe that Christ

ABOUT THE CHURCH

Below are listed representative indicators of five areas of congregational life related to faith maturity and loyalty. The more that each of these factors exists in a congregation, the greater the growth in faith maturity and loyalty.

	Youth	Adults
THINKING		
My church challenges my thinking	42%	46%
My church encourages questions	45	40
WARMTH		
My church feels warm	63	73
CARING CHURCH		
Other youth at my church care about me	38	—
Other adults at my church care about me	—	57
SERVICE TO OTHERS		
Congregation gets you involved in helping other people in your city	41	—
Congregation gets you involved in helping people who are poor or hungry	36	—
Congregation gets members involved in community service	—	43
Congregation gets members involved in peacemaking and social justice activities	—	14
Congregation helps members become more loving and compassionate	—	57
WORSHIP		
Congregation provides spiritually-uplifting worship services	—	70

—Peter L. Benson and Carolyn H. Eklin, Effective Christian Education: A National Study of Protestant Congregations (Minneapolis: a research project of Search Institute, March 1990), p. 49.

is God's Son can find it easier to believe that each of us can become God. I find it much easier to believe in a powerful Creator than that I am the Creator. I know my limitations, and I fall short of being all-knowing or all-powerful. A quick assessment of my life reassures me I am not perfect and have no way of being perfect.

The "you are perfect" saying is also part of the "you are God" mentality. Both concepts keep one from developing a relationship with the Creator. My wife and I visited a town in northern California where one person spends his days playing God. To everyone he meets, he says, "You are perfect." He believes that each person is perfect, but the problem is that no one recognizes the perfection. This is like the "I know it all, I just don't know I know it all" dilemma. His proclamation of perfection is supposed to free persons to discover their godliness, release them from their mere human limitations, and help them move to their heavenly state of existence. It is incredible how many people buy into the concept. "Buy into it" is a good description, too. Few are satisfied with the man's free proclamation. They pay hundreds of dollars to attend seminars where they are told they are perfect, they are powerful, and they are God.

You can't turn mortal man into God. You can't take a sinful person and make him or her perfect just through thoughts of perfectionism. A limited mind cannot know all or comprehend the eternal truths of the universe.

This is not bad news; it is a relief. We can end our frustration of trying to become perfect or powerful. God took care of that problem when He sent Christ to form the bridge between finite man and infinite God. It is easier to accept Christ's sacrifice for all than it is to accept the idea that all are free from the need for sacrifice. Each day our mistakes and difficulties reinforce the knowledge of our limitations. We cannot become God, but we can accept the means by which God has made a way to Him. His Son alleviates all need for perfection and power. Accepting His perfect sacrifice and the power through His Spirit into our lives, we no longer need to fake it or convince ourselves we can be who only God is.

Harmful beliefs are the bases of hurtful faith. Having just one

---

We can end our frustration of trying to become perfect or powerful. God took care of that problem when He sent Christ to form the bridge between finite man and infinite God.

HOW OFTEN DO YOU READ THE BIBLE?

Daily	11%
Weekly	22%
Monthly	14%
Less than Monthly	26%
Never	22%

—George Gallup, Jr., and Sarah Jones, 100 Questions and Answers: Religion in America *(Princeton, N.J.: Princeton Religion Research Center, 1989), p. 40.*

harmful belief can poison an entire relationship with God. Until each person has eradicated all of the harmful beliefs in the relationship with God, faith in God will not be what it can be. Pure faith is a rare thing in our world of many religions, cults, and mind benders. To possess pure faith, a person must come to believe in a source of knowledge, a point of reference held up as an authority. That authority for me and millions of others is the Bible.

Men and women distort what is there; they add to it, subtract from it, and make it say something it never intended. In its untainted form, it is the means by which faith in God is developed. All of the truth needed is within the Bible's covers. It is the Word of God. Faith in God cannot be developed without knowing God's Word. It may seem easier to make up our beliefs as we go, but relying on the source of faith that has been used for thousands of years has never failed. To heal the mind and purify faith, God's Word is the cleansing agent.

To possess pure faith, a person must come to believe in a source of knowledge, a point of reference held up as an authority.

TWENTY-ONE HARMFUL BELIEFS
OF A FAITH THAT HURTS

1. God's love and favor depend on my behavior.
2. When tragedy strikes, true believers should have a real peace about it.
3. If you have real faith, God will heal you or someone you are praying for.
4. All ministers are men and women of God and can be trusted.
5. Material blessings are a sign of spiritual strength.
6. The more money you give to God, the more money He will give to you.
7. I can work my way to heaven.
8. Problems in your life result from some particular sin.
9. I must not stop meeting others' needs.
10. I must always submit to authority.
11. God uses only spiritual giants.
12. Having true faith means waiting for God to help me and doing nothing until He does.
13. If it's not in the Bible, it isn't relevant.
14. God will find me a perfect mate.
15. Everything that happens to me is good.
16. A strong faith will protect me from problems and pain.
17. God hates sinners, is angry with me, and wants to punish me.
18. Christ was merely a great teacher.
19. God is too big to care about me.
20. More than anything else, God wants me to be happy.
21. You can become God.

CHAPTER 4

When Religion Becomes an Addiction

Religious addiction is often used as a means to avoid reality. One example is Rick, who was in our sexual addiction program. Because of a religious experience that had delivered him from his sexual compulsivity, however, Rick was leaving before the staff thought he was ready. His pastor had enabled Rick's harmful faith by repeatedly negating the need for psychological or medical treatment.

Rick was an exhibitionist who repeatedly acted out his compulsion on a weekly basis. While in prayer on the unit, he experienced "deliverance" from his sinful behavior. What Rick experienced—as do most addicts who have a diagnosis of religious addiction—was relief from feeling guilty and from feeling responsible for his sexually compulsive behavior.

His religious addiction allowed him to avoid having to take responsibility for working through his exhibitionistic behavior. His religious "fix" allowed him to avoid his exhibitionism as primarily an act of passive aggression. With a means of mood alteration provided him by harmful faith and prayer, he distanced himself from the undesirable emotions of anger toward women.

Rick used his religious addiction to avoid the reality that exhibitionism is a symbolic act of aggression toward women, a maladaptive way of expressing repressed anger.

Rick's addiction relieved him from dealing with the brokenness

---

WHAT DO PEOPLE THINK ABOUT THE BIBLE?

Here's how people view the Bible:

- 31% Literal word of God
- 24% Inspired word of God
- 22% Inspired word with errors
- 7% Human document
- 10% Ancient literature
- 6% No opinion

—George Gallup, Jr., and Sarah Jones, 100 Questions and Answers: Religion in America *(Princeton, N.J.: Princeton Religion Research Center, 1989), p. 8.*

---

that led to his exhibitionism. Many exhibitionists have repressed anger toward their mothers or female caregivers; their exhibitionistic behavior accomplishes two goals—to be seen, and to express anger toward females. These are complex, and often painful, issues for the addict to deal with. Compulsive behavior is an addiction to a strategy for circumventing angry, sad feelings. Rick's compulsive exhibitionism allowed him to skirt the real issue of his feelings of self-worth.

For Rick, some very real issues will go unaddressed. He will most likely return to to his previous well-established behavior—sexual acting out alternated with religious compulsivity. Like most religious addicts, however, Rick will put the responsibility for change on God. Rick believes that God delivered him. If he acts out again, he would feel that the reason was sin, not addiction, and that God can and will forgive and deliver him from sin. Once delivered from his "sin," Rick can continue with his denial intact. When he acts out again, the process repeats itself. Rick's behavior is not reality based. The reality is that his "sinful" behavior is rooted in addiction and is something he must take personal responsibility for.

People become addicted to drink and drugs for understandable reasons. The substances have addicting chemicals that lock a person's psychological desires into a physiological need that must be fulfilled. In the past few years the term *addiction* has been used to characterize behaviors that go beyond chemicals. Some have criticized a growing trend to label everything that is a problem as an addiction. They complain that rather than accept responsibility for their behaviors, people continue in those behaviors, justified in doing so because they are "helplessly" addicted. Others argue that persons focused on recovering from an addiction are less likely to look at the issues surrounding the development of the problem and more likely to concentrate on extinguishing the behavior. Instead of fixing a deep inner conflict or admitting a serious spiritual deficiency, they simply try to stop a behavior and miss out on God's power to completely change them physically, mentally, and emotionally.

Addiction and responsibility have never been mutually exclusive characteristics of a condition. Few people addicted to alcohol would say, "Of course I drink. I'm an alcoholic." The person is much more likely not to use the label of alcoholic because once it is admitted, the person must choose whether or not to accept responsibility to do something about the addiction. For this reason, alcoholics, drug addicts, and other types of addicts do all kinds of things to get around the label of addict. Their denial becomes complicated and well developed to protect themselves from the addiction indictment.

To use the term *addiction*, therefore, is an invitation to accept responsibility for the problem and determine to do something about it. The challenge is to break through denial and be willing to do whatever it takes to be free.

Sin and addiction are not mutually exclusive in a condition either. All of us, as much as we hate to admit it, sin. Whether we are alcoholic or not, our drinking anything is sinful if it does not honor God or if it leads another person into the same sinful behavior. A three-hundred-pound man who has never had a drop of alcohol sins when he drives up to a convenience store and orders a "Big Swallow," which is full of sugar, caffeine, chemicals, and more calories than most people consume in one meal. That is no less sinful than the man who downs pure vodka until he passes out. Whether either fellow is addicted to the substance is irrelevant. Neither behavior is honoring to God, and both are extremely negative influences on society and younger, impressionable people who are developing parameters for acceptable and unacceptable behaviors.

Sin and addiction exist simultaneously. Because of the demeaning manner in which the church has treated addicts, many people have overreacted and attempted to remove the issue of morality and sin entirely from addiction. Talk to recovering people about the behaviors

---

Addiction and responsibility have never been mutually exclusive characteristics of a condition.

Without a renewed relationship with the Creator, the feeling of being fully forgiven cannot be achieved, and the recovery becomes an act of compensation rather than a process of change.

that existed in the midst of the addiction, and most will not deny that they were involved in a multitude of sinful acts. The original addiction destroys the relationship with God, and then other areas fall prey to sin and cause further separation from God.

Many people feel so guilty about these sins that they don't do well in recovery. Fleeing the sins of the past had nothing to do with their use of the term *addiction*. Their recovery isn't based on the ability to deny their sins. Instead their recovery begins when they accept that they have been involved in many sins and can feel forgiveness for those wrongs. Without a renewed relationship with the Creator, the feeling of being fully forgiven cannot be achieved and the recovery becomes an act of compensation rather than a process of change.

The term *addiction* is not used to avoid responsibility, and it is not used to avoid the issue of sin. Then why is it such a desirable term for many current maladies, and what advantage is there in calling something an addiction? First, it is used so frequently today because persons who seem to be doing the most with their lives are those who have had addiction problems. The recovered addicts are leading the way toward personal change and growth. While the rest of the world is satisfied to deny and continue to compensate for their losses and ill feelings, addicts are busy doing an inside job on themselves to "devictimize" themselves from the addiction.

If something can be labeled as an addiction, our culture feels more hope for overcoming it because we know how to fight addiction. There are steps to fight addiction. God is part of addiction recovery. Families are expected to receive help when a family member is addicted. Groups of addicts band together to help one another with simi-

While the rest of the world is satisfied to deny and continue to compensate for their losses and ill feelings, addicts are busy doing an inside job on themselves to devictimize themselves from the addiction.

HIGH WEIRDNESS

Ivan Stang, America's leading connoisseur of crankdom, is a Dallas radio announcer and film producer. He "has spent 20 years compiling an exhaustive catalog of the inhabitants of what he calls America's 'zoo of beliefs.' . . . For starters, there are the publishers of the Flat Earth News in Lancaster, Calif., who don't believe all that Pythagorean nonsense about a round earth. Then there are the Breatharians (also—surprise!—from California), who argue that we can survive without food or drink. That health cult's faith was shaken when its founder was found to be sneaking out at night to buy junk food at convenience stores."

—Art Levine, "On the Trail of High Weirdness," U.S. News & World Report, November 14, 1988, p. 67.

lar addictions. In our society, it seems that addiction problems are the ones to have because help and support are available, there is hope for change, and many other people have had a similar problem. Addiction has become a label that invites others to the point of recovery.

The other advantage of the addiction label is that it identifies a specific condition with a specific set of symptoms. Often people are miserable without knowing the source of the problem. They feel hopeless because no one seems to understand. Others who haven't been through the same feelings and behaviors don't have the credibility to help. But when a person can relate to an addiction, that person discovers that others have had the same problem, the problem has many similar characteristics, and others have found relief for their misery. When overeaters find that they don't just overeat, that they eat addictively like thousands of other food addicts, they have a greater sense of hope. If a driven businessperson discovers work behaviors parallel workaholism, the isolation is over, and a greater tendency to find help motivates the person to find others who have overcome their addiction to work. Addiction's biggest benefit is in its invitation to stop the denial, accept the full dimension of the problem, and join others in the recovery process. This happens when the person locks in and identifies with the common elements of addiction.

Addiction's biggest benefit is in its invitation to stop the denial, accept the full dimension of the problem, and join others in the recovery process.

If people could identify their harmful faith behaviors as an addiction, they would be in a better position to identify that there is a problem rather than justify what they are doing. Some individuals have spent their whole lives in a world of religious fanaticism and fantasy, hiding in their compulsive behaviors and delusions. They believe they are honoring God, but they are only circumventing reality, easing their pain, and attempting to work their way to heaven.

Some are in dangerous cults, some are in denominational churches, some are attending a local church on the corner in your neighborhood, and others are seeking God in isolation. Some learned their harmful faith from their parents, and others developed theirs on their own. But because there are so many others like them, they do not believe there is a problem. They are unaware that they have completely missed God in their search for Him.

Until they look at their lives and see the parallels to a condition common to others, they may have little hope for change. If they can see that their practice of faith is off center, there may be great hope for change. If they perceive that what they have done with their lives is an addictive process, they may break through their denial and band with the others to pursue a pure relationship with God. With the power of God and the support of fellow strugglers, there is great hope for recovery.

A Definition of Addiction

When a person is excessively devoted to something or surrenders compulsively and habitually to something, that pathological devotion becomes an addiction. The presence of a psychological and physiological dependency on a substance, relationship, or behavior results in addiction. When a person would sacrifice family, job, economic security, and sanity for the sake of a substance, relationship, or behavior, addiction exists. When a destructive relationship to something becomes the central part of the person's life, when all else is sacrificed for the sake of that sick relationship, the person is said to be addicted.

Addictions develop when people seek relief from pain, a quick fix,

They believe they are honoring God, but they are only circumventing reality, easing their pain, and attempting to work their way to heaven.

TEN COMMANDMENTS

"A survey asking about the Ten Commandments found that 85 percent of Americans personally embraced them. But only 45 percent believed that the general public espoused them. 'People are still religious themselves,' Dr. McCready said, 'but they don't think society is.'"

—Kenneth A. Briggs, "Religious Feeling Seen Strong in U.S.," New York Times, December 9, 1984.

---

or an immediate altered mood. When a person develops a pathological relationship to this mood-altering experience or substance that has life-damaging consequences, addiction exists. The addict becomes devoted to the source of mood alteration and, by giving up everything for that change in feelings, comes to worship the addictive act with body, mind, and spirit.

Most discussion of addiction focuses on drugs and alcohol. They are the most widely known producers of instant mood alteration. More is known about persons who enter into a pathological relationship to alcohol and drugs than any other addiction. The life-damaging consequences are easiest to see with these chemical forms of addiction. However, even though chemical addictions are common, there is great confusion over them, especially when it comes to mood alteration.

Drugs and alcohol are both mood and mind altering, even in small amounts. Many people think of addictions only when connected to a condition of intense inebriation that comes from extreme overindulgence. This is a gross misconception.

Drugs and alcohol alter the way the mind interprets the perceptions the senses provide; they alter the mood or one's feelings and emotions. Even small amounts of a mood-altering chemical allow the user to flee the depths of feelings and pain. The addiction is allowed to flourish because of its ability to alter reality in small or large doses.

The addict, possessing little self-worth, forms faulty perceptions of God and the world in general. The mood- and mind-altering chemicals allow the false perceptions to somehow make sense and feel less of a burden. The more the reward from the chemical, the more likely the

---

When a person would sacrifice family, job, economic security, and sanity for the sake of a substance, relationship, or behavior, addiction exists.

person will continue to rely on the chemical as a translator of reality or an insulator from it. If a small dose can provide this insulation, a small dose can become just as psychologically addicting as a large amount is physiologically addicting.

Addiction is not just confined to chemicals in large and small quantities. Addiction goes beyond drugs and alcohol and branches into emotional and process addictions. They all serve the same purpose as the addictions of substance. They all are used to change reality into a more tolerable form. They all eliminate God or at least distort the relationship with God. Every form is just as destructive as another; all result in disillusionment and isolation.

Emotional Addictions

Some people become addicted to negative emotions. It may seem strange to think a person could become addicted to something that is painful rather than something that brings instant pleasure like alcohol or sex. As negative as the emotion might be, it becomes addictive be-

---

MULTIPLES OF CATALOGS

Many are the catalogs of New Age material, offering anything from New Age music to calendars of New Age events, including the following:

- *The New Age of Christmas*—a world premiere album of instrumental music [what about the actual foundation of Christmas: the birth of Christ, the Son of God?]
- *Mask Phones*—create an inner environment by blocking out sight and noise distraction
- *Deep Enchantment*—"A mysterious and subtle musical adventure into the realm of the Unicorn. Silvery sound effects and ethereal tonal textures take the listener through other worlds, where magic is everywhere, weaving in and out of the air itself. Marvelously evocative music to take you to a safe and timeless world of perfect clarity."
- *The Firewalk Experience*—a seminar and experience on changing fear into power. The ad includes two pictures of different men, surrounded by a crowd, walking barefoot on what you are led to believe is hot coals.
- *Calendar of Events*—an 80-page (8½" x 11") catalog of New Age events happening in the Los Angeles area, just for the month of December.

cause it is easier to manage than another more painful or difficult emotion. If sadness and depression become more tolerable than anger and rage, retreating into depression can become just as addicting as retreating into a drunken stupor.

From my own experience I know this to be true. I had a relationship with a wonderful girl I wanted to marry. When I caused the relationship to end, I should have grieved and expressed my anger and rage at myself until I rid myself of every ounce of the venomous emotions. Instead I lived with self-anger and self-hatred, masking them with depression and long bouts of profound sadness.

People like myself live with their negative feelings rather than express them. Then they retreat to less negative feelings in an attempt to cope. In our society men and women differ in what they have been allowed to express and what they have been asked to suppress. For example, it's not considered ladylike to be angry. Many women were never allowed to have anger as little girls. Getting angry would mean risking the wrath or perceived loss of love and attention of their parents.

To be pleasing to a power greater than themselves, their parents, the women-to-be had to sacrifice their anger. Without their anger, they cannot set boundaries and protect themselves from the violations that occur in life. Without their anger, they become victims to be violated, beaten, battered, and bruised. Without their anger, they cannot muster the courage to address their God. No matter how intense the rage at their plight in life, they cannot protect themselves or get those people who are the victimizers in their lives out of their lives. Their role is to be pleasing, and angry people are not pleasing.

Victims' anger did not just go away; it remained deep and hidden. To compensate for its unhealthy presence, some resorted to depression like I did. They exhibited the miserable personality syndrome: nothing is right, and everything becomes a source of misery and irritation.

Instead of expressing deep hurt, the wounded female lives a misera-

MENTAL HEALTH VERSUS RELIGION

"Nowadays, many religions seem more like secular mental health associations than Judeo-Christian sects. . . . Conversely, some branches of the mental health movement seem a lot more like religious sects."
—Peter R. Breggin, "Mental Health Versus Religion," The
Humanist, *November/December 1987, p. 12.*

ble existence and gripes and complains about everything. She becomes addicted to her misery because it allows her to forget about her anger or at least postpone dealing with it. Her dependency on misery is just as difficult to break as someone else's dependency on crack cocaine. Both are means to a different reality that allows for pain to be deferred.

In some expressions of the Christian faith, anger is a no-no for both men and women. Some believe that everyone must be completely loving and forgiving at *all* times and that anyone showing anger is not a good Christian and should work on the sinful attitude at the heart of the anger. But that belief is a distortion of how Christianity and reality are to be joined. Everyone, Christian or not, is going to experience anger. The sooner this anger is expressed and resolved, the better. Yet many angry Christians don't acknowledge they are angry, while they seethe with bitterness and resentment. And their denial of their feelings is ineffective and unnecessary.

Christ became angry, expressed it, and did something about it. His anger led Him to cleanse the temple of money changers. Without it, He would have never risen to the occasion to remove violators of the temple's sanctity. They were misled believers who had become mired in one part of activity around the church, exchanging animals for money so the money could be given to God. Their interest was not in God but in the money that could be made from buying livestock low and selling it high. Christ knew their hearts and was hurt and angry over their unwholesome faith activities.

Mrs. Jones is addicted to her depression. She uses religion to medicate her misery much like the alcoholic or compulsive overeater uses compulsive behavior to medicate and reinforce depression to avoid having to acknowledge repressed rage.

Mrs. Jones had a good portion of her retirement money sent to the church, which used it to buy a fancy sound system. She had given the money at her pastor's urging to help pay the church's rent. When she realized that she had been used by the church, she was unable to express her anger. She saw the situation as just another bad decision. *God will judge him* was her rationale, as if the fact that God will judge means she needs to hang in there to be used time and time again. Unable to get angry at those who used her, Mrs. Jones became more

---

Yet many angry Christians don't acknowledge they are angry, while they seethe with bitterness and resentment.

depressed, bitter, and resentful. To get angry with those in authority was a no-no, a lesson she learned early in life. She never learned that it is human to be angry with those who misuse and abuse authority and who take advantage of others.

Whether it was her church, children, friends, or family members who used or abused her, she would *put it in God's hands* rather than confront the abuser or set some boundaries. What she was really doing was making God responsible for her inability to use her anger in a healthy way, to be assertive, to set boundaries, and to say no.

Mrs. Jones's use of the Scripture to rationalize her persecution and to justify her position served to avoid having to set and maintain boundaries. She operated under the principle that if all persecution is ordained by God, there is no need to say no. Without a healthy sense of anger, she didn't have the ability to be assertive and protect herself from being violated. Without her anger, she didn't have the capacity to defend herself in a world that is quite often unsafe.

If Mrs. Jones became angry, she would have to take responsibility for the shame connected with an angry child of God. Her shame is bound with her anger. She learned early in life that if she was angry she would experience the shame of being unacceptable. This connection, which is not reality based, causes her to be dysfunctional in her relationship with God, herself, and others.

Her harmful faith has nothing to do with God. Her religious addiction provides her with only an illusionary relationship to God. Her god of religion provides her with a false sense of acceptance for playing the role of the miserable martyr in the hurtful system. Mrs. Jones needs to take responsibility for her own life.

Without our anger we are unable to cleanse the temple of God and maintain its sanctity. Without our anger, we cannot get those people who violate the sanctity of our beings out of our lives. Without our anger, we are relegated to playing the role of enabler and victim in the harmful religious system and in life.

Without anger, people must allow themselves to be defiled and victimized without objection. Anger can be a mechanism for self-defense; those who deny its presence are vulnerable to manipulation and all forms of exploitation. People who don't have the right to be angry become powerless, unable to stand for what is right.

People who don't have the right to be angry become powerless, unable to stand for what is right.

Men are supposed to deny a different set of emotions. In our society big boys don't cry. Without our grief and sadness, we can't release our sense of violation. The pain and shame that come from abuse have no way of being processed. A common axiom is "that which cannot be processed is repressed." We stumble through life without understanding our feelings, completely out of touch with our emotions. We are deeply grieved by our lost expectations and sense of inadequacy, but we don't feel safe acknowledging our sadness.

We show our anger but never the deep hurt and sadness underneath it. When we feel sad, anger becomes a safe retreat. It causes the adrenaline to rush through us so the payoff is not just that we avoid looking weak, but we also feel differently because of the chemicals pumped through our bodies. The more adrenaline we pump through anger, the less sadness we are forced to feel.

This lack of grieving is a poison to our existence. There is no biblical precedent for men not expressing openly their deepest hurts and sorrows. The Old Testament depicts many real men showing their real emotions. The men of the nation of Israel would rip their clothes, sprinkle themselves with ashes, wear black arm bands, and spend time in mourning and grief. They would wail before the Lord to process their sense of shame and pain. That extremely freeing experience allowed them to express their emotions to the full degree and then move on without the needless baggage of building negative feelings. Without the ability to "wail before the Lord," we are forced to repress our disappointments and sadness and find ways to compensate for these emotions by replacing them with others less threatening to express.

The unfortunate development of the aggressively virile American male is the result of a man's unwillingness to grieve. The macho image is a defense against life and the possible situations of vulnerability that would leave him open to be controlled or ridiculed by others. Macho men, without their grief, must find a way to gain power and control over their environment. They have a unique way of rationalizing and justifying their behavior and violations of others, and they are driven to perform to gain the prestige needed to command the respect of others. Many times what is seen from the outside as giftedness or "anointing" is simply an overcompensation to defend against a posi-

We stumble through life without understanding our feelings, completely out of touch with our emotions.

tion of vulnerability. Many driven to power by their anger are full of grief and sadness that are unfelt until a crisis or breakdown brings all these emotions to the surface.

It is incredible that so many men in our churches today are out of touch with their emotions when the Christ they say they follow was so in touch with His. From Scripture we can see that Christ did not deny the depths of what He felt. In the Garden of Gethsemane, with His soul "exceeding sorrowful, even to death," as "His sweat became like great drops of blood" (Matt. 26:38; Luke 22:44), Christ was able to grieve the unfairness of His impending persecution. He did not withhold the expression of those emotions out of fear that others would no longer follow Him. He honestly expressed the full degree of what He felt as He was feeling it. Many emotionless followers are not using Christ as a model.

If Christ walked the earth today, some people in our churches would be uncomfortable with His open display of emotion. There is a good chance they would shame Him for that conduct. "Where is your faith?" and "Rejoice always, . . . in everything give thanks for this is the will of God" would be their admonitions (see Luke 8:25; 1 Thess. 5:16, 18). I can just hear some religious addict saying, "Come on, Jesus. You need to have real peace about this." The shaming of His feelings would be rooted in His not living up to their image of a man of God or how easy faith in God is supposed to make life.

The people in our churches are not the only ones who would have problems with Christ's honest and open display of emotion. Many in the mental health profession would be just as likely to have a poor response to His grief. They would perhaps say He was having a nervous breakdown or an anxiety attack. They would perhaps suggest He be involuntarily restrained until the crisis passes. His open and honest display of emotion would be too much for them, too threatening to their inner worlds of hidden feelings. When Christ walked the earth, He set a great example for us to follow. He didn't leave out the emotional realm. It's too bad so few choose to live after His example and choose to deny their emotions and the need to express them.

Rather than accept their negative feelings and resolve them, emotional addicts become addicted to the emotions that make life bearable, the emotions that are familiar and appear easier. These emotions

He honestly expressed the full degree of what He felt as He was feeling it.

Rather than accept their negative feelings and resolve them, emotional addicts become addicted to the emotions that make life bearable, the emotions that are familiar and appear easier.

are the ones the hurtful family tolerated. To be accepted, addicts were forced to find or create a delusional reality that allowed them to avoid what they never learned to handle. That way, they could hide or kill the feelings of shame of being unacceptable. They became addicted to the pretense and the emotions they relied on to survive.

We have become an emotionally addicted society with many emotional addicts. We are walking paradoxes of what we are willing to show and what we are actually feeling. We are in a constant state of denial when it comes to our emotions. Women, though angry on the inside, feel safe only if they show their misery and depression. Men, feeling sad and depressed, will not risk being labeled weak by expressing their sadness. They push people around through their anger that masks their depression on the inside. An angry female without her depression could not exist. A depressed man without his anger could not cope. Both become addicted to the emotion that appears to be more tolerable and acceptable. Fortunately, many are breaking through the denial and living comfortably and honestly with their emotions.

Process Addictions

In addition to chemical addictions and emotional addictions there are process addictions. Process addictions such as work and religion are more pervasive in our society than the more commonly recognized chemical addictions. Work becomes the means by which persons establish a sense of self and acceptability to themselves, to others, and to God. Process addicts focused on work believe they are valued only for what they can accomplish rather than for who they are.

Behind every workaholic is a person who feels inadequate and is driven to compensate for lack of self-worth. Compulsive achievers defend against the day when they might be forced to admit inadequacy or inferiority. Workaholics are actually quite spiritually focused persons. They attempt through work to find God. If god is money, the work is intended to bring them closer to that god. If they have a relationship with God the Creator, they work to gain favor and be pronounced good.

Workaholics follow after a god that is a fabrication of the true God. They become addicted to the sense of power attained from the work and the striving to excel above others. People addicted to a process such as work become addicted to pursuit after a god of their own making. They lose the real God and worship the fruit of their labor, be it money, fame, or whatever earthly pursuit they value.

Addiction as Idolatry

All addictions have one element in common: worship of the process and worship of the outcome. The worship aspect of addiction is easily seen in the lives of most addicts. An extremely overweight friend of mine would not stop eating excessively, even for the sake of his family. He loved food and had some with him most of the time. He could go hours during the day without touching food, but when he was home in the evenings, he spent most of his time eating. It was a reward for his hard work. It was compensation for his deprivation as a child. He lived to eat.

It didn't matter that he was an embarrassment to his children. It was insignificant to him that his cholesterol level was in a very dangerous category. He didn't react when his wife threatened to leave if he didn't lose weight. Food was too much a portion of his life to do without. He was always thinking about what he would eat next. While he was eating, nothing else mattered but how good he felt as he ate. No follower of any religion had a more devoted member than this man who served the god of food.

Worship is built into addiction. The addict serves the act of addiction with every element of existence. Initially, a drink alters the person's mood, bringing a brief, temporary change. As the problem progresses, however, the person becomes a slave to drink and gives up everything for it. Upon the altar of alcohol are placed family, friends, work, and self-respect. Everything is offered up as sacrifice for what was once a drink but has now become an idol of worship. In the end,

---

Process addictions such as work and religion are more pervasive in our society than the more commonly recognized chemical addictions.

all addictions become a form of idolatry, that is, the worship of a relationship, substance, or behavior instead of God. The object of idolatry stands in place of and in the way of God.

It may be drink, sexual encounters, or work, but all addicts find a means to make life tolerable. These objects of addiction allow the avoidance of pain and real internal conflict. It may kill the person in the long run or destroy all relationships, but the object of addiction must be maintained for survival. The addict will live for the addiction and die for it in the ultimate act of worship and devotion.

Religion as Addiction

A person with harmful faith can worship a false god just as easily as an alcoholic can worship a bottle of booze. The person with harmful faith is just as likely to be willing to die out of devotion to that false god as a drug addict is willing to die out of devotion to drugs.

The misled faithful adhere to a hurtful religion to dodge the emotional turmoil that comes with facing the reality of their circumstances. Their lives focus on the religion and not on God. The religion engulfs them, and they lose themselves to the practice of it.

Van grew up in an abusive home, the son of an alcoholic father who became belligerent when he drank. Van remembers vividly the fighting between his mom and dad. And he remembers his older sister secreting him and his two brothers in the closet until all was clear. It was not unusual for Van's mother to wake the children in the middle of the night and go into a tirade about his father. Other times the children would be wakened by his dad coming home drunk, yelling, screaming, breaking things, and beating his mom. Van and his brothers and sister would go to bed each night in fear of what might happen.

If Van's father wasn't venting his anger on his mother, he was venting it on the children. When the father came home, he was often greeted by the mother relating how rotten the kids—especially Van— had been that day. Van's father would stop them in the middle of what they were doing or drag all the children out of bed and beat them. Many times at his mom's insistence he would line up the kids, tell

These objects of addiction allow the avoidance of pain and real internal conflict.

them to drop their drawers, and spank and humiliate them. Van remembers the pain and the shame inflicted on him and his brothers and sister. The siblings reported the fear and terror they felt being forced to watch the beatings. The threat "This is what is going to happen to you if you kids don't straighten up" has an all too familiar ring for Van and his siblings.

All Van knew was that he wanted to escape the pain and shame of his family. He wanted someone to care for him and not hurt him. He needed someone to be nice and protect him. He needed someone or something to make his life safe and worth living.

One of Van's friends introduced him to a church where he heard how God loves him, how the fruits of the Spirit could be his, and how upon his acceptance of Jesus Christ God would fill him with the Holy Spirit.

Van became a Christian. He spent all his time in Bible studies, worship services, ministry outreaches, home fellowships, and other work of the Lord. Van found his escape from the pain of the past. Van's relationship became more dependent on religion than on his God.

Van found the affirmation he always wanted in church. Van was unaware of the fact that his teaching the word of God to his friends had more to do with his need to be affirmed and accepted than with his love of God. Van relished the mood alteration he experienced when

---

MAKE YOUR OWN FAITH

"Americans, never quite satisfied with their options, and rarely pleased with old traditions and old rules, will create their own religions. They will mix and match the best of each faith to which they are exposed and emerge with a synthetic faith.

It will be fascinating to watch people develop these new religious philosophies. In all likelihood, they will seek a blend of elements that will give them a sense of control over life, personal comfort and acceptance and a laissez-faire life-style philosophy. It is likely that from Christianity they will borrow Jesus' philosophy of love and acceptance. From Eastern religions they will borrow ideas related to each person being his or her own god, the center of the universe, capable of creating and resolving issues through his or her own power and intelligence. From Mormonism they will extract the emphasis upon relationships and family, toward establishing a greater sense of community."

—*George Barna*, The Frog in the Kettle *(Ventura: Regal Books, 1990), p. 141.*

those around him esteemed his ability to teach. But Van was unable to generate self-esteem for himself or to feel worthy of God. He valued and was valued for what he could do rather than for who he was. All Van realized was that he had found a way to experience the joy of being valued. He was hooked.

Van began to find himself at odds with the sister who once had protected him and the brothers who had shared his pain and shame. He began to berate his siblings for their rebelliousness toward God. He preached and "Bible-bullied" and shamed them. But they just didn't measure up to Van's expectations. Just as his father had berated them because of his alcohol, Van began to berate and shame those around him because of his religion.

It became clear to Van that he had the answer and that he needed to abandon those who loved him the most; they just didn't measure up. Van dove into the only thing that seemed to bring him a sense of relief and comfort—religion. Religion made him feel like he was somebody. He had found a way to hide those feelings he desperately needed to rid himself of.

Van got married and things went well, at first. After a while, however, he began to notice his wife's shortcomings. He would constantly condemn and demean her for her lack of commitment. Altering his mood with his sense of righteousness, he would constantly throw the Scriptures on submission in her face any time she complained about his insensitivity and her need for a caring husband. His father's abuse to his mom lay in the abuse of alcohol. Van's constant belittling and badgering of his wife lay in the abuse of religion.

His wife finally had enough. No longer able to endure his sense of self-righteousness and his religious abuse, she filed for divorce.

Having to endure the loss of marriage, Van dove further into his harmful faith for relief. He would do anything he could to be involved with religion if it allowed him to keep his focus off his own problems. He would stay up all night with street people and not be able to show up for work the next day. His employers became more and more irate with his tardiness and absenteeism and gave him an ultimatum: if he continued to be late or absent, then he would have to find employment elsewhere. Van responded indignantly and continued to preach the "godly" lifestyle to his fellow workers and to show up late, if at all. Fed up with his behavior, his employers discharged him. Van had deluded himself into believing that there wasn't anything wrong with his behavior and that his employers were persecuting him for his faith.

Divorced, unemployed, and feeling abandoned by the "god" he

tried so hard to please, Van came to us depressed, lonely, and suicidal. We talked about how many times the children of alcoholics become obsessive-compulsive and we looked at the characteristics of harmful faith. Van began to realize how he had used religion like a drug to alter his mood and justify his behavior. He identified how much of his behavior was like his dad's. He was as insensitive, demeaning, abusive, and irresponsible as his father had been, except Van had used religion instead of alcohol to distort the reality of his behavior.

Van was able to talk about his abuse as well as his abusive behavior with a group of caring people who understood what he had gone through. He is now in the process of healing his own wounds, making amends, and working with a twelve-step program that allows him to adopt a healthier faith.

Like any other addiction, the practice of religion becomes central to every other aspect of life. All relationships evolve from the religion. Like an alcoholic entering a favorite bar, the religious addict feels total acceptance in the company of other like-minded believers. They offer support and encouragement. They permit a diversion from responsibilities and growth. Any sign of pain or conflict becomes an excuse to retreat back into the assembly of other deluded followers who reassure the addict that everything will work out.

The religious addiction becomes tied to these people who support the addiction. The addict depends on the rituals and the others who go through those rituals. The dependency on the religious practice and its members removes the need for a dependency on God. The believer becomes hooked on a substitute with others who will not let go. The religion and those who practice it become the central power for the addict who no longer is in touch with God.

While I attended seminary, I worked in a counseling center on campus that allowed all the rookie counselors to practice counseling skills. One evening I met a couple who had been having difficulty with their daughter. She had gotten pregnant at age sixteen and moved in with the baby's father. The parents were respectable members of the local church, and the experience had been humiliating for both of them. When it happened, their relationship changed dramatically. They grew apart and existed without intimacy. They rarely talked when they were together, and the times they were together were less fre-

---

The dependency on the religious practice and its members removes the need for a dependency on God.

quent. They came to counseling because the wife wanted the relationship to change.

The woman had fled to a new church when she became too embarrassed to attend her old one. The pastor incited the congregation to screams and howls every time he preached. He was quite a change from her staid pastor of twenty years. Everyone welcomed her, and she felt as if she had found a new home. That her husband was not with her made it even better for her; at least for a little while she could forget about her responsibilities and struggles at home. A lot of attention was thrown her way because everyone wanted her to become a member of the church.

The wife's dedication grew more and more intense. She attended on Sunday mornings, Sunday nights and Wednesday evenings. On Tuesday mornings she baby-sat for the young mothers' class, and on Thursday afternoons she attended a women's Bible study. Almost every day she was at the church. She started doing some volunteer work around the church office, and that was when the pastor noticed her and began to develop a relationship with her. When he suggested that each Friday afternoon they have a counseling session, she was thrilled to be able to spend the time with him. She thought of it as a totally innocent involvement.

Her first uneasy feelings occurred when he suggested that she leave her husband. She was angry with her husband, but she had no intention of leaving him. A bolt of reality struck her, and in a moment she realized that the minister was unhealthy, the church was unhealthy, and her involvement was unhealthy. She had become fanatical in her church activity. God had nothing to do with it. It was all out of a motivation to relieve the pain from the situation with her daughter. She was able to communicate in our session together that her involvement had become an addiction.

Many others have become trapped in an unhealthy involvement with a church. Conviction turns to addiction, and pain is eased with excess activity. Most are not able to see for themselves that the involvement is unhealthy. If someone is not able to point out what they are doing, they continue in their compulsive actions, believing God is honored. Like this woman, they allow the intimacy to fall from their

---

Many others have become trapped in an unhealthy involvement with a church. Conviction turns to addiction, and pain is eased with excess activity.

relationships, and they become vulnerable to other unhealthy relationships. The warmth of the other followers melts away the ability to objectively evaluate the experience. Before the experience is over, the addict is lost inside the organization that looks good to most but is actually a wall between the follower and God.

Compulsive Churchaholism

In the case of the bereaved woman who lost her daughter to pregnancy and an undesirable boyfriend, religious addiction took the form of activity much like workaholism. A compulsive churchaholic is an accurate description of a person obsessed with the need to do more and more through church work. Like the workaholic who invests everything in work, eluding the responsibilities that come with relationships, the religious addict creates an atmosphere that revolves around church work. Any interpersonal relationships are developed as a result of or a part of the service to the organization. At any sign of conflict the compulsive churchaholic retreats into church work. All intimacy can be avoided by spending increasing amounts of time doing what appears to be dedicated service. In times of great pain and disappointment the religious addict has church work for protection from the rejections and abandonments in life. Dependency is not on God; it is on the work and the comfort that comes from being too involved to have to cope with problems.

Peace is found in activity. Just as alcoholics drink to find relief, religious addicts find relief in work. However, what is labeled as peace is actually avoidance. The hard work is the enabler for avoidance. Essentially, they work so hard in an attempt to outrun the pain. Real people are lost and replaced with those who will assist in carrying out the charade. Busyness becomes the goal, and religious compulsivity provides for misled believers a false presence of God. The compulsive working out of their religion gives them the mood alteration necessary for the illusion of being okay. Though those feelings of being okay may be fleeting, it is still better than living without a moment of rest or relief from the conflicts of life.

Dependency is not on God; it is on the work and the comfort that comes from being too involved to have to cope with problems.

However, what is labeled as peace is actually avoidance.

Churchaholics have embraced a counterfeit religion. God is not honored, and the relationship with Him is not furthered. Work is the focus of everything. It—and not God—allows the persons to feel safe. Rather than retreat to the loving arms of God, they literally bury themselves in their compulsive acts. The harder they work, the better they feel because they convince one another that God is applauding their efforts. They are so entangled in the world of the church that they no longer have time for the family. They are trying to work their way to heaven or pay the price for their guilt. Without intervention, they lose all sense of reality and rarely come to understand God as He really is.

Addictive Components of Religion

Anyone can become addicted to just about anything. Anything that hides or kills the pain of not being able to process the conflicts of life and relationships will serve well as an addiction. The practice of faith and involvement in religion offer many potentially addictive components. One can become addicted to the feelings of righteousness or the feelings that come with finally being right about something; one can become obsessed with prayer; one can become addicted to the emotional highs resulting from worship and praise; one can become addicted to the feelings of being a part of something exciting; one can become addicted to the feelings of belonging to something big. Being a part of other believers produces wonderful feelings. Those feelings of relationship should be enjoyed. They are addictive only when they become the purpose of the endeavor rather than a wonderful by-product of worshiping God.

Worship provides an example of how an unbalanced practice of faith can cause problems. Many people who worship God in song and praise achieve emotional highs. In God's presence they feel better

Rather than retreat to the loving arms of God, they literally bury themselves in their compulsive acts.

Anyone can become addicted to just about anything. Any-thing that hides or kills the pain of not being able to pro-cess the conflicts of life and relationships will serve well as an addiction.

about themselves and their future as they focus on the wonder of God. If they lose focus, if the feelings, rather than God, become the central part of the worship experience, the worship is harmful and addictive.

Many retreat into a religious group in times of stress or disappoint-ment. They seek the safety of God's church when their powers are exhausted and they continue to feel lonely, abandoned, and scared. Security is found with other believers focused on God. Often the per-sons feel so welcomed and safe that they desire to continue in the faith because of the people. God is not the primary factor. The addictive emotions are feelings of acceptance and warmth. These believers think they are growing in faith, but they closely resemble the busi-nessmen who go to church just to make contacts. Sometimes, though, the involvement will continue until reliance is placed on God and not on the feelings of belonging.

Addiction Replaces God

True addiction always results in separation from God. It starts as a substitution for God and eventually becomes a wedge between the person and God. The alcoholic feels unloved and rejected by God. The booze efficiently destroys the presence of God and blocks a per-son's knowledge of God, and the person becomes overwhelmed with-out tapping into the power and strength of the Creator. Where God would be potentially found becomes off limits for the alcoholic. A reli-gious addict replaces God with a caricature of God. The addict sees God with a score card writing down every wrong thing that has hap-pened. To the addict, the only way to erase the sins from the score card is hard work. The work and the feelings derived from it replace God completely.

One form of replacing God with a caricature of God is the use of

True addiction always results in separation from God.

The comfort of God is pushed aside by the self-induced comfort of superiority that comes from being able to rattle off a verse rather than connect with another human being as Christ did.

Scripture. This comment seems strange because most people use the Word of God to grow closer to Him. Meditation on God's Word and memorization of God's Word align persons with God. But for some people, the Word can become a god unto itself. Memorization can become an addiction rather than an act of devotion. Persons become obsessed with verses and in the process forget that the verses are about a God who communicated with people.

The churchaholic obsessed with Scripture stops communicating because every conversation is so filled with verses and sermonettes that no one wants to listen to or even be around the person. It becomes a form of religious intellectualism; someone is so immersed in an aspect of faith that real faith is replaced by that one aspect. The comfort of God is pushed aside by the self-induced comfort of superiority that comes from being able to rattle off a verse rather than connect with another human being as Christ did.

A family member abuses Scripture in this way. Every relationship turns into a student-teacher dynamic. She holds herself above others, ready to set them on course with a helpful Scripture she has memorized. She has alienated everyone in the process. If her faith was pure, it would be attractive to others. Instead it is repulsive and drives people from her and from wanting to pursue a relationship with God. As she builds up her image with this "admirable" form of communication, she puts God down in the eyes of those who see her faith. Her position of "teacher" brings with it a sense of power, prestige, and control while it alienates all others. She uses her sermons of superiority to gratify her need for security. She is safe because people don't dare come too close lest they be chewed up by her Scripture-quoting tongue. The Word of God has become her god.

Adrian Van Kaam states that "addiction is a perverted religious presence that has lost its true object."[1] All addicts in all forms of addic-

All addicts in all forms of addiction seek something spiritual when they first begin to tangle with the addiction.

tion seek something spiritual when they first begin to tangle with the addiction. They seek relief or, to use a more spiritual term, *peace*. The interaction with the addiction actually becomes a religious experience with its own rituals and rules surrounding the behavior. The less relief the addiction provides over time, the more intricate the rituals become to heighten the experience. As the rituals and rules increase, God is left further behind, and the true object is lost.

Van Kaam further describes addiction:

> The object . . . of my striving will be a situation, object, or experience which promises me the deepest and most lasting experience of wholeness and fulfillment with the least possible responsibility, mastery, decision, or commitment. . . . I am addicted only when one or the other type of addiction becomes a central mode of life for me around which my personality organizes itself and when every other mode of life becomes subservient to this addiction.[2]

Alcoholics and drug addicts are not the only ones who reach a point where the personality organizes itself around the addiction and every other mode of life becomes subservient to it. Religious addicts do exactly the same thing. Rather than become more filled with the Spirit of God, they become filled with the activities of the church. Rather than become more like Christ, the individuals become more like the church wants them to be or more like they want to be perceived by others. The personality changes as it revolves around the compulsive behaviors of religiosity. Nothing is more important than the distorted practice of faith, and nothing must deter the addicts from practicing faith in this driven manner. It becomes everything; God and others are second to it.

All addicts crave something that will grant them the experience of wholeness; the experience of being significant, of having meaning and purpose; the experience that offers fulfillment for an ever-more-fleeting moment. Those who refuse to risk throwing themselves wholly in the arms of God find it safer to pursue religious activity. The activity of religion becomes a drug, the quick fix of choice. It appears to be so admirable that it makes the addiction more deceptive than most. The ones who rise to the top of the organization are provided with the meaning and purpose, or at least feelings of meaning and purpose, that they long for. The ones who cannot find fulfillment at home with their families attain it at the church every time the doors are open. The practice is a false significance with a false god known as ego.

All addicts crave something that will grant them the experience of wholeness; the experience of being significant, of having meaning and purpose; the experience that offers fulfillment for an ever-more-fleeting moment.

The true presence of God in one's life doesn't provide an escape from reality and personal responsibility. The presence of God should provide a firmer grip on reality and a hope that reality can be faced with all of its pain and sorrow. Comfort is provided by a caring God who offers an interlude in time for refreshment, restoration, and re-creation. These interludes never replace God or others. They are involved with God and God's creation.

True faith enriches the believer and those who know that person; it doesn't form an offensive wall between the believer and God and others. Faith is never an excuse to escape, pack the bags, and head for the hills. Faith without addiction is an invitation to develop a relationship with God and enrich the lives of others through that relationship. All of this is quickly destroyed when the practice of faith becomes a compulsive addiction.

The presence of God should provide a firmer grip on reality and a hope that reality can be faced with all of its pain and sorrow.

——— **N o t e s** ———

1. Adrian Van Kaam, "Addiction: Counterfeit of Religious Addiction," *Studies in Formative Spirituality* 8 (May 1987): 243.
2. Van Kaam, "Addiction: Counterfeit of Religious Addiction," pp. 246–47.

CHAPTER 5

Religious Addiction:
The Progression

When religion becomes an addiction, it is very difficult to identify in the early stages. It looks so good. As the addicts serve themselves, they appear to serve God. No one guesses that they are playing out dangerous roles that will deprive them of faith and hope. As the addiction progresses, it does so along a predictable course. Like other addictions, it grows in its destruction as it becomes worse over time. The addiction intensifies as the abusive behaviors and harmful beliefs produce less and less relief. Addicts get hooked on the false hopes, mood alteration, and ability to distort reality. Those who fall deepest into the addiction deny reality altogether.

Addiction comes from the desire to escape. Addicts will destroy everything else to maintain the ability to escape into the addiction of choice. Nothing else matters to them. But as relief becomes more difficult to achieve and escape is no longer possible, addicts will turn to other addictions in an attempt to feel better. They eventually will eat, drink, steal, lie, have illicit sexual encounters, or engage in many other compulsive behaviors that will also eventually control them. Everything that can become a form of escape is used to run from feelings and the brutal reality that religious addicts face.

No one guesses that they are playing out dangerous roles that will deprive them of faith and hope.

Addicts will destroy everything else to maintain the ability to escape into the addiction of choice.

The harmful faith system is all too willing to have religious addicts join because it is created to take advantage of those who seek escape rather than faith. They escape into the accepting arms of those who want to see more and more new recruits. They escape into an unreal world where people, ideas, and rules replace a relationship with God. The farther they drift from God, the more desperate the addicts become, until they are willing to lie, cheat, steal, or kill for the harmful faith organization or its leader. They become so hooked that they are almost unreachable or unapproachable because their denial is so strong. They hit bottom and change, go crazy, or kill themselves. Those are the only three alternatives for religious addicts who have progressed through all of the addictive stages.

Religious addiction doesn't occur overnight. It is a long progression that subtly captures every aspect of the addict's life. It rarely begins in adulthood. Most of the time the roots of addiction can be traced back to a difficult childhood. In the early years the seeds of hurtful faith are planted that eventually grow into an addiction. Those seeds can be anything from rigid parenting to ritual abuse involving children in the occult. Whatever the source of the harmful faith seeds, the future addict is on a course in search of a god that does not exist, a god that is a creation of man, like any other idol created in our own image.

Just as a foundation is laid, it can be ripped up. No one is doomed to a life of religious addiction and harmful faith. If a person is able to go through the painful process of breaking through the denial and

MIND CONTROL

In a book discussing the use of mind control by cults the author states, "Put a person into a situation where his senses are overloaded with non-coherent information, and the mind will go 'numb' as a protective mechanism . . . it gets confused and overwhelmed, and critical faculties no longer work properly." It's no wonder that seemingly smart people can be deceived.

—C. B. Harris, "A Test of Faith," Orange Coast Magazine,
April 1990, p. 95.

If a person is willing to go through the painful process of breaking through the denial and seeing the addictive progression, there is hope for change.

seeing the addictive progression, there is hope for change. The following section traces one woman's addiction from the foundation through the late stages.

The Foundation

Faye Stanley was an only child born into a dysfunctional family. Although she survived emotionally, her family's problems affected her entire life. She never escaped the destruction that came from her father and the family he created. Her father was a rugged man who worked in a machine shop. It was a dirty job, and he would come home with grease on his work pants and black grease under his nails. He would enter the house after work, grab a beer, head for the shower, and then spend the rest of the evening walking around the house in his pants and a sleeveless undershirt. Rarely was he clean shaven except on Wednesday nights and Sunday mornings when he would take the family to church. He was mean, uncaring, and miserable to be around. Feelings were not allowed as a part of the family experience.

Faye's mother was an unskilled woman who never graduated from high school. She would have left Faye's father long ago, but she had no way of making a living. She feared that she and Faye would starve on the streets. She stuck by her husband and tolerated his abuse partly because of her feelings of dependency and partly because of her belief that a woman should not leave her husband. So, while Faye's mother prayed for her husband to change, Faye and her mother suffered his abuse. He hit his wife and abused his daughter verbally. His feelings of inadequacy were projected onto the two females as he demeaned them in all sorts of ways. By the time Faye was ten, she felt totally inadequate and inferior to her friends; she especially felt inferior to men.

Faye developed physically quite early. Her father was the first to notice the shapeliness of her hips and the budding of her breasts. Her menstrual cycle started when she was eleven—and so did her father's sexual abuse. One night a week Faye's mom met with the other women at church. It became a time of terror for Faye as "Daddy's special time" came around each week.

Faye stopped facing life as other little girls did. She crawled into a complex world of fantasy to survive the abuse. She felt as dirty as her father smelled when he came home from work. Her guilt was extreme. For two years the sexual abuse continued until Faye's mother came home early one night to find the two of them in Faye's bed. None of them talked about it again, but Faye's mother never left her alone. They lived with the nasty little secret, each one rationalizing it away.

The verbal abuse continued throughout adolescence. Faye was always ridiculed for less than perfect behavior. Her parents' expectations of her to excel above them drove her to work hard and make something of herself. She did well, but that was never good enough. Her parents rarely affirmed her efforts. They commented about how something could have been better or how someone else appeared to be working harder and doing more than Faye. She was driven in her attempts to meet their needs. It was an incongruous setup to have two underachieving parents demanding more than Faye could possibly deliver. The pressure became so intense that shortly after graduation from high school, Faye married and moved out. Within a month she was pregnant.

· · • · ·

At the age of twenty-four Faye Stanley was fed up with the way her life was going. Her husband had left her three years ago, and she was miserable raising her daughter alone. Between her job at the phone company, her housework, and the care of her daughter, she had little time for herself or a social life. She became deeply depressed and wondered if life could ever be any better. At times she thought of suicide and probably would have done it if not for her daughter.

LUTHERAN BABY BOOMERS

A fifty-eight-page report based on a study of baby boomers between twenty and forty years old in 111 Lutheran Church in America congregations states that "baby-boom church members 'seem to prefer a community of believers that helps them feel wanted and needed, offers a friendly atmosphere, accentuates the positive [and] at times challenges them physically, spiritually, intellectually and financially.'" This is opposed to such things as "denominational pedigree, rightness of doctrine or constancy in the practices of piety."

—Washington UPI, "Baby Boomers Found Short on
Commitment," Los Angeles Times, January 24, 1987.

FOUNDATIONS FOR RELIGIOUS ADDICTION

- Abusive parent, often the father. Abuse is physical, emotional or sexual.
- Child deprived of nurturing. Neither parent meets the basic emotional needs of the child.
- Feelings of alienation. Child feels detached from the family and what is perceived as a perfect world for others.
- Attitudes of perfectionism from imperfect parents. Demanding parents inflict the child with an irrational desire to be perfect and make no mistakes.
- High expectations. The parents are relentless in demanding the child be what they were not and attain what they did not.
- Low affirmation. Although the child exerts tremendous effort, the parents are never satisfied and rarely provide positive feedback to the child.
- Parents' addiction problems. Frequently, one or both parents will be alcoholics or sex addicts, or they will exhibit some other obvious compulsive behavior.
- Absent father. A child of divorce may have little male influence.
- Feelings of being dirty. Abuse and negative attention leave a child feeling guilty and dirty.
- Poor peer relationships. Afraid to share personal reality with others, the child feels cut off emotionally from friends and often seeks destructive relationships.
- Vivid fantasy world. Reality becomes so difficult that the child creates a fantasy world and retreats to it frequently.
- Feelings not shared. The home has provided little freedom to express emotions, and the child never learns how this is done or why it is helpful.

She had few opportunities to fix herself up and feel good about the way she looked. The only time she dressed up was to go to church, which she rarely did because she felt so alienated by the people there. When she married, they were her best friends. When she divorced, they treated her like she was a threat to their marriages and images. In her loneliness she became a seething caldron of unresolved emotions. Every area of her life seemed to be gradually drifting out of control.

The Early Stage

The First Experience

In Faye's darkest moments she cried out for God. She felt a deep emptiness that she knew was a lack of spiritual growth. It was hard for her to completely trust her life to God since she had never resolved some of her childhood faith problems. She was distraught over how a loving God could allow her to be abused. It made no sense to her that her father could be so evil and continue to be part of the church. Her spiritual journey was hampered by her many doubts. She longed for a relationship with God, and she longed for a relationship with a man. Any attention would be better than the loneliness crippling her.

One day at work a fellow worker saw that Faye was depressed and provided her with a listening ear. When she was in the middle of expressing her pain and explaining her extreme stress, he asked her to attend a meeting with him. She was more than happy to go. She arranged for a coworker to keep her daughter, and off she went on the closest thing she had had to a date in three years. She felt like a little girl in the presence of the man. She giggled and talked nervously while he silently drove the car to the meeting. She admired a strength and calm about him. She was pleased that they were going to a religious meeting their first time out.

They arrived at a church building that had no name on it. As they entered the rear of the building, the people were in silent prayer. At the front of the church a woman dressed in a colorful robe was chant-

She longed for a relationship with God, and she longed for a relationship with a man. Any attention would be better than the loneliness crippling her.

ing. As she chanted, she motioned with her hands in small circles, and she kept her middle fingers touching her thumbs. There were no crosses or Bibles in the church; it was very stark and plain, unlike any other church Faye had been in. The minister asked the followers to raise their heads and slowly open their eyes. The flutist who had been playing during the prayer stopped, and the minister began to speak.

Faye was mesmerized by the minister's voice. She felt warm listening to the words and being next to her friend and the others in the room. The minister instructed the people to hug one another and express something positive about the person being hugged. Faye hugged her friend and told him she admired his calm strength. He then told her that she was very beautiful and obviously a very smart lady he was proud to be with. She almost melted at his words. Later she would remember that during the hugging time she began to feel wanted. She felt good, and a wonderful sense of relief came over her. She felt like she belonged, like she had found a home.

When the hugging was over, the minister began to speak about a life free of pain and disappointment. She talked about the incredible faith that must be developed to find the level of living where even the death of a friend is seen as something good. She said that the suffering of the most sincere believer is accompanied by gratification in the midst of the crisis.

Faye saw the evil in her life and how she had been so negative. The woman was speaking right to her, it seemed. It was the first time a minister had communicated so directly to her need. She told her friend she wanted to join the group. He told her it was too early. He encouraged her to return a couple of times before she made a decision. She agreed that she would come back.

Faye was astonished that they didn't ask for money. They encouraged people to come for a month before deciding to give anything. That made a great impression on her. She was tired of the money-hungry ministers always begging her to give more than she had. She felt it was a true sign of their integrity and sincerity that they would not immediately be interested in money. Before she left, there was another hugging session, and the minister gave her a special blessing. She felt great and looked forward to coming back again.

There were no crosses or Bibles in the church; it was very stark and plain, unlike any other church Faye had been in.

In her glorious feelings of euphoria and belonging, she never stopped to realize that no one had ever mentioned God.

On the way home, her friend was more talkative. He told Faye that she fit in well with the group, that she seemed to be one of them from the beginning. He went on to say that the minister had spoken to him on the way out and expressed her desire for Faye to be part of the group. Faye was overwhelmed with his comments and the evening. Before he had spoken to her that day, she was depressed and lonely. Within a short eight hours she felt loved, accepted, and part of something very good. In her glorious feelings of euphoria and belonging, she never stopped to realize that no one had ever mentioned God.

Intoxication of Belonging

A first experience with a harmful faith system can be intoxicating. There is a rush in breaking away from isolation and into the arms of several others who appear to care deeply. The leader's attention only enhances the intoxicating effects of finding a place to belong. The hurting person reaches out and needs are met, attention is paid, and the potential addict becomes hooked on the warm fuzzies of the worshipers. That a person feeling so left out could feel so wanted is an amazing emotional leap hard to forget. The victim equates sincerity with attention and wants to belong to something that provides such a sense of belonging. If the victim was depressed before hooking up with harmful faith believers, the relief from the depression is so dramatic that he or she often feels emotionally healed just from being with others who care so much. Rational thought and objective evaluation are discarded to enjoy the emotional rush that comes from breaking out of isolation and joining others in spiritual pursuit. It feels so good that the victim is convinced it must be right and it must be of God.

As in any addiction, the initial experience during the first stage alters the mood. A person tries something and feels better. God

Rational thought and objective evaluation are discarded to enjoy the emotional rush that comes from breaking out of isolation and joining others in spiritual pursuit.

doesn't have to change or heal the person's emotions. The group's affirmation is the only thing necessary. Although some people feel uncomfortable in the presence of other followers, a susceptible victim, full of pain and disappointment, doesn't evaluate the experience or feel threatened by the others involved with it. He or she simply feels it, and it feels wonderful. The religious experience, intensified by contact with the religious leader, is just as powerful as a shot of tequila or a hit of cocaine. It radically changes how the person feels, and that person will come back for more.

The susceptible religious addict doesn't realize that every aspect of first exposure to a harmful faith system has been premeditated. What happens and what is said to that potential follower are not accidental. Everything works together so the person is easily manipulated into liking the group and wanting to return. Having physical contact, hearing a special word from the leader, statements that make the victim feel exceptional, no plea for money, and delaying a decision to join—all are tools calculated to win the person into the group. The leader wants control of the victim's life and provides a very addictive initial contact to lock the person into the harmful faith experience.

Sometimes the initial experience is not in a worship setting. It can occur over the telephone. My wife and I were watching television one day when we flipped the dial to a program featuring a man who had a local group and was trying to build his following over television. I wondered aloud to my wife what would happen if I offered to give money to the organization. I called the number and acted as if I was a susceptible victim to the get-rich-through-God plans that were being preached. I told the woman that I wanted to give money. She astounded me by saying that she did not want a first-time caller giving money. She was there to help me and suggested I listen further before giving money. If I believed the fellow was a wonderful man of God, I would have thought that he had a sincere heart for ministry. I suspected he was a fraud, however, because I recognized the organization's strategy as a very clever scheme to hook a person into the hurtful faith system. Every day, susceptible victims enter the early stages of addiction by naively aligning themselves with a harmful faith system because of a remarkable initial experience.

The susceptible religious addict doesn't realize that every aspect of the first exposure to a harmful faith system has been premeditated.

Growing Attraction

Faye's initial experience was followed by a visit from the group leader. Their time together bonded Faye to the group. Faye thought the leader was very spiritual. Faye was told that she, too, possessed many spiritual powers that would be developed as she participated in the group. The leader assured Faye that they were there to meet her needs and she should call on anyone in the group at any time. Having this person come to her house made Faye feel very significant. She loved the sense of belonging and the special attention.

Before leaving, the woman spent a few moments with Faye's daughter. She told Faye that she sensed some very deep spiritual rumblings within the center of the child. These needed to be calmed, so she asked Faye to bring the girl to their next gathering for a special time of spiritual cleansing. Faye had worried about her daughter, and she was relieved to discover that there would be a cure for her withdrawn and listless behavior.

At the next gathering Faye became hooked. Her daughter was prayed over, hummed with, touched by everyone in the group, and hugged until her clothes were wrinkled. Also the group prayed that Faye would find a special man and that her spiritual guide would lead her out of despair and into the life she wanted. By the evening's end, she realized she was feeling something she had not felt for some time. She was feeling hope.

It was obvious that the people weren't worshiping God as she had worshiped Him in church when she was growing up. They rarely mentioned God, and they never brought up the name of Christ unless they were referring to a teaching compatible with their beliefs. Because she was caught up in the ecstasy of acceptance, their beliefs didn't seem to matter. She had found a home and people who seemed to love her. Those incredible feelings of belonging seemed to matter most. There was so much affection and love that she really didn't care how the beliefs differed. To her, being with the people and sharing in their worship experience were direct gifts from God. She wanted what they had, and she wanted to be a part of what they did. That they cared equally for her daughter made them all the more attractive.

Because she was caught up in the ecstasy of acceptance, their beliefs didn't seem to matter. She had found a home and people who seemed to love her.

Anytime people with lingering pain and a growing sense of emptiness are not focused completely on God, they are likely to fall for a counterfeit experience or become dependent on a compulsive behavior for relief.

Faye is like many other addicts from dysfunctional homes. Instead of growing from the dysfunction, she fell back into it. The early experiences left her (and other addicts like her) hurting and distrustful, searching for a way out of the pain. Whatever is convenient and available that will provide hope or just a change in the drudgery of everyday responsibility can become a source of dependency.

Anytime people with lingering pain and a growing sense of emptiness are not focused completely on God, they are likely to fall for a counterfeit experience or become dependent on a compulsive behavior for relief. They can be attracted to the most unattractive things, such as prostitutes, anonymous sex shops, smelly bars, and repulsive behaviors. Anything becomes attractive as desperation grows.

In the case of religious addiction, the attraction is not so difficult. The desperation does not have to reach the same depths. The people look good and smell nice, and all the activity is supposed to be for a glorious purpose. It's no wonder so many people can become attracted and then addicted to a harmful faith system.

WORLD WAR III

Guru Ma, Elizabeth Clare Prophet, invited "all her faithful, who may number some 30,000 worldwide, to move to Montana and escape the coming doom. Followers have begun to converge on the region and lease homes in a church-owned subdivision. At the main headquarters, dubbed the 'inner retreat,' the group is constructing a system of tubular underground shelters for 756 people." They own 33,500 acres and have launched extensive construction projects. The group has been found to hold a large amount of weapons for defense. Guru Ma's daughter "has joined a growing phalanx of outspoken defectors and accuses her mother of pursuing an opulent lifestyle, dining on lobster and prime rib, while keeping her followers in a constant state of austerity as they prepare for World War III."

—*Michael P. Harris, "Paradise Under Siege," Time, August 28, 1989, p. 61.*

Religious addicts don't worship God. They use spiritual highs to satiate the need to experience something other than the boredom and pain of their existence.

Perversion

Religious addicts don't worship God. They use spiritual highs to satiate the need to experience something other than the boredom and pain of their existence. They use activity to distract themselves from their tough reality. They pervert what God intended for good. Seeking faith in God, they become so diverted by the experience and activity that they miss God.

Just as sex is good and draws marriage partners together in a richer relationship, religion can be good and draw people closer to God. But anything that is ordained by God can be perverted into an experience of ecstasy used only for relief. Both the act of sex and the worship of God can be perverted into the worship of self. Relief of the painful self becomes the entire focus of the endeavor.

Perversion becomes possible in the worship of God and the practice of religion because of the addict's neediness and brokenness in coming from a dysfunctional family. The foundation of dysfunction allows for the distortion of something good into something negative, self-centered, and exploitative. The severe dependency needs of the adult child of dysfunction turn faith into a practice of rituals, beliefs, and

The intended focus of real faith is distorted and perverted, lost in the trance and delusional reality that the religion drug can provide.

doctrine as a way to make life tolerable. The intended focus of real faith is distorted and perverted, lost in the trance and delusional reality that the religion drug can provide. The victim continues to practice the rituals of the religion and falls out of love with God and in love with the compulsion. The perverted faith looks good and feels good, but it is a counterfeit of a true love for and faith in God.

Transition from God

The religious addict begins a gradual transition away from God. Church attendance is no longer based on the need to know God; the addict attends church to feel significant and secure in a system of faith. Prayers are no longer ways of communing with God; the addict prays to have an experience as a person of God and takes pride in being able to talk of the hours spent in prayer. He or she uses the church to avoid life rather than find the strength and guidance to encounter all that life has to offer—good or bad. What could have been a place to find shelter from the storms of life becomes a place where the religious addict "sets up camp" to stay out of life. Being there is the priority over worshiping God.

Sacrifice for the church completed in the name of God sacrifices the family and the addict's relationship with the family. Attendance at church becomes excessive to the point of being obsessive. Every spare moment is devoted to a church-related activity. Other family members become concerned because when they are together, the addict is at church; the noble cause of serving on committees is not to be questioned by the seemingly less faithful other family members. The faith grows more harmful as religion becomes a hindrance to the intimacy needed to maintain significant family relationships. Each family member starts to take a separate path away from the religious addict. Unfortunately, those paths are often also away from God.

What could have been a place to find shelter from the storms of life becomes a place where the religious addict "sets up camp" to stay out of life.

Rather than recognize the personal areas that need work for growth and maturity, the addict refuses to change and becomes increasingly locked into the behaviors that maintain the religious addiction.

Eventually, the addiction directs the addict's focus back to self and away from God and others. Initially, the addict judges himself harshly and wishes he could be as good as the rest of the world. As the addict's compulsive nature develops he starts to negatively judge others and defend himself. Rather than recognize the personal areas that need work for growth and maturity, the addict refuses to change and becomes increasingly locked into the behaviors that maintain the religious addiction. The addict loses all humility; he or she no longer embraces the imperfections of humanity or acknowledges personal shortcomings. Living in denial and self-justification makes life without God easy, and the transition becomes a very rapid slide away from Him.

False faith becomes an excuse to hurt others when addiction robs the believer of faith. Scripture is used as a weapon. The addict quotes it to justify and rationalize her problems while she contorts it to shame, dismiss, and disqualify all others. The "us versus them" mentality of the harmful faith leader becomes part of the addict's mentality. As dependency on the hurtful faith grows, the addict becomes more hostile and isolated. A new family replaces the old one. The new family of believers does not confront and allows the addict to live according to her delusions. The old one becomes too reality based to tolerate.

The addict's entire perspective on life changes. Simplistic answers replace explorations of all the dimensions of a problem. The difficulty of a true walk of faith is replaced with the magical belief that all is well for the faithful. Pleasing the other faithful takes priority over pleasing God. The addict is forced to conform to the other misled believers; pressure mounts to not disappoint those who are the new source of love and encouragement. True faith is destroyed as a new faith grows in people, principles, and a place to feel needed.

The difficulty of a true walk of faith is replaced with the magical belief that all is well for the faithful.

CHARACTERISTICS OF THE EARLY STAGE OF RELIGIOUS ADDICTION

- Extreme stress. Increased stress impairs judgment and obscures warning signs of harmful faith.
- Repeated disappointments. Feelings that nothing works out right lead a potential addict to seek quick fix solutions to lost expectations.
- Miserable existence. The addict has turned in many directions for hope and found none.
- Feelings of insignificance. The addict starts to believe life does not matter and there is no productive part to be played in it.
- Spiritual search initiated. Out of despair the addict seeks spiritual answers as a last resort.
- Loneliness. Any attention from any source would be welcomed.
- Hoping for someone to solve misery. Solving the problems seems too difficult; there is a need to be rescued.
- Increasing doubts about God. Wondering if God cares or if God is real, he or she is more vulnerable to variations of traditional faith.
- Increasing dependency on others. Association with others allows for delusional thoughts and existence in an unreal world.
- Feelings of guilt. Nothing can be done to overcome powerful guilt feelings.
- Feelings of insecurity. A terrible disaster seems to be lurking, and everything seems to be a potential sign of doom.
- Geographic cures. In an attempt to solve problems, the addict believes a fresh start will make life better but discovers it has further complicated the problems.
- Loss of other interests. Family, friends, and other activities are replaced with the compulsive activities surrounding the practice of hurtful faith.

- Abandonment by friends and family. Associates become so irritated by obnoxious behavior that they no longer spend time with the religious addict.
- Unwillingness to discuss problems. The individual becomes unapproachable about increasing out-of-control behaviors.
- One-sided sermons. Edicts, Scriptures, and judgments so fill the dialogue with the person that all conversations cease.
- Faith attached to a person. A comforting person becomes the link to harmful faith.
- Intoxicating affiliation. First experiences in new harmful faith group produce immediate mood alteration.
- Growing attraction. Every new meeting, person, and experience increases the attraction to the harmful faith group.
- Heavy church attendance. Attendance becomes a means of avoidance and a way to be part of the group with little relationship with God.
- Conformity with other addicts. The person starts to look, dress, and talk like others in the group.
- Lack of intimate relationships. Intimacy with friends and family is sacrificed for the sake of religion.
- Growing denial and self-justification. The person becomes blind to problems and justifies behavior.
- Scripture as a weapon. Verses are quoted to judge others and justify self.

The initial stage of religious addiction is a difficult one to spot. Many who do the same things as religious addicts are actually involved in a real faith, but their motives and foundations are different. Many faithful followers would be wrongly labeled first-stage religious

There was nothing she would not do for the group. That included giving about 30 percent of her salary to the leader.

addicts; many addicts would be considered faithful followers of God. Only in the second stage does the differentiation become marked as the addiction rises to the surface to reveal the poisonous faith of an addict.

The Middle Stage

Complete Attachment

It wasn't long until Faye's growing attraction turned to complete attachment. She became deeply immersed in the group. Their identity was her identity. She belonged and felt valuable and significant. She wanted to be the strongest member possible, so she talked about her religious experience at every opportunity, gathered faithfully with the others, and read books that explained how to develop spiritual powers.

There was nothing she would not do for the group. That included giving about 30 percent of her salary to the leader. Upon receiving every paycheck, she wrote out a check to the group first. Sometimes her daughter had no milk for her cereal. Sometimes they had to eat beans every possible way beans can be eaten. She didn't think it was too much for her to give, even though the leader drove an expensive foreign car. Some months if the group needed more money, Faye went beyond the usual 30 percent. She was so attached to the group that she almost felt it was a commune where everyone should share everything. Her attachment to the group was complete.

Faye stopped all relationships with anyone outside the group. She didn't trust people who didn't hold her views, and she cut herself off from them. The only outsiders she spent time with were the ones she tried to recruit into the group. She was so attached to the philosophies she learned and the practice of faith with the group that she burned with desire to bring others into the group. She saw every person she met as a potential member. She would listen to an individual, searching for a point of need she could address. Once she found it, she prom-

What looks to be a supernatural encounter with God is nothing but a chemical reaction; it's not as powerful as heroin, but it's just as destructive. Addicts search for the high—not for God.

ised her group would meet it. Many were turned off by her pushiness, but others were attracted to the group because Faye was so strong in her beliefs and association with the other members.

Religious Self-Medication

Addiction usually begins from a desire to self-medicate pain and suffering and to remove the weight of being a responsible person. Where meaning and purpose are lacking, where spiritual strength is deficient, the developing addict will find some means to drug the pain and emptiness. The religious experience is the source of medication. The repeated search for the ecstatic experience becomes a quest much like the heroin addict looking to score a new supply of drugs; sometimes it is successful, sometimes not. When it isn't successful, the hunt for ecstasy continues.

Religious addicts work themselves up into a frenzy to experience a religious catharsis. They swoon, fall over, scream, yell, faint, jump up and down, and do anything that will pump adrenaline through the blood. They learn how to induce the euphoric rush when excitement

---

CHRISTIAN SCIENCE HEALING

- "On June 18, 1977, fifteen-month-old Matthew Swan awoke with high fever and vomiting. His mother, Rita, called on a practitioner of Christian Science healing. Rita and her husband, Doug, believed in the power of Christian Science to heal through prayer. But Matthew grew worse every day, suffering pain and paralysis. On the 13th day of his illness, the Swans sought medical help—too late. Today, Rita blames the church for admonishing her to stay away from doctors. But, most of all, she blames herself." Rita and Doug were led to believe that "their fears about their baby's health were making him ill." That's a terrible load of guilt to carry for the rest of their lives.
- "During the evening of April 3, 1986, Ginger and David Twitchell's younger son, two-and-a-half-year-old Robyn, had stomach pain followed by vomiting. For the next five days, the Twitchells and their Christian Science practitioner prayed for Robyn, but on Tuesday, April 8, he died." Although the Twitchells are on trial for manslaughter, "if faced with the same situation today, however, they say they would again begin by praying. 'Who are we to trust?' asks David. 'God or man?'"

—Rosalind Wright, "A Matter of Life and Death," Good Housekeeping, March 1990, p. 68.

turns to hormones flooding the system. What looks to be a supernatural encounter with God is nothing but a chemical reaction; it's not as powerful as heroin, but it's just as destructive. Addicts search for the high—not for God. They feel inadequate and incomplete any time they walk away from a gathering or service in which they did not have an incredible rush of their own chemicals through the bloodstream.

All of the pent-up hurt and depression must find a source of release. Anyone could sex it out, drink it out, or gamble it out on a temporary basis. Religious addicts choose to ritual it out. Each session of worship becomes a repeat of the behaviors that led to the emotional catharsis the previous time. If it doesn't occur, the emotions remain imprisoned and continue to seek a source of release. Anger and rage may result from the unexpressed emotions that are without a release valve. The addicts are so deluded, they function at such an unemotional level, that they are unable to see they are out of control and their emotions are set to self-destruct. If the service or worship experience does not manufacture the fix, religious addicts may look elsewhere to find it. This leads to the development of other addictions alongside the religious one.

Dual Addictions

Religious addicts cannot find relief from a religious source every time. Because they become frustrated that they are not experiencing the same intensity as they did in the early days of their faith, they turn to other sources to supplement the addiction of choice. Some drink and become dependent on the secret times of drunkenness. These usually follow some of the most intense worship times with the group. However, most commonly religious addicts are food junkies. They love sugar rushes, and they love the hours they take up eating everything they can find. The leader of the group, who is often overweight also, never speaks against overeating. Too many people would feel abandoned and potentially not return to the church. The leader will yell and scream against alcoholics, but he or she will never insinuate that someone is committing the sin of gluttony.

Sexual sins and sexual addictions also can surface as the intensity of the religious experience weakens. Secret and shameful sexual experiences produce a high similar to religious ecstasy. The tightly wrapped addict, afraid to break any of the organization's rules, is afraid to admit frailties and desires that would be labeled unholy. Unexpressed lust is coupled with the intense need for relief. The need for relief lands the addict in the arms of the first person willing to participate in meeting special needs. The forbidden sins of faith saturate the body with mood altering substances as the adulterer is lost to a fantasy world of secret sex and irresponsibility. Many are hurt by it, and no one understands how such a dedicated person could commit such an offensive act.

Recruiting Others to the Faith

In the middle stage the religious addict is destined to recruit as many people to the group as possible. A day without an attempt to attract someone into the group is a wasted day to the religious addict. The true Christian shares faith in God with others. A person with the gift of evangelism loves to talk with others about faith. But the religious addict is more interested in sharing the experience. Each new person who is willing to share the experience becomes a reassurance that the addict is doing the right thing. Each new recruit affirms the decision to affiliate with the group and becomes a motivation to work even harder. The addict is compelled to tell others of the pleasure that comes from the group, its leader, and the practice of the faith.

Anyone refusing to participate is shamed, ridiculed, and labeled ungodly. The addict's beliefs must be reinforced; anyone rejecting those beliefs must be discounted at all costs. The more entrenched the person is in the system, the bigger the threat when he or she is rebuffed by someone. Anyone who communicates why the group is not practicing true faith must be rejected as swiftly as that person rejects the beliefs. Each rejection, interpreted as rejection by God, produces tremendous pain and insecurity. It motivates the addict to try harder, talk to more people, and grow spiritually so people will be more attracted to the group.

All-Encompassing Harmful Faith

During the middle stage of religious addiction, dependency on religion encompasses each aspect of the misled believer's life. Time is consumed by the church or group activity and the compulsive acting out of faith. Like a junkie whose life is consumed with his next score,

Anyone who communicates why the group is not practicing true faith must be rejected as swiftly as that person rejects the beliefs.

the religious addict, obsessed with the next crusade, worship service, street-witnessing extravaganza, or whatever the ritual that sets up the addict's next religious high.

Addicts band together and get high by acting righteous and above all others. They inflate their feelings by perceiving that they merit God's acceptance. They continue their high by endeavoring to please others so that they look superior to those who observe the acts of sacrifice.

Everything must involve the practice of faith. Every trip to the grocery store is an act of faith and an opportunity to recruit others. A walk down the street can result in a scriptural shouting match that the addict believes will win others to God. Friends are in the group, or they are not friends. Family members are supportive, or they are avoided. Social events must involve people of the faith.

Anyone outside the group of believers is viewed as contaminated by the world and unfit for interaction. Nothing exists outside the realm of other faithful followers who have forsaken all earthly ties in attempts to please God. They have become so focused on their concept of heavenly good, their world is so saturated with their harmful faith, that they are of no use to anyone outside their group.

The harmful faith becomes a ritual of sacrifice reaching into the pocket and the relationships of misled believers. Religious addicts give sacrificially to merit the "blessings of God." They sacrifice their time, finances, and their intimate or significant relationships to please their God. They make whatever sacrifice necessary to obtain their fix—like a cocaine addict who once used the drug out of desire or choice but now is forced to spend money earmarked to meet the family's basic needs. Religious addicts will spend vacation savings, retirement savings, Social Security checks, grocery money, or anything available to gain favor from the leader of the group. Nothing is so sacred that it cannot be devoured by the all-encompassing practice of harmful faith.

Special Gifts

The emergence of special gifts may become the means by which the religious addict evaluates the quality of the relationship with God. When special talents are claimed, such as the ability to predict the

---

Nothing is so sacred that it cannot be devoured by the all encompassing practice of harmful faith.

Some religious addicts become so focused on the gift that they forget about God, the Giver of all gifts.

future, the addict merits the acknowledgment of other followers and prestige within the group. The addict becomes more and more dependent on exercising the gift in public to achieve the mood alteration necessary to feel loved and accepted.

Many people have very real spiritual gifts to minister to others. Some have the gift of compassion, which is a supernatural ability to reach out to others, to make them feel accepted, and to meet their needs. Others might have the gift of teaching, causing God's Word to be absorbed into the hearts of students. These spiritual gifts differ from the counterfeits of self-manufactured talents used to exploit others and elevate self-importance. Even these spiritual gifts can be perverted and exploited. Some religious addicts become so focused on the gift that they forget about God, the Giver of all gifts. They use their gifts to rise to the top of the organization, claiming to be specially anointed by God. True spiritual gifts are exercised in humility for the service of the body. They are never used for self-elevation.

Increased Pressure

With increased involvement in the harmful religion comes the added pressure of responsibility. The honeymoon eventually ends, and the religious addict becomes aware of the demands of the leader. The greater the demands, the more compelled the addict is to perform up to the standards of the one in spiritual authority. As the leader holds the follower accountable, the religious addict responds with more intense effort and the desire to please. The stakes are placed higher; the addict is asked to sacrifice self-identity, family, and what is known to be right and wrong. The leader's views are promoted in place of right and wrong. The addict is so saturated with harmful faith, nothing seems unreasonable. The more that is asked, the more that is given. The goal is not to please God; it is to please the leader.

The stakes are placed higher; the addict is asked to sacrifice self-identity, family, and what is known to be right and wrong.

The religious addiction has become a trap not easily sprung. What was once an experience of liberation now enslaves the religious addict.

What once brought relief from the pressures of life is now depended upon for survival. Without the group and its rules, the addict fears being set adrift. The religious addiction has become a trap not easily sprung. What was once an experience of liberation now enslaves the religious addict.

Attendance and involvement used to bring a sense of belonging. Now absence or lack of involvement brings tremendous feelings of guilt. The addict is now caught up in having to remain obsessively and compulsively involved to defend against any sense of not measuring up. Hope becomes less a prospect than ever imagined. Tough reality starts to blot it out as it was blotted out before the religious addiction developed. The addiction diminishes in its ability to provide relief. The addict begins to act out; the behavior becomes more bizarre and ritualized to maintain the illusion of hope the harmful faith provides.

Deepening Denial

By the time religious addicts are in the middle stage of the progression, they have created their own world with their own rules and are unwilling to be with anyone who does not abide by those rules. They insulate themselves from those who challenge the harmful faith system. Their denial of reality and their problems deepen as they hang on to their harmful faith and their distorted reality. They lock into the system and their beliefs and go through the motions, waiting for a major spiritual breakthrough.

They want God to perform a miracle, just for them, to prove He is real. Their faith has died, and without some type of tangible evidence, they cannot go on. In their denial, they claim that coincidence is a miracle of God. They claim healing for problems that never existed. If these proofs do not come immediately, they wait. Some religious addicts have sat atop a hillside for months waiting for the Second Coming. The predicted date passes, but they stay put, denying the reality that their date was wrong. Rather than come down the hill and rejoin society, they live in the protection of their denial and their false hopes of divine intervention. They become like compulsive gamblers waiting for the long shot to come in. Neither gambler nor religious addicts see the price they are paying for their denial and magical thinking.

As the denial deepens, addicts eliminate all doubts about their faith and no longer question the validity of anything within the practice of the faith. The harmful faith makes them blind to truth. Everything else is questioned in light of the hurtful faith. Personal interpretation of Scripture becomes the standard of truth, and all judgments of others are based on those self-conceived interpretations and standards. All problems are flatly denied. Denial prevents discussion on any issue that might crack the facade of perfection. Others' problems are addressed with pat answers and little concern. The clock of despair ticks swiftly, bringing addicts closer each day to the point when financial problems, illness, or emotional distress can no longer be denied.

The middle stage of religious addiction is full of activity and diversions from God. The addict is able to function, believing the harmful faith is the real thing. God is lost, and there is little chance of finding Him until the addict hits bottom in the last stage of religious addiction.

The Late Stage

When Faye reached the last stage of her addiction, it did not take long for her to hit bottom. She gave all of her savings to the group, and she lived from paycheck to paycheck. She felt that she was trusting in God to provide for her and her daughter if problems arose. The problems came and destroyed her. First, problems developed at work. No one at work could stand to be around her because all she did was rant and rave about her group. Then when her work was in a bind, she was unavailable because she was at a group gathering. Finally when she started arguing about religion, it ended in a shouting match and her supervisor fired her.

She felt good about being fired. It was the price she had to pay for her faith. She loved playing the martyr. She lived on her severance money for two weeks, and then she was broke. That was when her

---

As the denial deepens, addicts eliminate all doubts about their faith and no longer question the validity of anything within the practice of the faith. The toxic faith makes them blind to the truth.

CHARACTERISTICS OF THE MIDDLE STAGE OF RELIGIOUS ADDICTION

- Immersed in the system. The person becomes an active member, identifying completely with the group.
- Knows propaganda of the group. Many pieces from the leader's writings are readily quoted.
- Outspoken. Little regard is shown for offensive comments made in the name of faith.
- Giving unusual amounts of money. Basic needs of the family are sacrificed to have gifts noticed by the organization and win favor.
- Relates to few people outside the group. Relationships are limited to other misled believers.
- Recruitment of others. Motivated to recruit others to the harmful faith, the addict does not attempt to bring others closer to God.
- Self-medication. The religious experience becomes an intoxicating high that medicates the addict's pain. Each new day is a search for a new religious high.
- Disappointed if ecstasy does not occur. Longing for the emotional catharsis that brings relief, the addict searches for other forms of relief when the harmful faith does not produce it.
- Dual addictions. Other addictions develop, such as eating, drinking, and having illicit sexual encounters, as the pleasure from religious ecstasy wears off.
- Difficult to handle rejection. Those refusing to join the group are discounted to overcome the feelings of rejection.
- All-encompassing practice of faith. Every area of the addict's life is affected by the destructive faith.
- Always searching for ways to further the faith. Every activity is used as a means to talk about the group and its beliefs.
- Discovery and use of special gifts. Self-manufactured

and authentic spiritual gifts are used to exploit and manipulate.

- Claims of special anointing. The addict believes God has provided a more unique mission and more unique gifts than the less faithful have.
- Increased pressure. The drive to perform and please does not stop.
- Involvement for survival. The addict becomes trapped in the system with no choice but to conform or risk mental upheaval. The addict is totally dependent on the system for survival.
- Deepening denial. Unable to see the price being paid for the magical thinking, the addict refuses to question the reality of the faith.

daughter became ill with a kidney disease. With no money to go to the doctor, and her child's fever raging, Faye called the leader of her group and asked for advice. The leader told her to bring her daughter to the gathering that night so they could pray for her. She took her daughter there and everyone prayed and touched her, but she did not get better. They told her to have faith, and God would take care of the girl.

As the days of hoping for a miracle passed, Faye watched her daughter drift in and out of consciousness. She questioned whether to trust the group. She questioned their motives from the beginning. She realized she had no money because of the group. Her thoughts of doubt were merely passing suggestions, but they finally became strong enough to motivate her to take the girl to the county hospital. When she arrived, the girl was unconscious and lifeless. The doctors hooked her up to a dialysis machine, but by noon the next day the girl was dead.

Faye became hysterical. God had failed her; the group had led her the wrong way; now her daughter was dead. Her family knew the reason was that she did not take the girl to the doctor in time. Faye was humiliated, depressed, and ashamed. Her family tried to console her, but she did not want to be with them. She gathered enough strength to have a funeral for her child. Each person there was someone who had disappointed her in some way. She felt hopeless and alienated from the world. When the last shovel of dirt covered her daughter's grave, she drove home, sobbing as she made her way back to where the memories of her little girl lived.

At the house, a calm came over her. She regained her poise, and her tears dried up. She felt a new peace about what had happened. It didn't matter what the others thought of her. It was irrelevant that the group had been a farce. She didn't care that they took her money. All that mattered to her was her little girl and being near her. She cleaned up the house, took a bath, and prepared for bed. Before entering the bedroom, she went to the medicine cabinet and took down the bottle of sleeping pills that had been there for over a year. Faye went to the kitchen, poured a glass of water, and took all thirty pills. She calmly walked to the bedroom, wrote a note to those who would find her, said her prayers, lay down, and never woke up again. She became another tragic victim of harmful faith and religious addiction.

Religion Stops Working

Faith stops working for all religious addicts, just as it did for Faye. When religious addicts reach the last stage of the progression, they are consumed by the addiction and isolated from anyone who is not part of the harmful faith system. Anyone not accepting the delusions of the addicts is considered weak in faith or at times even the enemy. The enemies can include family members. No one is allowed into the private world of misled believers. Only those who are also consumed by the addiction are trusted. The addicts will not listen to reason, and they base all their decisions on what the faith leader says or what they believe God has told them. Eventually, the isolation and the false beliefs create a crisis that cannot be overcome by more denial.

Life does not feel good in the last stage of addiction. All is not fun, and every religious experience is not enjoyable. The highs still come, but they are fewer and shorter. The less relief that comes from them, the more the addicts rely on another addiction such as eating to provide the pleasure lacking from the religious experiences. When the religious highs diminish, feelings of despair and distress replace them. The addicts try harder in hopes of working up relief. When relief does not come, they feel abandoned by God, and the original guilt and pain they tried to cover begins to resurface. They feel lost and hopeless,

Eventually, the isolation and the false beliefs create a crisis that cannot be overcome by more denial.

The weight and burden of continually acting as if all is well compound the stress and disappointment already there.

abandoned by the group because the image of perfection is destroyed by their obvious despair. The religion they invested so much in stops working, and they don't know where to turn.

It is never easy trying to act like everything is working when it is so badly falling apart. The weight and burden of continually acting as if all is well compound the stress and disappointment already there. Under the strain, the addict experiences suspiciousness, distrustfulness, confusion, and psychological and emotional deterioration. Feeling the victim, feeling persecuted and hopeless, the addict works to prove the blessings will come. When they do not, the addict is convinced that the role of martyr is a good one to replace the role of superior faith warrior.

Resentment and Anger

Resentment and anger become increasingly evident as little works out as expected, and every day becomes a bigger disappointment than the day before. If the person has preached against a sin that continues to surface, the sermons fill up with bitterness and resentment. Growing feelings of inferiority produce anger toward others who appear to have their lives well ordered. There is no one to share the feelings with because the group will reject the misled believer for not having strong faith. This intensifies the emotions. Rage often overpowers the rational thoughts of the addict, and everyone near is put on the defensive.

Anger and rage are the first signs that the harmful beliefs are starting to fall apart. When the anger emerges, there is no longer an ability to fool others with a look of false peace or serenity. There are problems, and they are obvious. The root of the anger is the disappointment that the faith leaders, beliefs, and system did not deliver. The relief did not come. The addicts are enraged by how they look to the rest of the world and the fact that now reality must be dealt with, unprotected by delusional thinking.

Rage often overpowers the rational thoughts of the addict, and everyone near is put on the defensive.

DECEPTION

Oftentimes it is hard to understand how someone could ever end up as a cult member. The cult's beliefs may seem so obviously off-base to an outsider. But what many don't realize is that "what you see up front is not what you get inside; there is a consistent pattern in cults and cult-like groups of withholding information normally needed to make informed decisions or give proper consent. . . . The ends justify the means. Whatever deception and abuse it initially takes to bring someone into the fold is all right. . . . One crucial thing that cult members do is to get people to suppress their ability to critically analyze."

—*An interview with Father William Kent Burtner, O.P., "Don't Be So Sure You Could Say No To A Cult,"* U.S. Catholic, *April 1990, p. 18.*

The cults can see persons ripe for "conversion," and they will lure them into the fold with half-truths and other techniques to skirt the blatant truth. Cult members are not dumb; they are deceived.

The addicts are angry with themselves but throw that anger at everyone else. Problems are attributed to the devil, unbelievers, sin, lack of faith, lust, greed, and anything else that can be preached against those outside the faith. Although the dogmatic beliefs start to falter, they are preached to others more dogmatically than ever before. The angry addicts are so miserable to be around that most choose not to associate with them. This increases the pain, heightens the isolation, and moves the persons closer to despair. As long as the anger continues, the hope for change continues with it.

Projection

With everything falling apart, someone must be blamed. The addict will not accept responsibility, so a scapegoat must be found. That scapegoat will be the recipient of all of the anger and disappointment. The pain will be projected onto that person or institution as if that entity was the cause of the addict's problems. Every consequence of

The addicts are enraged by how they look to the rest of the world and the fact that now reality must be dealt with, unprotected by delusional thinking.

Anything other than self is used to be a recipient of the rage and blame.

the compulsive religious behavior is depersonalized, considered to be the result of someone else's actions. If a person didn't cause the trauma, it must be sin, the spirit of lust, or the world. Anything other than self becomes a target of the rage and blame.

If addicts recognize a need for change, it will be in the area of behavior, not the heart. They will try to do things differently rather than change any thoughts or beliefs. By identifying the problem as a behavior, such as lack of prayer, addicts can hold on to the harmful faith until the very end. They will try everything to produce the spectacular desired result. They are so grandiose about their faith that they see no need for a change in heart, maturity, or development of character. Since addicts believe they possess the truth, they are convinced that different behavior will isolate them from whatever is the source of oppression.

Crumbling World

Disappointment, anger, rage, and more determined effort are results of the world starting to crumble around addicts. Troubles come from many sources, and each one is an affirmation that the faith system will not come through for them. It could be financial collapse that begins the fast slide toward hitting bottom. Some have contributed and pledged so much to the group that they bankrupt themselves. Some sign notes, use their homes as collateral, and then have to give up their homes when the truth is known about the shady dealings of the ministry.

As the world becomes more confusing, the addict searches out ways to change behaviors to fix the problem. Often too much time is spent away from work. Needed overtime is turned down so that compulsive religious activity can be continued. Because work can be converted into a time of sharing his harmful beliefs, a car salesman will witness rather than sell cars, or a hairdresser will talk about the faith so much that no one will come back for hair care. This, along with alienating other employees with irritating sermons, may cause a job loss and a financial disaster.

Home life starts to crumble as the finances do. The angry addict

WOULD YOU JOIN A CULT?

Along with the deception involved in a cult's push for new recruits, there is the emotional and psychological status of the potential recruit. "One point that I want to make is that anyone can be gotten. Not all the time, but we're all vulnerable at some point in our lives. . . . You're a raw nerve. Along comes a warm, caring, nonthreatening individual—usually a member of the opposite sex—who says, 'I understand. I've been there, too. I go to a group that has really helped me.' Often your circumstance may not even be extreme, but you're just slightly off balance."

—*An interview with Father William Kent Burtner, O.P., "Don't Be So Sure You Could Say No To A Cult,"* U.S. Catholic, *April 1990, p. 18.*

becomes so caught up in God's work that all family responsibilities are neglected. Relaxing with the family or taking a child to Little League or ballet class is stopped so that the religious disaster can be worked out. This situation produces fertile soil for affairs and often leads to divorce. After living with an addict for years, the family finally becomes fed up and refuses to exist with the addict anymore.

Faith also starts to crumble. The addict, no longer able to maintain the denial, slips into brief moments of understanding. Glimpses of the reality of the foolishness briefly enter the addict's mind, but they are quickly brushed aside with a frenzy of activity. The thoughts produce tremendous feelings of guilt, confusion, and pain. Still, the addict starts to realize that there has been abusive enforcement of rules and that the rigid doctrines of the group have hurt, not helped, people.

Thus disillusioned, addicts begin to doubt. For the first time since becoming involved with harmful faith, they doubt themselves, their beliefs, and the existence of God. They doubt the sincerity of the leaders they follow. Confusion overwhelms them. Unable to trust their perceptions and unwilling to trust anyone else, they lapse into deeper and deeper depression as they realize they are powerless to control their lives.

For the first time since becoming involved with harmful faith, they doubt themselves, their beliefs, and the existence of God.

At the end of the progression is desperation so intense that it forces change. Mental and emotional breakdowns are common among religious addicts when the magic wears off.

Hitting Bottom

At the end of the progression is desperation so intense that it forces change. Mental and emotional breakdowns are common among religious addicts when the magic wears off. Some attempt to take their lives. Some take the lives of others and then their own. They do desperate things because their minds can't handle the incongruity between their beliefs and what they know to be real. They feel betrayed by God and the world, and they don't care who they hurt as long as they don't have to suffer further humiliation. Many see the only way to guarantee this is to die or be forced to be admitted to an institution, such as a mental hospital or a prison.

In the end, the presence of a false god denies the addicts what they desperately need, a loving relationship with a loving God. Unfortunately when they finally put down their work, performances, rituals, and need for perfection, there is often no motivation to seek the true God who could heal their broken hearts.

CHARACTERISTICS OF THE LATE STAGE OF RELIGIOUS ADDICTION

- Despair. The addict begins to sense hopelessness because the harmful faith is not producing the desired results.
- Erratic behavior. Knowing something is wrong and refusing to change beliefs, the addict attempts to fix the problem by changing behavior rather than the heart.
- Resentment and anger. As the addict's world falls apart, everyone else is to blame, and everyone else is a source of rage.
- Obsession with beliefs. Continually wondering what is

wrong with the faith, the addict questions, ponders, and thinks through each belief until the addict is completely unable to concentrate.

- Deep depression. Collapse of beliefs leads to the inability to function.
- Physical deterioration. Depression and stress take their toll on the body, resulting in fatigue, lack of appetite, and medical complications.
- Stagnation. Once faith is lost, all else seems lost, and the addict is unable to do anything but obsessively ponder past mistakes.
- Searching for another fix. Other addictions such as food, drugs, and sex intensify as the addict seeks relief from other sources.
- Fear. Experiencing major insecurity, the addict becomes afraid of everyone, seeing each person as a threat. The addict is afraid to continue in the hurtful faith system and afraid to get out.
- Financial collapse. Work-related problems and financial irresponsibility often result in financial collapse.
- Family deterioration. Stress and distrust destroy family relationships, resulting in affairs and divorce.
- Hitting bottom. Running out of self-will and manipulation, the addict must give up the addiction and turn to God.

Hope for Change

The ultimate stage for religious addicts is the recovery stage. People who have released themselves from the trap of addiction will find a

Unfortunately when they finally put down their work, performances, rituals, and need for perfection, there is often no motivation to seek the true God who could heal their broken hearts.

loving God ready to receive them. They will also find loving people in traditional churches ready to forgive them and invite them back into the fold. The end of religious addiction does not have to be a disaster. It can be an experience of coming back into a relationship with a very patient God.

God allows us to become totally dependent on ourselves. He allows us to become totally dependent on other things, such as chemicals and rituals. He even allows us to be dependent on religion that leaves Him out. He will let us exhaust all our resources and explore every area of dependency outside His plan for each life. While we try to live every way except His way, He continues to wait. No religious addict has wandered so far that there is no way back to this loving, patient God. One step toward a godly dependency is all it takes.

The end of religious addiction does not have to be a disaster. It can be an experience of coming back into a relationship with a very patient God.

CHAPTER 6

Ten Characteristics of a Harmful Faith System

It is not hard to tell a healthy faith system from a harmful one. The harmful faith system stands out with its obsessive people who victimize family members and destroy their own faith in God. The following comes from a journal of one who knows hurtful faith from personal experience. Nothing worked for this young man until he worked out his faith.

I accepted Jesus Christ as my Lord and Savior in April of 1974. I was sixteen and a sophomore in high school. Being raised in the church I knew all the stories, but I did not know Jesus personally. A Sunday afternoon in the park changed all that. Then the fun really began.

My parents were busy looking for a deeper teaching, not a closer walk. This led them to a cult church. Like all cults it had some good, right-on Bible teachings. It also had even more inter- pretative twists, false teachings, and power-abusive leaders. There was even a seasonal prophet. By that I mean "HIS" prophecies always had something to do with what time of year it was. Easter had a bunny, Thanksgiving had a turkey, Christmas had a tree, etc.

Most of all the decisions for the church and congregation were made at the weekly men's meeting. This was great if you were a man. Women did not enjoy many liberties, if any at all. They were constantly told to just submit, and obey without question.

SUPERNATURAL PHENOMENA

"Americans are a nation of believers in supernatural phenomena, according to a national public opinion poll commissioned by *Parents* magazine.

Sixty-five percent of those polled subscribe to at least one of nine beliefs regarding the paranormal. What, exactly, do they think is true?

- 34 percent believe some people have the consistent ability to predict the future;
- 33 percent said there are spirits or ghosts that make their presence known to people;
- 25 percent, certain people have mental or psychic powers to bend spoons and make objects move;
- 22 percent, certain numbers are either lucky or unlucky;
- 14 percent, a person's spirit or soul can be reincarnated in another body in a later life;
- 14 percent, there are physical objects (lucky charms) that can bring good fortune;
- 11 percent, astrology can accurately predict the future;
- 8 percent, quartz and other crystals can increase one's mental and physical abilities."

—Ingrid Groller, "Do You Believe in the Supernatural?"
Parents, *October 1989, p. 32.*

The pastor, or shepherd as he was called, had final say in everything in the lives of his flock: whether to buy a house, take a vacation, get married, and even whom to marry. Two of the women in the church were given permission to marry. One to her boyfriend, who was a member of the church, and the other one to an appointed gentleman in the church who had a small boy but had no wife to help raise him. Many people sold everything they had and gave it to the church. Then they would share housing with others in the church. My parents would later do this and live with the shepherd and his family. This eventually led to them leaving the church. It's one thing to go to church with somebody; it's another to live with them.

My spirit told me that this was wrong, yet I could not prove it when biblically challenged. It's sad that we sometimes need to be challenged before we start to read the Bible. But for me it was God taking a bad situation and making it good. People from the church (usually men) started stopping by the house unexpectedly with a word or correction for me. Everything I said or did was questioned and analyzed by my parents or their friends. I started asking God questions. Why me? What did I do to deserve this? Am I out of the will of God? God does not want His children fighting, does He? As I became more familiar with the Bible I was able to answer many of my parents' and their friends' questions or statements with what was truly in the Bible and show them where it was in the Bible. I soon became known as the black sheep of the family. Unfortunately my mother told many a tall tale about what was really going on in our house to my grandparents and other relatives. She rationalized that they didn't have as deep a walk as she had therefore they wouldn't understand.

Discipline was many times handled at the men's meeting. The child offender would have to pull his or her pants down and be spanked with two male witnesses present. This was very upsetting to the young girl teenagers of the group. Fortunately, my younger sister and I were never disciplined in this manner. Being in our late teens and very strong willed (we would not submit) we were just verbally reprimanded or grounded.

One month before I was to turn 18, I had a best friend chosen for me. It was the seasonal prophet. I was also informed that I was no longer allowed to date until I was 18. I could not date girls except those in the church, and I could not date them until I became a member of the church. Dating was also something the girls had no control over. You see, if a boy wanted to take out a girl, he didn't ask her. He asked her father. The girl had no choice.

Upon my 18th birthday I was given three choices:

1. Join the church, and live at home.
2. Move out and live on my own.
3. Move into the single men's home.

I had felt this coming on, so I had already accelerated my studies to graduate early from high school. This was not easy because I had to work 30 hours a week from the time I turned 16 to pay for my own rent, gas, and car insurance. Also 25 percent of my income went to the church. This was not by my choice but by my parents. I never complain now about giving ten percent.

Two days after my 18th birthday I moved out of my parents' home with the help of four friends. My parents had gone out to a meeting making this the most opportune time to leave without a fight. The next morning, though, I got my fight. My father had come to the grocery store where I worked. Before I clocked in he asked me if I would step outside so we could talk in private. We got outside and as I turned around he "sucker punched" me. Being 60 pounds heavier and 4 inches taller, he was able to knock me down with one punch. He then informed me that they (mom and dad) had given my soul over to the devil for the cleansing of my spirit and that I would be dead in six months. I did agree to talk with one of the elders from my parents' church. At the time, he was living in a trailer up on a nearby mountain. I prayed the whole way up that if I wasn't sure of discipleship being right or wrong that I would just drive off that mountain. Not a real healthy thought. Well I did go into that meeting all prayed up (the only way I knew to get some good answers). After three and one-half hours I was sure God was real. I looked at the elder and saw right through him. In fact I was able to share with him about our loving God, the one we can call Father. I left rejoicing. Later, when my parents left the church, one of their friends informed me that the purpose of that meeting was to pluck my eyes out. They felt my eyes were causing me to sin. It pays to go into battle with your armor on.

Over the next eight months I lived with friends and other members of my family. I thought about joining the military, but I felt I was needed more as a witness to my parents than in a barracks somewhere else.

Then just before Christmas my parents left the church. I wish I could say that we all lived happily ever after, but I can not. Not yet anyway. My dad and uncle no longer talk to each other. In fact my uncle won't even mention God now unless he is swearing. My parents feel that I deserted them when I left home so they have very little to do with me or my family. I have tried to reconcile, but they do not wish to talk about it. But who knows, prayer does and will change things.

What a sad account of an actual experience with harmful faith. Too few understand that people are being exploited in this way every day. Religious addiction is developed in a harmful faith system. It flourishes there where other addicts build the system. Without the system that feeds into and off the addiction, the addiction would die. Every hurtful system has identifiable characteristics that set it apart from healthy systems. These characteristics allow the individuals stuck in the system to play out their distinct roles in a predictable manner.

The characteristics of a harmful faith system differentiate it from systems, churches, and ministries committed to growing people in faith and developing their relationship with God. Knowing the characteristics of a hurtful system can be helpful in evaluating whether or not a ministry or group is poisonous or pure, addictive or freeing. Since we are all prone to addiction, it can also aid us in staying on track or bringing us back into balance.

*The characteristics of a harmful faith system differenti-
ate it from systems, churches, and ministries committed
to growing people in faith and developing their relationship with God.*

"Special" Claims

Characteristic #1: *The members of the harmful faith system make
claims about their character, abilities, or knowledge that make them "special" in some way.*

Members of harmful faith systems reach a point in their addictive
progression where they make claims about themselves to set themselves apart from others. They may attempt to support these claims
with Scripture. Each time Scripture is used, some followers are more
motivated to serve, feeling God's special hand on the ministry and the
people involved with it.

Some of the most clever deceivers of our time, and of times past,
have used Scripture to foster their hurtful faith. Satan had no problems in quoting Scripture to back up his temptations of Christ. Matthew wrote about the incident as follows:

> Then the devil took Him up into the holy city, set Him on the
> pinnacle of the temple, and said to Him, "If You are the Son of
> God, throw Yourself down. For it is written:
> 'He shall give His angels charge over you,' and 'In their hands
> they shall bear you up, lest you dash your foot against a stone'"
> (Matt. 4:5–6).

He attempted to control Christ, manipulate Him, and motivate
Him to do something outside the will of God. Scriptures from the Old
Testament were used as tools for evil. The good guys are not the only
ones who use Scripture.

One pastor asserted his "specialness" by quoting the book of Revelation, where John writes

> To the angel of the church of Ephesus write, "These things says
> He who holds the seven stars in His right hand, who walks in the
> midst of the seven golden lampstands" (Rev. 2:1).

OLDER FOLKS AND THE CULTS

Although cults usually appeal to people in the teens and twenties, a new trend is the luring of older people into cults: "Middle-aged and older women make particularly attractive prospects for fringe groups. They frequently have clear titles to houses, cars, savings accounts and social-security checks. In many cases—alone, lonely, separated from family— they also are susceptible to a good line."

—Bill Barol, "Getting Grandma Back Again," Newsweek, October 23, 1989, p. 71.

Now, follow this reasoning: his assertion was that the angel mentioned of in this quotation was the pastor at the church of Ephesus. Because he, too, was a pastor of a church, the Lord speaks directly to him, much like He did to the pastor (or angel) at the church of Ephesus. And so, since God spoke to the pastor at the church at Ephesus in order for him to pass on God's word to the people, God likewise speaks to him to communicate to the people of his church. Thus, he justified his special communication link with God.

This type of rationalization of direction by God is very dangerous. It places the leader at a level above all others in the church. Challenging the authority or correctness of the leader is equated with challenging the very Word of God. How could anyone disagree with a leader who says he has a direct link with God? Who would want to be pitted against the Word of God? The leader knows this and uses this as a clever manipulation of the "unknowledgeable" followers who believe in the sincerity of their harmful leader. Members of that organization are placed in a vulnerable position if, when they challenge the motives or actions of the leader or persecutor, they are put off with statements like, "I was only doing what God asked me to do." For those under that type of manipulation and persecution, there is no way to challenge the persecutor's position. They either agree and obey or suffer the consequences. And religious addicts are more than eager to agree and obey.

Members of that organization are placed in a vulnerable position if, when they challenge the motives or actions of the leader or persecutor, they are put off with statements like, "I was only doing what God asked me to do."

In a healthy church, a pastor will encourage persons to minister as they discover talents and gifts that can be used for the service of God.

The Claim of a Special Anointing or Calling

A terribly poisonous misconception is that God has a special calling only for certain people and everyone else needs to find something "unspecial" to do. According to the misconception, the business-person who tries to do God's will on the job is not as special as the leader of a church. This premise goes against the teaching that God has a special plan for every person's life. In a healthy church, a pastor will encourage persons to minister as they discover talents and gifts that can be used for the service of God. The minister of pure faith will encourage all people to consider themselves special in the eyes of God. Each person has a very special place of service designed by God, and each person should be encouraged to find it.

In the harmful system, the minister will set himself or herself up as having a special destiny or mission that can be performed by no one else. This special anointing or calling many times is nothing more than the pathological need to be valued or esteemed. It also takes some of the power that should be attributed to God and gives it to the minister. It is a way to usurp God's authority, and it is a way to discredit anyone who disagrees with the direction of the ministry. If others will not value the minister enough to submit to the dictatorial rule, God's anointing is called in to make sure everyone understands that any waver of support for the persecutor is seen as a waver in faith in God. Those who feel or have felt this type of manipulation should leave that church or organization immediately. Most religious addicts don't feel it; they thrive on it.

This claim of a special touch has caused problems for people I know. The abuse of a high position to build a self-serving ego has

If others will not value the minister enough to submit to the dictatorial rule, God's anointing is called in to make sure everyone understands that any waver of support for the persecutor is seen as a waver in faith in God.

FALSE ADVERTISING

The advertisement is on a half sheet of paper. In the upper corners there are pictures of the Holy Bible and praying hands. In the center of the paper is a picture of what you would take to be Jesus with hands outstretched and the word *prayer* in large letters arching over His head. Above the picture is the statement "God only helps those who help themselfs" [misspelling theirs], and this is where the ad begins to go astray. In using this statement that is commonly, but mistakenly, attributed to the Bible, "Madam Elizabeth" has shown her true colors. She is using the guise of the Christian spiritual trappings to promote herself and her special powers, "blessed by God to heal all people."

The copy in the ad reads, "Are you sick in your stomach or any other part of your body? Divorces, health, love, alcoholics. Let ELIZABETH help you. Why suffer when you can be free of problems? Guarantees work in 3 days. . . . I can help you overcome your problems, no matter how big or small. Are you worried about money debts, jobs, or your loved ones? . . . Just one call can convince you that she will help you with any problems right away. Don't delay, call right away."

The ad has two testimonials of people helped by Elizabeth, one had a broken heart and another an incurable disease. The ad promises a lucky charm to anyone who responds as well as your lucky day and numbers. A strange mix, to say the least!

caused unhealthy marriages to be continued without healing, finances to be wasted, time to be spent in hours of futile work, and people, left feeling forsaken by a God who does not seem to care. Under the guise of special direction from God, people have compromised their faith and fallen into a trap that did nothing but establish one person's authority above and beyond any earthly accountability.

The religious addicts at the top seem to always profit from this misguided loyalty by being able to spend more, build more, or sin more, depending on the area of their lives that has deteriorated. The victimized followers—seeking a closer relationship with God but focusing

Under the guise of special direction from God, people have compromised their faith and fallen into a trap that did nothing but establish one person's authority above and beyond any earthly accountability.

more on the addicted leader than on God—lose contact with God and often fall away from faith permanently. Misguided loyalty allows the delusions of the leader to grow and destroys the faith of the loyal. The result may be financial bankruptcy for some and spiritual bankruptcy for others. The only hope for everyone involved is for the leader who claims to be God's special officer to be forced into accountability or dethroned to protect other potential victims.

Power often corrupts persons. When organizations are developed with little or no accountability for the leader, there is tremendous potential for the leader to fall into corruption. One church I was involved with in Texas confronted a minister about his behavior. Many issues led to the question of whether the minister should stay or go. The minister's response was that he had started the church and that anyone disagreeing with him should leave the church. He claimed that God had given him the vision for the church and the means by which the church had grown. The leaders knuckled under the pressure of the minister, and he retained his position. He continued with no means of accountability, and it was only a matter of time until he was in trouble again. When ministers practice absolute authority over a group of people, everyone loses, especially God. This is always the case when religion serves a person instead of a person serving God.

The Claim of Special Powers from God

The claim of special powers from God is another way for a person to feel valued, regardless of whether or not they have anything to do with God. This claim is often used to manipulate people into believing the gifted one is a great person of God. One of the scariest Scriptures for these ministers is found in Matthew 7:21–23:

> Not everyone who says to Me, "Lord, Lord," shall enter the kingdom of heaven. . . . Many will say to Me in that day, "Lord, Lord, have we not prophesied in Your name, cast out demons in Your name, and done many wonders in Your name?" And then I will declare to them, "I never knew you; depart from Me, you who practice lawlessness!"

When organizations are developed with little or no accountability for the leader, there is tremendous potential for the leader to fall into corruption.

The problem comes when some people use God's healing power to manipulate and exploit believers.

No more notorious abuse takes place than in the area of faith healing. At times God rips through the normal bonds of the universe and moves against the forces of nature to heal people miraculously. On some occasions He uses people to facilitate that process, and on other occasions He does not. The problem comes when some people use God's healing power to manipulate and exploit believers.

A perfect example is the faith healer from California who claimed to know people's afflictions, their names, where they lived, and other personal things that only a miracle worker would know. Once he had established his credibility through those feats of knowledge, he would claim to heal the people of what he knew was wrong with them. The religious addicts who followed him loved to watch his magic and believed it was all for real. He deceived the devoted followers into believing God revealed the needed information to him. In fact, supplied with a tiny hearing device and radio receiver, he got the information from his wife who had gathered it before the "performances." Confronted about the practice, he admitted that it had been part of the family tradition passed down from his minister father.

Not only did he mislead loyal and would-be followers into believing that he was hearing God, but he deceived them into believing he healed those people with the power of Jesus. The power of modern technology was portrayed as the power of the Savior of the world. The supposed special power was used to prove he had a favored position with God.

His exploitation of the terminally ill, the sick, and the afflicted and his ability to reportedly laugh about the exploitation of their finances are unconscionable. Few things are more cruel than exploiting the search for hope of those in desperate need. These are the people to whom God may well say, "I never knew you." The addicts who follow them may never know God, either.

There is no room to compromise since the dictatorial leader believes that everyone should submit to his or her rule without question.

Authoritarianism

Characteristic #2: *The leader is dictatorial and authoritarian.*

Every church or ministry must have a strong leader if it is to meet the challenges of hurting people and help them grow in their faith. The stronger the leader, the stronger the ministry throughout, whether the person holds all the power or chooses to delegate everything. Problems arise when the leader takes the leadership role as license to dictate whatever he or she feels is right or wrong. Those who work in this setting find themselves either agreeing with the direction of the ministry or leaving. There is no room to compromise since the dictatorial leader believes that everyone should submit to his or her rule without question. Those who fear for their jobs or feel they may not be able to find similar jobs will comply with the leader rather than challenge certain decisions or actions that appear to be wrong.

Often a strong leader mistakes the position of leadership for a position free from accountability. The leader will set up a harmful faith system that allows for free rein and no accountability. There may be a board of directors, elders, or deacons, but when the authoritarian ruler picks them, he or she picks people who are easily manipulated and easily fooled. What appears to be a board of accountability is a rubber-stamp group that merely gives credibility to the leader's moves. These board members become the coconspirators of the persecutor and permit the leader to persecute without interruption. Then when a practice is called into question, such as an extremely high salary, the persecuting dictator justifies it by saying the board made the decision or approved it. The illusion of accountability becomes more dangerous than those organizations that are blatant in their disregard for accountability.

In harmful faith systems, the organization is built around a dynamic leader whose vision for the ministry launched it. Many solid ministries have been started by the vision of a dynamic leader, and they are able to continue or reorganize when that leader relocates, retires, dies, or is asked to leave the organization. In harmful faith systems, the organization would sink or discontinue without the authoritarian ruler to tell the people what to do. His or her name is all

Often a strong leader mistakes the position of leadership for a position free from accountability.

In a harmful faith system, the organization would sink or discontinue without the authoritarian ruler to tell the people what to do.

over the ministry. Without the talent and charismatic personality of that leader, there would be no reason or motivation to continue the mission. The ministry is a short-term project centered on one individual, not God. When that individual chooses to exploit and manipulate the followers, the exploitation goes unabated since there is no accountability. And when for some reason the leader leaves the ministry, it dies.

Persons who gather around a ministry of true faith use their talents to reach out to people and serve God. They fit in their talents and abilities where God can best use them. In a harmful faith system, talents and abilities are used to meet the needs of the authoritarian leader. His or her needs come first and must be met for the ministry to continue. The persecuted victims, blind to the manipulation and egotism of the leader, line up to assist in serving the persecutor. When the victims find out they have not served God or other followers, they are usually very angry and often must deal with feelings of betrayal and abuse similar to recovery from an incestuous relationship.

Underneath the raging ego of the persecuting leader is a suffering person who fears being unimportant. The position of leadership may have been the first and only time the minister has had any authority. He or she uses the authority to prop up negative feelings of inadequacy. Anyone wanting to advance in the organization must never challenge the authority of the harmful faith leader. Additionally, complete support for the leader and the leader's style of management must also be given without criticism. Any negative comment or action is perceived as a threat that the authoritarian leader cannot handle. The threat is eliminated so the ministry can survive and the mission can be accomplished.

The authoritarian leader comes to power because a driven personality accompanies tremendous talent and charisma. The individual has no problem establishing spiritual and emotional authority over the followers and religious addicts by using persuasive and manipulative talents. Seeing the dynamic presentation of beliefs and behaviors that are

Underneath the raging ego of the persecuting leader is a suffering person who fears being unimportant.

VARIETY OF BELIEFS

Which of the following do you believe in?

Angels	74%
Astrology	58%
ESP	50%
Witchcraft	29%
Bigfoot	22%
Ghosts	22%
Clairvoyance	21%
Loch Ness Monster	16%

—*George Gallup, Jr., and Sarah Jones,* 100 Questions and Answers: Religion in America *(Princeton, N.J.: Princeton Religion Research Center, 1989), p. 34.*

part of the leader's faith, rather than part of true faith in God, the followers willingly accept the teachings, doctrines, and dogma with unquestioning loyalty and allegiance to the leader. The more they accept the teachings of the leader, the more the leader feels the people's dependency, and so the more license the leader takes in controlling the thoughts and beliefs of the followers. As long as people are willing to follow, that leader will feel supposed support from God for ministry and manipulation. The leader is completely unaware that the entire exercise is being conducted to build ego rather than serve God.

The authoritarian and dictatorial style is not found only in some harmful faith churches. It can also be found in harmful faith families. Tim's story is similar to others where power takes control of a parent.

Tim came from a rigid religious background. His earliest memories were of his father taking him to hear someone preach who sounded more angry than godly. At home his father was as dogmatic as the preacher was at church. He was a general in the army of God, and his family was going to fall in line. Authority was not to be questioned, children were to be seen and not heard, mom's place was in the kitchen, and no one was allowed to express any needs or desires. His

The more they accept the teachings of the leader, the more the leader feels the people's dependency, and so the more license the leader takes in controlling the thoughts and beliefs of the followers.

father held God up as the omnipotent Overseer who was waiting for His children to make mistakes so that He could punish them. God was portrayed as a tyrant. His father would justify his absence in the home and the intensity and fear he instilled in the family by blaming God for his behavior. Dad could rail on the family since he was the priest of the family and the voice of God for all those who were in "submission" to him, but for everybody else anger was one of the seven deadly sins.

Tim was not allowed to watch television or play with any kids outside the church. His world was filled with rules and regulations that were to be obeyed at all costs or the wrath of his father and God was to be borne. There was no hugging or kissing in his family, especially between father and son.

Tim would wonder why he couldn't be like the other kids and have fun. What was wrong with him? Why did dad and God not like him? Why was he different? These were Tim's thoughts as he was growing up. As Tim got older, he felt that he wasn't able to live up to his dad's or God's expectations. Though there was a part of him that wanted to be close to his father and God, it was just too painful to get close.

Tim drifted away from God and the family. Tim was a very timid and frail man, always fearful of "screwing up." He felt that he didn't fit in with his family, the family of God, and society in general.

Tim finally found that he could find relief from his pain, loneliness and boredom in drinking and in sex. Tim had found a "god" that could meet his need to numb out his feelings of insecurity and inadequacy. I met Tim in a chemical dependency unit.

Tim was a victim of his father's harmful faith, religious abuse, and addiction. His destructive family system allowed his father to perpetrate the delusion that God was a God only of wrath. This left Tim with a hole in his soul, a hole that Tim filled with alcohol and numerous one night stands with other men. For Tim the alcohol killed the pain of never measuring up, and the sex filled the need for male attention and affirmation that he never got. The alcohol gave Tim the false sense of security; the sex and the absence of insecurity gave him the false sense of significance. If someone wanted him, even if only for sex, he still mattered. Someone finally cared for him in some way, even if it was only to use him for sex.

In Tim's recovery, besides addressing the alcohol abuse and sexual compulsivity, we had to address the religious abuse of his past. Tim at this time was afraid to call out to God. Fearful of his heavenly Father's wrath, he ran from Him. Tim had been running from God for a long time, and there was no reason for him to believe that God wanted anything to do with him.

In Tim's recovery he was able to identify the harmful characteristics of his family's faith. He saw how all the family members played their hurtful roles to a tee. He saw that he was not "crazy" but a victim of craziness and harmful faith.

Tim not only gained control over alcohol and sex, he also learned the characteristics of true faith. He was able to finally establish a relationship with God, free from the fear of punishment and grounded in respect and love. His father's tyranny stopped affecting his life when Tim refused to be victimized by it.

An "Us Versus Them" Mentality

Characteristic #3: *Religious addicts are at war with the world to protect their terrain and establish themselves as godly persons who can't be compared to other persons of faith.*

In their attempt to maintain and protect their beliefs, religious addicts line people up in two camps. There is no middle ground. A person is either part of the harmful faith system or against it; a person is either supportive or destructive. This mentality is fostered within the organization until the followers believe that people on the outside are threats to the ministry, have no understanding of what is "really" going on, and must be ignored if they challenge the beliefs of the religious addicts. At the point of any new threat, the leader and the religious addicts are ready to go to war to protect what they have invested their lives and souls in. Individuals who have not made a similar investment will be perceived as enemies ready to strike at any moment.

The "us versus them" mentality is evident throughout the organization and its teachings. Religious addicts will go to great lengths to stress the church's or organization's uniqueness. Other followers will be told of ways that each of them possesses special knowledge and insight that others do not have. Some ritual or practice could be utilized as the center of that uniqueness and superiority.

This mentality is fostered within the organization until the followers believe that people on the outside are threats to the ministry, have no understanding of what is "really" going on, and must be ignored if they challenge the beliefs of the religious addicts.

$2 BILLION

"Celebrity preachers on TV offer diverse services—solace or salvation, cures or charitable works—to 13.5 million Americans. But the medium's common commercial message is: 'Send money.' The electronic faithful do, almost $2 billion a year."

—*"God's Green Acres, at Home with the Televangelists,"* Life, June 1987, p. 54.

An example could be a teaching such as baptism. I was immersed and prefer this form of baptism. But theologians have disagreed on this subject for centuries. At times it can become the focal point of disagreement between groups. God is more interested in the heart than in the form of baptism. Rather than accept the different concepts and realize that God will honor the act of public dedication, whatever its form, religious addicts will demand their way is better and the other is a tragic mistake. This attitude will be carried over into other areas as well.

The form of baptism is just one practice that separates denominations from one another. Each denomination is based on certain differences that allow people to affiliate with congregations and worship styles they are most comfortable with. When those differences are used to support an attitude of superiority, they become a source of manipulation to keep people from deserting the organization. They condemn others, not from a fundamental foundation of belief but from judgment over a simple act of using water to sprinkle or to immerse.

Religious addicts are sometimes viewed as being on fire for God when they propagate the "us versus them" mentality. Railing against the evils of the world, they make personal attacks on the sinners and glorify the existence of the saints. They imply that they are above the mundane sins of the world. The message is often that this group of compulsive addicts has come to a new level of life that others do not possess. When the addicts are finished with the "us versus them" teachings, no one is attracted to the group by faith. People enter into it only by manipulation.

Religious addicts often cease to react and operate like human be-

---

Sinners feel alienated and hated by zealous addicts.

As the ministry grows, it will be subject to closer scrutiny, and some of its harmful beliefs will be revealed as such by those who suspect the motives of the leader, the addicts who follow, and the entire organization.

ings. They exhibit no compassion for those who are hurting and those who feel trapped in sin. Sinners feel alienated and hated by zealous addicts. The attractive, gathering nature of Christ is lost in religious addicts' desire to set themselves above and apart from all the rest. Their self-righteousness replaces the humble service to God that was probably apparent at the beginning of the walk of faith.

The more harmful the belief system becomes, the stronger the "us versus them" mentality of the organization becomes. The larger the system becomes, the more the addicts will have to protect. As the ministry grows, it will be subject to closer scrutiny, and some of its harmful beliefs will be revealed as such by those who suspect the motives of the leader, the addicts who follow, and the entire organization. When these investigations into the ministry begin, religious addicts are manipulated into believing that they are being attacked by the enemy. The prudent course would be to admit the mission has gotten off track a bit, and confess the wrongs and bring it back in line with biblical teachings. But religious addicts would never do that until every other option had been taken away by those who are perceived to be the enemy.

Religious addicts build an exclusive society of harmful faith believers. People prosper and succeed by supporting the beliefs and practices of the persecuting leader. Like any other society, its rules govern and control every aspect of the society and its people. Anyone not adhering to the rules is an enemy of the society and everyone in it. Religious practice loses its focus on God and becomes a complicated process of furthering the society and its rules. Those in the exclusive society believe they are serving God, but they are serving a person and that person's concept of what should and should not be. Unwillingness to serve that concept will bring on the wrath of all the religious addicts who do not see the reality of the creation of an exclusive empire.

Those in the exclusive society believe they are serving God, but they are serving a person and that person's concept of what should and should not be.

Punitive Nature

Characteristic #4: *Harmful faith systems are punitive in nature.*

Harmful faith systems don't have to be big to be damaging. In small churches across the world congregations are led by ministers just as manipulating and controlling as the head of a harmful mega-ministry. When a minister gains control of a small group of people, it seems that control can produce some of the most punitive forms of faith practice in existence.

One example comes from a small church in southern California. The minister was a small man who saw himself in a big way. He wanted total control over his congregation, and they allowed him to have it. The control was often very negative and punitive.

An unmarried woman told the pastor she had been involved in an affair with a married man in the church. She felt terrible about it and had broken off the relationship. She felt guilty and wanted to confess this to the minister and receive his help in moving back to a close relationship with God.

He was willing to help—but only after he had put her through some very stressful situations. He forced her to go to the man's wife and confess the sin to her. He forced her to go before the congregation and confess her sin before them. He forced her to agree not to date for one year as a sign of true contrition for her acts of adultery. Rather than offer her hope, he offered her a set of very difficult hoops that destroyed her personally as she jumped through each one, thinking they were the way back to her relationship with God.

Contrast that to the approach Christ took when confronted with the adulterous woman. He told those who brought her to Him to search themselves and anyone who was without sin could start the stoning process. No one did. Then He did not provide a punitive system for the woman. He simply told her to go and sin no more. The woman felt the compassion of God, not the wrath, which too many ministers take upon themselves to inflict.

Another incident in the small church occurred when a group questioned the minister's morality and his relationship with a woman in the church. He was not accused of adultery; the group was concerned

---

The minister addicted to power punishes and purges the system of anybody who would upset the status quo.

They are demanded to sign up and sacrifice their families and friends to meet the system's needs.

about the undue attention and affection he obtained from the woman. The pastor attacked the accuser and demanded that anyone having anything to do with the man be removed from the church. Sides were drawn immediately to support those who were faithful and punish those who doubted the integrity of the ministry.

In the name of righteousness, this and other minicrusades have been carried out in the church. Each punitive action taken against a member or group of members divides the congregation and removes those who would attack the minister's power. The minister addicted to power punishes and purges the system of anybody who would upset the status quo.

On the inside, everyone believes God is tough to follow. The leader is willing to go to great lengths to ensure the congregation pays the price to follow. From the outside, the whole ministry appears negative and punitive, out of balance, and distorted from the love, acceptance, and forgiveness freely given by God and His Son.

Overwhelming Service

Characteristic #5: *Religious addicts are asked to give overwhelming service.*

The harmful faith system does little to counter the compulsive workaholism of career seekers. It refuses to do this because it is so guilty of the same sin within itself. Religious addicts are requested to serve, serve, and serve some more. They respond by becoming involved in numerous groups, committees, and meetings. They are demanded to sign up and sacrifice their families and friends to meet the system's needs. They believe they serve God, but they serve their egos as they seek greater notoriety within the system's hierarchy.

This level of service often becomes overwhelming. People become so drained that they can't think clearly. Their emotions become dis-

Deep depression, extreme anxiety, and a general numbness are common in overwhelmed religious addicts.

They fight to deny their physical and emotional conditions, often until it is too late to provide effective treatment.

torted. Deep depression, extreme anxiety, and a general numbness are common in overwhelmed religious addicts. Activity takes precedence and dries the souls of the addicts, leaving many feeling hopeless and some the victims of total breakdowns. Leaders in the system wonder why so many become involved but then fall away from the faith. They are burned out by the service demands of the system.

It is hard for addicts to see that activity has become central to the practice of faith. They are caught up in doing things rather than serving God. Not everyone is Mother Teresa. Not everyone has her gifts or her support system. Leading lives of overwhelming service does not put addicts in the religious hall of fame; it puts them in the hospital or breaks their relationships. Only when the whirlwind stops can God reenter as the focus of faith.

Followers in Pain

Characteristic #6: *Many religious addicts in the system are physically ill, emotionally distraught, and spiritually dead.*

Many harmful systems claim to solve all problems: emotional, spiritual, and physical. The irony is that the systems accomplish just the opposite. Yet religious addicts are determined to hide their real feelings and thoughts and present a happy, peaceful glow. All discomfort is suppressed to maintain the image of perfection.

The pain that is buried is buried alive, so it surfaces in the form of emotional despair and physical illness. Religious addicts often suffer from chronic back pain, headaches, eye problems, arthritis, asthma, and hundreds of other complaints. They fight to deny their physical and emotional conditions, often until it is too late to provide effective treatment.

It is not easy living in an unreal world. People have to do drastic, desperate things to maintain unreal beliefs. Denial becomes a quick and easy tool to live a lie until both physical and emotional trauma break religious addicts' facades of perfection. The followers in pain find relief only when they break down and are forced to examine their true condition and limitations.

Denial becomes a quick and easy tool to live a lie until both physical and emotional trauma break religious addicts' facades of perfection.

Sharon came from a rigid religious background and was a pained follower. Throughout her life she was reminded of her "total depravity," which she interpreted to mean that she had no worth or value and that all she needed was Jesus. Unfortunately, the only Jesus she knew was the one of religion. The more she was unable to find emotional relief in her life, the more she was convinced by her harmful faith that it was because of her sin and depravity. The more she tried to be perfect, the more she failed to measure up. The more she ate, . . . Her religion highlighted her inadequacies rather than taught her about the Christ who loved her. Her hurtful faith was performance oriented rather than relationship oriented.

Sharon numbed her feelings with overeating. The more she ate the more she repented and asked Christ for deliverance. The more she sought Christ's acceptance, the more she invested herself in her harmful faith. She worked hard at the church to find her salvation. The more she tried to be perfect to merit her God's intervention, the more she saw the hopelessness of ever being good enough. The more she saw the fruitlessness of ever being good enough, the more she ate. The more she ate, the more she believed that she needed Christ to deliver her. The vicious cycle of addiction was in place. Like the hamster on the hamster wheel, the more she tried, the faster she went nowhere, until she was exhausted and began to look for help outside her harmful family of faith.

When Sharon initially sought help for her eating disorder, she had no idea that her faith was harmful and that it was a major factor in her feelings of inadequacy and hopelessness. She was firmly convinced that if she could get her eating under control she could be "more perfect" and that God could then accept her. Her destructive thinking told her that if she could get this "sin" out of her life then God could love and accept her.

Part of her treatment, since her eating disorder was firmly entrenched in religious addiction, was to address her harmful faith. It was most difficult for her to acknowledge the fact that she was hurt and angry with God; that she was bitter at having to perform for Him to merit His acceptance. Breaking through her denial about her feelings toward God allowed her to be open to the idea of a loving God.

She began to realize that the God she knew was the god of religion, the god of her harmful faith who demanded performance for acceptance, the god who demanded that she clean up her act before he would hear her petitions.

We explored how her faith was full of harmful thinking. Sharon's thinking was all or nothing. She was either in or out of His will with no gray areas. She was totally out of touch with the reality that as we learn how to live life and know God, we are going to make mistakes—and that it isn't bad, it's human. Much learning is the process of trial and error. The issue is to learn from our mistakes and not judge them.

Though she knew the Scriptures on grace, she never was able to experience it. For Sharon, grace was dependent upon her behavior. She was immensely relieved when she began to realize she didn't have to earn God's grace. Since she was able to reach out and find someone who understood and could help, she realized that God had heard her petitions and had extended His grace by directing her to a place where she could get help.

Sharon was able to find comfort in her eating disorder group and found that many of its members were also running from the same feelings. Some shared how their harmful faith had incapacitated them and kept them in bondage.

She began to explore how her hurtful faith had kept her in bondage. She began to question. She began to identify, with the help of others and a trained professional, the harmful characteristics of her faith and how they tied into her need to alter her mood, to stuff her feelings. She began to see how her faith was not freeing but was, in fact, condemning, which made her feelings of inadequacy worse.

Sharon, with the help of others, began to identify how the twelve-step process could help her understand and gain freedom from bondage. For the first time, Sharon began to experience unconditional acceptance from those in the group and from the loving God of the Bible. She gained strength and courage to live life more freely and fully, no longer a pained follower.

Closed Communication

Characteristic #7: *Communication is from the top down or from the inside out.*

Communication in harmful faith systems isn't a two-way interaction. Information is valid only if it comes from the top of the organiza-

*With an attitude of spiritual superiority, religious ad-
dicts reinforce that they are always in greater touch with
God's truth, more sensitive to God's will, and more worthy of being listened to than anyone else.*

tion and is passed down to the bottom or from within the organization
and shared with the outside. Religious addicts stake out their positions
and are unapproachable on differences of opinion. Those at the top no
longer hear of the perceptions and needs of the people. The addicts on
the inside no longer care about the needs of people on the outside.

Religious addicts develop very selective hearing and will respond
only to those things perceived as important to them. Anything that
doesn't fit into what they already believe to be true will probably go
unheard. With an attitude of spiritual superiority, religious addicts
reinforce that they are always in greater touch with God's truth, more
sensitive to God's will, and more worthy of being listened to than
anyone else.

The same system of closed communication exists in many families,
and religious addicts often come out of these family systems. Closed
communication is especially common with fathers and children. A
father may not take the time to communicate with his children because
he views what they have to say as insignificant. A father with "more
important things to do" will not plug into the needs, thoughts, and
feelings of his children. So he remains ignorant of them. He values
only his words to direct them and punish them. The children feel
inadequate to express themselves and their desires. The religious addict raised in this type of home re-creates it in the organization. The
organization eventually becomes ineffective because it loses touch
with the people it is designed to serve—just like a father loses touch
with his children.

Many harmful organizations have someone there to close off the
communication for the leader. The job is to placate those who disagree
and satisfy those who want a direct voice into the leader. The person
running interference knows that his or her job is to never tell the

*In closed communication, the top of the organization
loses touch with people's needs because those at the top
do not care about the people they are supposed to serve.*

leader anything other than what is desired to be heard. The harmful system discounts the importance of each individual who is part of the organization.

Open communication is a valuing process where people are heard and feel heard. They are treated as equals, and the organization or ministry listens so its function can be centered on those needs. In closed communication, the top of the organization loses touch with people's needs because those at the top do not care about the people they are supposed to serve. The religious addicts who follow also cease to care for people in need.

Legalism

Characteristic #8: *Rules are distortions of God's intent and leave Him out of the relationship.*

When religious addicts create a harmful faith system, God is lost in the process. In God's place, rules are implemented that serve only to further the empire of religious addiction. As new people come into the hurtful faith system, they are indoctrinated into the rules rather than strengthened in a relationship with God. The rules reinforce addiction, not faith. Addiction leads to conformity to a predictable pattern of behavior, often blocking faithful following of God.

One harmful faith system takes great pains to ensure that dress and hair styles conform to the antiquated rules and beliefs of what is becoming to God. All people dress the same, wear their hair the same, and look the same. There is no room for individuality. An adolescent's desire to find uniqueness and develop a separate personhood from parents is squelched. Conformity is the number one priority. There is so little room for individuality that the kids rebel by the droves. When they do, they are considered outcasts and of little importance compared to the few who are willing to stay inside the system, follow the rules, and reproduce the addiction structure.

A harmful faith system may place less value on what you look like than on what you do. They believe their rules are accurate interpreta-

---

As new people come into the hurtful faith system, they are indoctrinated into the rules rather than strengthened in a relationship with God.

It becomes a faith system based on "don'ts" rather than a faith centered on God. What you do is valued more than who you are.

tions of God's standards, and they expect others who participate to adhere to the rules. It becomes a faith system based on "don'ts" rather than a faith centered on God. What you do is valued more than who you are. Because many young people do not discover who they are, they develop as robotic duplicates who believe life is found in the implementation of rules.

It is hard for these harmful faith practitioners to realize that Christ put down the rigid, legalistic system of religion of His day. He was a rebel who picked grain on the Sabbath if it meant meeting a need. When the rules said not to heal, He healed anyway to bring a person closer to God and to make a person stronger in faith.

Faith has always been more than a list of do's and don'ts. Standards are only one part of faith. When they become the main focus, faith grows rigid and legalistic.

No Objective Accountability

Characteristic #9: *Religious addicts have no system of objective accountability.*

This one aspect of harmful faith is a central theme for all areas of harmful faith. If religious addicts were in healthy, accountable relationships with others, hurtful faith would not be allowed to flourish. Anyone who proclaims to be so tied into God that he or she does not need to be tied into people is a religious addict guaranteed to fail in faith and fail in ministering to the needs of people. God never intended anyone to be so focused on Him that there is no need to stay connected with people. No one has a faith that can be free from accountability to others. Lack of accountability is a clear sign of lack of faith in God and the presence of a faith in self built on self-assertion and ego.

If religious addicts were in healthy, accountable relationships with others, hurtful faith would not be allowed to flourish.

A person accountable only to God is a person out of control.

When harmful faith practices come under scrutiny, the religious addict reacts predictably: "I am accountable only to God." No one is accountable only to God. We are all accountable to the government. A married person is accountable to a spouse. Anyone asserting singular accountability to God either is not thinking clearly or has a terrible sin to hide. When a religious addict makes this assertion, people should clear out of that ministry if change is not implemented immediately. A person accountable only to God is a person out of control. The religious addict defines God in his or her terms, creates a religion around his or her needs, and then remains accountable to a false god of religion created in his or her image.

Under the reign of a leader with no accountability, religious addicts tend to avoid accountability, also. They become little generals in a misled army that they say no one understands outside the organization. This cuts off all others who would question the beliefs and practices and arms them with the right to do as they please. These little generals follow orders from their leader, believing they are on a mission from God, and refuse to listen to any input from concerned others. Severing accountability eliminates much of the possibility of someone's turning misled believers away from the organization and back to a true faith in God. They continue as part of the system as misguided believers and at times are driven into total disbelief in God.

Labeling

Characteristic #10: *The technique of labeling is used to discount a person who opposes the beliefs of the religious addict.*

Labeling attempts to dehumanize persons so that dismissing them or their opinions is much easier. Choosing not to address someone individually who has doubted the harmful faith, the religious addict places a blanket negative label on all who would disagree with his or her personal habits. Rather than say that John Smith has made a negative statement, the addict proclaims that there are "detractors," "traitors," or "malcontents" who would destroy the ministry or organization. The labels become rallying points under which the other followers can be moved to action to squelch a revolt. Once the label is

Labeling attempts to dehumanize persons so that dismissing them or their opinions is much easier.

---

in place, it becomes more difficult to see that person as a human with real needs and the potential for good judgment.

Although John was a Sunday school teacher, he was labeled a troublemaker. He had been with the church since its beginning, and all was fine until he began to disagree with the pastor about interpretations and applications of Scripture. The pastor labeled him a troublemaker and silenced him. It was obvious to the pastor that John wasn't capable of having legitimate concerns. And because the pastor called John a traitor, the church staff forgot they were dealing with a person who had been a part of that family of God since the beginning. If what John believed was contrary to what the pastor believed, they felt that John's belief was traitorous. What this harmful faith enabled was the delusion that each person has a right to his or her own relationship to God, as long as it lines up with the system's guidelines.

John had written a letter to the pastor about his concerns with the ministry. He had shared the letter with one of the elders to get his response. The elder went to the pastor with information about the letter's contents before John had decided what to do. That was it! The pastor felt that John had gone too far, that he was trying to undermine the ministry. The fact that he shared his concerns with one of the elders was proof. The pastor immediately called John at his place of work and informed him that he was no longer going to be allowed to teach and that he wasn't welcome there any more. He was a traitor and he needed to repent of his rebellious spirit.

The pastor had privately interpreted John's concerns as rebellion.

RELIGIOUS EXPERIENCE

Have you ever had a religious experience—that is, a particularly powerful religious insight or awakening?

☐ Yes   33%

☐ No   63%

—*George Gallup, Jr., and Sarah Jones,* 100 Questions and Answers: Religion in America *(Princeton, N.J.: Princeton Religion Research Center, 1989), p. 160.*

RELIGIONS AROUND THE WORLD

"Africa south of the Sahara has religions numbering in the thousands. We're still in the hundreds here. There are thousands of religious groups in India that haven't made it here yet. There are four or five hundred in Japan."

—Jay Kinney and Kevin Kelly, "Why Cults Flourish, Interview with Gordon Melton," Whole Earth Review, Spring 1987, p. 52.

From the pulpit he preached on how a little leaven spoils the lump and how the congregation needs to expel those who would corrupt them. John and his family were no longer friends of those with whom they had fellowshipped over the years. They were "traitors" who had "betrayed" the pastor and therefore needed to be expelled. What John had done was simply to disagree with authority. At no time had he disqualified anything the pastor had preached, and he had shared his concerns with only a select few in leadership.

John and his family were devastated. Their lives had revolved around the church for so long that they had very few friends outside the church. Rejected and abandoned by those they had trusted and cared for, John's family was broken and in pain because the system could not tolerate difference. John was no longer a person with feelings and intellect but a traitor with a rebellious spirit. By labeling John and by persuading other church members to believe that label, the insecure pastor was able to avoid having someone disagree with him.

The military uses labeling to enhance the "killability" of the enemy. The last thing a military leader wants a soldier to think about is that the person in rifle sights may be a father of five little girls who will starve after daddy is killed. All Asians are labeled as gooks or some other slang term so that dehumanization is possible. The soldier is better able to kill one hundred gooks than one father or husband or real live human being. Religious addicts use the technique well, and when they use rumor and innuendo to kill the reputation of a sincere person who disagrees, other followers are more apt to go along if a label has dehumanized the dissenter.

The purpose of labeling is to separate and divide. In our society someone who has conservative beliefs is labeled a fundamentalist. The label no longer describes the approach by which that person evaluates life; it now describes the person. Someone who thinks that fundamentalist views are narrow focuses on the holder of those views and labels him narrow-minded. The approach is transferred to the person's individuality. The person is shamed and demeaned for beliefs that have little to do with the person's value or the person's unique gifts from God. Disqualification by labeling is a poisonous practice that hurts the victims and allows persecutors to continue in their harmful faith.

When it comes to abortion, I believe it is a sad option. I'm not for it. Caring about this issue greatly, I have been sensitive to the use of labeling within the abortion debate. Those who are prolife are labeled antichoice and antiwomen by those who want the female's right to decide to be the priority of the issue. Those who are prochoice are labeled proabortion or prodeath to rally against them. The technique works well to form sides and maintain the troops. However, the labels don't reflect the true depth of beliefs on either side.

Most people labeled proabortion really don't think it's a good method of birth control. Some will even admit that they consider it a form of killing. They believe a mother should not take illicit, addictive drugs during pregnancy so they naturally would not agree to kill the child during pregnancy. Abortion is not actually the issue they fight. They perceive a world where men make all the decisions for women, and they want out of that world. Proabortion is the stand they take representing that move to independence from a man's thinking. What is held as most dear is not choice or abortion but the independent existence of a female's body.

Those labeled antichoice for the most part don't believe a man should make a decision about a woman's body. They wouldn't condone a man force-feeding a birth control pill down a woman's throat. They are not out to use submission as an excuse for exploitation. They believe in choices for women. But just as they do not believe that a

---

EMOTIONALLY DAMAGED

"The Christian Church is the only institution or body poised to provide meaningful answers to the emptiness and self-deception of our nation. The people of our country are severely damaged emotionally. We are a population of active, affluent people suffering from inner turmoil and strife that we try to hide even from ourselves."

—George Barna, The Frog in the Kettle (Ventura: Regal Books, 1990), p. 164.

Because it is difficult to rally against rational-thinking people who have distinctly different views, labels must be used to polarize the opponents and energize the followers to fight against those opponents.

child should be murdered when it is one week old after birth, they do not think a life should be terminated before birth. The freedom to choose is eliminated by the law after birth, and they want it eliminated before birth. The complication comes because the child grows within a female's body. They would say they are not antichoice, but all choices must have restrictions, this one being the taking of life.

Because it is difficult to rally against rational-thinking people who have distinctly different views, labels must be used to polarize the opponents and energize the followers to fight against those opponents. The enemy is disqualified so the underlying issues that need to be considered can be avoided. The potential to find the truth in the opposing argument is destroyed when the labels are put in place. For example, calling someone narrow-minded may produce the desired effect. No one wants to follow a narrow-minded person or even be associated with one. A narrow-minded person challenging your position is of no consequence so that person is eliminated as a competent opponent.

Labeling discounts and dismisses the opposition and establishes the superiority of religious addicts. It does not invite the exploration of the beliefs of others to better understand those persons; it reduces them so the victims will be better able to fall in line with other religious addicts who demand defiance against those who have been labeled. It becomes the perfect weapon to attack the enemy or defend the harmful faith system, its beliefs, and addictive practices. Labeling allows religious addicts to define truth, uphold that truth as defined, and destroy anyone who would dare to question that truth.

Knowing the characteristics of harmful faith systems enables people to evaluate the characteristics of the church or organization they are affiliated with. When people of harmful faith systems identify

Labeling allows religious addicts to define truth, uphold that truth as defined, and destroy anyone who would dare to question that truth.

them as such, there is hope that multiple generations of abuse will discontinue. Followers can see and feel it when they are being manipulated by religious addicts. The persecution will stop when they refuse to be victimized. The move away from the system by many of the victims may force the leader to become accountable and other addicts to recognize the reality of their compulsions. It may force religious addicts back into a real relationship with God, free of ego, manipulation, and the victimizing of those outside the system.

The move away from the system by many of the victims may force the leader to become accountable and other addicts to recognize the reality of their compulsions.

HARMFUL FAITH CHARACTERISTICS

1. "Special" claims about character, abilities, or knowledge
2. Dictatorial and authoritarian leader
3. An "us versus them" mentality
4. Punitive in nature
5. Overwhelming service
6. Followers in pain
7. Closed communication
8. Legalism
9. No objective accountability
10. Labeling

CHAPTER 7

The Roles of Harmful Faith

Harmful faith exists when one or more dysfunctional systems provide false concepts of God, faith, and the individual. It often develops when a person comes from a dysfunctional family and derives erroneous beliefs from that family system. It also develops when a church, denomination, religion, minister, or televangelist teaches half-truths that the individual from the dysfunctional family comes to believe. Encountering the promises of harmful faith, the wounded individual is easily caught up in the system that promotes the harmful faith principles to the point of victimization and addiction. In a dysfunctional system, whether it is a family or a religious organization, roles evolve to support the system. Each person must be willing to play the roles that become more keenly defined as addiction intensifies in the dysfunctional hurtful faith system.

In a dysfunctional system that breeds harmful faith, each person, no matter what role he or she plays, becomes addicted to the system, the beliefs, and the behaviors. The individual becomes trapped in predictable behaviors that remove God and faith, replacing them with a

In a dysfunctional system that breeds harmful faith, each person, no matter what role he or she plays, becomes addicted to the system, the beliefs, and the behaviors.

dependency on a set of rules and dictates. As a person's behavior lines up with one of these predictable roles, any deviation from that role is a sign of rebellion from the system and is dealt with quickly through shaming and rejection. Although each role is difficult to maintain, it is even more difficult to leave the safety and predictability of the role and act independently. A person who takes this step back toward reality becomes an outcast of the harmful faith system.

When people are admitted into New Life Treatment Centers, they rarely identify their problems as religious addiction. They come to us depressed, anxious, or with some other major dependency that has gained control of their lives. As we work with them, we often find that below the presenting problems are layers of family dysfunction, hurtful faith, and religious addiction.

One man stands out as a classic religious addict whose faith poisoned his relationship with God. He grew up in a very rigid home where things were done his father's way or not at all. His dad was a demanding, disciplined workaholic who counted on his son to live up to his expectations. However, his son never could, so he carried deep feelings of inferiority into adulthood.

In our patient's attempt to measure up to God, he transformed his dad's workaholism into his own churchaholism. He did everything he could to serve God. He was careful to abide by the rules of no drinking, no smoking, and no dancing; he avoided anything with the appearance of evil. He considered himself pure in every way. He felt he was measuring up.

After being married one year, he and his wife had their first son. A year later they had their second. He was determined not to be as tied to his work as his father was so he could be with his sons. However, the hours he worked at the church took just as much time away. When the boys entered high school, they both became drug abusers, and one died from a drug overdose.

Two years later the man came into New Life Treatment Centers, a broken and hurting figure. He couldn't forgive himself for his son's death. He believed it was a result of his sins passed to the next generation. His obsession with thoughts of not measuring up put him in a

---

Although each role is difficult to maintain, it is even more difficult to leave the safety and predictability of the role and act independently.

major depression. He victimized himself with his unrealistic expectations until finally he could no longer perform.

In this sad case a father turned a son into a victim. That son took the dysfunctional core of family relationships and passed them to his family. His rigidity victimized them. When death from an overdose took a boy's life, the father further victimized himself and taunted himself with thoughts of guilt and shame. He couldn't live up to his dad's, God's, or his own expectations. His self-defeating behavior almost destroyed him.

The roles of a harmful faith system indelibly mark personal development. They are often repeated in various forms from one generation to another. Unless help is obtained, there is little hope to break the chains of dysfunction and stop the multigenerational trend. The roles of the system are powerful predictors of a future generation of problems and trauma. Only when a person hits bottom and evaluates the level of self-destructive behavior does that person begin to see the alternatives of thoughts and feelings available.

The man who came to us worked through many layers of grief to crawl out of his distorted role. He grieved over never having the father he wanted or needed. He grieved over his son's death. He grieved over the loss of his perfect image of himself that was shattered by the problems with his boys. When he was through the grieving process, he was ready to look up again and find God's love without conditions or unrealistic expectations.

In a harmful faith system such as a church or a family, the person with the role of persecutor heads the group. The persecutor is supported by coconspirators, enablers, and victims. These people have one primary function: allow the persecutor to function, insulated from reality. Each person in each role believes the system, organization, or family must continue, and it is each person's job to distort, manipulate, hide, or deny reality so the hurtful system can go on. Each person in a different way protects the persecutor from outside disruptions that could stop the achievement of the persecutor's vision.

These people create a false reality by distancing and isolating the persecutor from contact with the real world. As they grow more committed to the persecutor and a harmful ministry, they become addicted to the behaviors of the role and the feelings derived from partic-

These people have one primary function: allow the persecutor to function, insulated from reality.

PRAYERS ANSWERED DAILY

The picture at the top of the advertisement shows Rev. Dr. John standing, Bible in hand as if he were preaching. Standing behind him, with a hand placed on his shoulder is none other than Jesus. Rev. Dr. John claims that he is a true disciple of Jesus, with faith so strong, his prayers are being answered daily. In his advertisement, you are encouraged to send him your prayer requests. When you do he says, "When I receive your prayer request, I will rush you this beautiful, engraved, antiqued, golden keepsake that contains the seed of faith Jesus preached about. It has been blessed in prayer by me and I want you to carry it, knowing God will meet your needs. This gift is free but if you can find it in your heart to tuck in fifty cents, to help with first class postage, it would be warmly appreciated."

Now it seems that stating that his prayers are so strong that he is seeing them answered daily is a claim that any Christian with a very active prayer life could make. Clearly, this is a man who is claiming to have a special connection to Christ.

—*"Truth Is Stranger than Fiction,"* The Wittenburg Door,
no. 92, August/September 1986, p. 28.

ipating in the false reality of the hurtful system. Once they stop supporting the false reality that allows the persecutor and the ministry to continue, they are no longer needed by the system and are thrown out.

Persons connected with a harmful faith system must be able to work under the authoritarian, manipulative rule of the head of the family or organization. They become order takers and must exhibit blind faith in the leader. The leader, the persecutor, becomes so strong that he or she replaces God in the lives of those in the dysfunctional faith system. This poisons everyone's faith. It also poisons the organization or family and everyone who comes in contact with it. The job of each role in the system is to process the poison into a palpable form that is sweet and seductive enough for the victims of the persecutor to swallow. Anyone not willing to help with dispensing the poison becomes a threat to the authoritarian rule, is no longer needed, and is removed from the organization.

The job of each role in the system is to process the poison into a palpable form that is sweet and seductive enough for the victims of the persecutor to swallow.

Jim Jones provided a tragically graphic example of how people become involved in a poisonous system, even to the point of death. He took hundreds of people to Guyana to create their own world where they could practice their own brand of religion. He poisoned his people with lies, deception, false hopes, and dreams that would never come true, and finally, he poisoned them with cyanide. He manipulated, brainwashed, and controlled the minds of his followers until they believed anything he said and would do anything for him. Somehow, the women justified having sex with him because he was in need of it and their duty was to provide it. How Jim Jones distorted the Bible to make it appear right, only those women knew. Somehow he was able to poison the values of everyone who made the trip with him. Before he was finished with them, he had robbed them of their God, of their faith and, for many, of their very lives.

The colossal power of a persecutor was vividly illustrated at the end of the reign of Jim Jones. An investigation into the ministry began as authorities became suspicious of all of the money and property that had been donated to it. The more threatened Jim Jones felt, the more desperate he became. His followers believed that the investigators were sent from hell to destroy what God had created. They believed so strongly that they were willing to kill a congressman to protect the ministry.

With his back to the wall and his options at an end, the desperate and suicidal Jim Jones convinced his followers to join him on a trip that was supposed to end in heaven. His loyal coconspirators and enablers lined up the victims to take a drink of "eternal life." When it was finished, hundreds of bloated bodies lay dead from the poisonous cup of Jim Jones.

That a man like Jim Jones could poison his flock with a toxic chemical leaves little doubt that other deluded leaders can poison their followers and fanatic parents can poison the faith of their children with toxic beliefs and ideas. But they cannot do it alone; they must have the help of coconspirators and enablers.

In a harmful church system, a persecutor dictates the rules to the rest of the followers. He or she uses a strong inner circle to carry out the mission. In a typical church, this could be made up of associate pastors, deacons, and elders; cardinals, bishops, and priests; members of the board, directors of ministry, or assistant directors. The titles vary from system to system, but in harmful faith systems, the structure is always the same and it propagates the poisonous beliefs of the persecutor.

The persecutor establishes a rigid hierarchy so that everyone knows

With the faithful followers willing to do anything to support the persecutor, the organization becomes dysfunctional and unbalanced, leaning heavily toward the top.

his or her role in accomplishing the mission. As each person fits into the structure, identity and individuality are sacrificed to meet the demands of the system. With the faithful followers willing to do anything to support the persecutor, the organization becomes dysfunctional and unbalanced, leaning heavily toward the top. The more unhealthy the system, the more unbalanced it becomes—guaranteeing that it will not last forever. It will fall apart unless enough people force the persecutor and others in the system to turn from their egocentric plans and move back to a focus on God.

Harmful faith in a family produces a dysfunctional system that destroys a relationship with God and traps the family members in unhealthy roles. Dysfunctional systems have been around ever since the first family. The first family was so disturbed that one son, Cain, killed the other son, Abel. Because the world is not a perfect place, every system, family, or organization has the chance to function in an unhealthy way. A look at the roles of the hurtful faith system indicates that they are consistent with the roles traditionally identified within dysfunctional families. If a person can come to an understanding of how dysfunctional families work to protect and uphold an addicted family member, it is easy to see how the misguided organization works to protect the persecutor.

A healthy system is made up of individuals with a full range of emotions, intellect, volition (or free will) and the ability to function independently. In a dysfunctional system, each individual plays out a characteristic or role needed for the system to function. Since individuals lack the capacity to function independently, they depend on one another to play out their roles and allow the system to continue. Those roles have to be played so that those in the system can remain in their denial and avoid the overwhelming fear of insignificance. Persons seek a relationship with God, but on the spiritual journey they become snagged in a system that takes away the relationship with God and poisons the faith of all who participate in it.

The Whitcombs exemplify how harmful faith can be handed down from generation to generation. One generation reacts to the dysfunction of another but is so locked into the unhealthiness that the same problems are repeated in a similar form. This story begins with a de-

A healthy system is made up of individuals with a full range of emotions, intellect, volition (or free will) and the ability to function independently.

---

ceased grandfather. This grandfather is the father of Lee Whitcomb, the central figure in this dysfunctional family. When Lee Whitcomb's father died, he did not leave his grandchildren money or property; he left them a legacy of abuse and family instability.

Grandfather Whitcomb was a farmer who worked hard to feed his family of five children. Lee was the oldest child and worked the closest with his dad. They plowed the fields and harvested the crops together, doing whatever it took to feed the family and make enough money to plant again the following year. As Lee reached his fourteenth birthday, he witnessed changes in his father. He became more moody and detached. There were fits of rage and horrendous arguments with Lee's mother. It grew worse and worse until everyone was terrified of the elder Whitcomb and what he might do if he ever lost complete control.

Lee's father did lose control. It was a gradual descent into abusive behaviors and violence. He began by grabbing Lee's mother and shaking her when he was in a fit of rage. He would do the same to Lee. One night Lee heard an argument between his dad and mother that climaxed in yelling, screaming, and then physical abuse. When Lee heard his mother being slapped, he ran into the room and stood between the two. His father hit him and broke his jaw. Afterward Lee's father ran from the house. Lee and his mother went to the hospital to have the jaw fixed. It was wired up and set, causing Lee extreme pain and discomfort.

Lee had never been extremely fond of himself, but the broken jaw removed the self-esteem he had left. He loved and hated his father at the same time. His father's pleas for forgiveness did nothing to restore Lee's feelings about himself or the relationship with his father. He felt that he was getting what he deserved, that somehow he must be very bad and in need of terrible punishment. Although his father was remorseful after the jaw-breaking episode, his remorse led to more anger, more depression, and more incidents of abuse. Each time Lee was hit, it reinforced his beliefs that he was unworthy to have a good life because he wasn't a good person.

Lee felt that much of what he experienced must have been because a God somewhere was trying to punish him for being a bad person.

A DEEPER RELATIONSHIP WITH GOD

When asked the importance of growing into a deeper relationship with God, here's what people said:

- 56% Very important
- 26% Fairly important
- 10% Not very important
- 6% Not at all important
- 2% No opinion

> —*George Gallup, Jr., and Sarah Jones,* 100 Questions and Answers: Religion in America *(Princeton, N.J.: Princeton Religion Research Center, 1989), p. 178.*

Each outburst of anger represented the anger of God toward Lee. The God he created in his mind was void of love and kindness. He was vengeful, and Lee felt he was the victim of God's wrath in addition to his father's problems. Lee's concepts of God were his own fashionings of God, his own interpretations of events as they related to God. He didn't get them from Sunday school because Lee's father never took the family to church. He didn't believe in God, and he left the rest of the family to develop their beliefs in the absence of biblical teachings. Each child, especially Lee, developed a tainted view of God that affected every aspect of life.

Lee and the rest of the family lived in terror of their father for three more years. When Lee was seventeen, his father had one final fit of rage over a tractor part that had worn out. When he discovered it, he became enraged, blaming Lee for not taking better care of the machinery. He held the worn metal piece in his hand, shoved it to Lee's face, and yelled at him. He took the metal piece and withdrew it as he cocked his arm. The moment he lunged forward to hit Lee with the evidence of his incompetence, Lee struck first. Lee slugged his father so hard he dropped the tractor part and fell to the floor of the barn. Angry and humiliated, he lunged at Lee again only to be thrown back to the floor. At seventeen, Lee was too big to be physically abused. He fought back and overpowered his father.

Lee's father ran from the barn to the car to escape. He drove the car fast down the dirt road to the highway. Lee watched the dust cloud spiraling behind the old green Chevrolet. As Lee saw his dad approach the highway, he also saw a huge truck coming down the highway. Obviously, his father's rage blinded him from seeing the truck.

He pulled in front of it and in an instant a huge ball of flame rose from the road.

Racing toward the wreck, Lee knew his father was dead. The car and the truck were engulfed in flames with the two bodies ignited beyond help. Lee was full of both guilt and relief. The terror for the family was over, but he felt he had led to his father's death. His feelings of relief only confused him more about himself, his feelings, and a God who would allow it all to happen. At seventeen, he was hurting and in search of answers.

Lee struggled with his guilt feelings about his father for many years. After his dad died, he picked up the responsibilities of the farm and worked it as his father had, but his brothers and sisters grew up and moved out. At age twenty-three he married a young high-school dropout who he felt would be satisfied to live on the farm. They had four children and raised them while they took care of Lee's mother until she had to be moved to a skilled nursing facility. When she left, an exact replica of the family she started remained behind to produce food from the farm and turmoil from an abusive upbringing.

At the request of a friend, Lee attended the local church as a favor. He agreed to give it a try and felt comfortable there once he did. The old organ sounded like a dying cat on certain notes, the preacher fumed with anger as he poured out his message, but Lee liked being there. He found something he missed as a child, and he felt a void being filled. Some of the guilt pangs that occasionally rattled him seemed to be quieted in the pews of that small church.

Lee became a Christian about a year later, and his involvement with the church increased greatly. He began as an usher and then served on the Sunday school committee; within three years he had become an elder. If there was a meeting, he was at it and probably running it. Other than the pastor, he became the most prominent personality in the church. People would comment to him and to others that they were amazed such a faithful follower had come from the likes of his unbelieving father. He loved the attention he received as a poor farmer boy made good. He loved the power he felt from being a leader. He loved the work and the feelings he had from serving God.

Because of Lee's background, his faith became unbalanced, and his family suffered from it. As he poured everything into the church, it wasn't long until Lee was serving his ego rather than God. It was as if each hour he spent at church was an attempt to erase some of the guilt over his father's death. Additionally, his involvement was in such contrast to his father's that church seemed to be a guarantee that his own kids would not turn out like their grandfather or like himself. So he worked off his guilt, worked off his father's old ways, and as he worked in the church, lost in the frenzy of activity, he could deny his own problems.

Lee's ego became so fixed on his image as a church leader that everything he did revolved around the facade of wholeness. Lee felt empty, even as a Christian, but the church work made his life look rich. He suffered as many adult children of abuse suffer, but no one could tell that as he worked each week in church service. He looked good to everyone, especially to himself.

Lee's four children all felt abandoned by a distant father. The children felt tremendous resentment over often being without a father for school events because he was too busy to be there. When they complained to their mother, she always responded with the demands that the children stop being selfish and that they be grateful to have such a wonderful father, a true man of God. It was evident that the children's feelings were irrelevant. All that mattered was the church.

As the resentment of the church and Lee grew, acts of rebellion began to surface. One son started getting in trouble at school. A daughter started dating boys whom Lee labeled "sleazy." As these embarrassments continued to erode Lee's image of himself, his demands on the kids' behavior became rigid. He demanded compliance and had a long list of "don'ts." He would not allow his girls to be seen out of the house past 9:00 P.M. He would not allow his boys to hang out with other boys in a corner of town. He demanded Bible study and family prayer time. Nothing would stand in the way of Lee creating the perfect family.

No one could live up to Lee's rules and the rules of the church. Every time a child did not meet his expectations, Lee became enraged and demanded adherence to all his rules. Each time a child stepped out of line, he saw it as a personal affront and beat the child in the name of disciplining the transgressor back to the faith. He had an image, and any family member not willing to support and protect that image was punished severely.

Discipline was replaced with total punishment, and punishment involved severe beatings of all four kids. As their father's anger increased, their resentment and bitterness grew. Each year each child fought to survive while longing to be free from the perpetrator of terror.

Each family member handled the father's anger and rigidity in a different way. Each one locked into a survival role to protect against a complete emotional and spiritual meltdown. The mother knew there was a problem but refused to deal with it. She would patch up the hurts of her children with little regard for their dysfunctional futures that were being constructed within the home. She paraded her crew through church and upheld the false image of a wonderful husband who was raising his children well. She was as hooked on the facade as Lee was, and while she was keeping his image in place, she lost touch with her needs and identity. Eventually, numerous illnesses put her in bed. At age fifty she lived like a sickly eighty-year-old woman.

The oldest son became a very successful businessman. He excelled in school and college and worked his way to the top of a large manufacturing company. He was a classic workaholic who shunned anything that had to do with the church. If there was ever a child out to save himself, it was the oldest boy. His drive and perfectionism made him difficult to live with. All three of his ex-wives would attest that he was extremely rigid on the outside while out of control on the inside. As his years increased, he became more withdrawn from family and friends, content to spend almost every waking minute absorbed in his work.

The oldest daughter reacted to the problems in a very unusual way. She grew up quite normally with a strong faith in God. Rather than avoid church, she used the church as a healthy bridge back to a real God, not the demanding God of her father. She married and had children and would be considered by most as living a blessed and fulfilled life. She was the exception to the other kids of her family and other religious addict families. The one common bond to the others was her avoidance of her father and mother. She understood them and forgave them, but she chose not to be around them.

Her sister didn't make the same wise decisions. She rebelled as her younger brother rebelled. At sixteen she dropped out of school and out of the family, moving in with one of the "sleazy" boys her father hated. She was a regular drug user and quite a boozer. Everything her father stood for, she did not. Every facet of his facade was the extreme opposite of her image. She became the child from the other side of the tracks. Her jobs were menial, and she never turned from the environment of filth she created. Each day she lived was an insult to her father who never had time to love her. Her only pleasure came in knowing how he seethed with repulsion each time she came to mind.

The rebellious son was in constant trouble with school officials until he finally managed to graduate a year late. The summer after his senior year of high school, he seemed to mellow and mature and enrolled in the local junior college. There he found some new friends who supported his more mature lifestyle. He graduated from college with a degree in sociology and went to work in a health clinic doing assessments. He had no place for God because his father was his image of God. He was a good man, but he never tapped into the saving grace of the Creator. He married, had children, and did all the things middle-class families do. He never filled the spiritual void left by his father's problems. Life was incomplete, and although he knew the realities of sociological problems, he did not know how to fix his spiritual one.

The example of the Whitcomb family shows how religious addiction is born out of family dysfunction. The addicted create their own dysfunctional families full of individuals who will do whatever it takes to survive. Unfortunately, survival involves unhealthy roles that are difficult to change. They separate the members, break the family apart, and produce individuals who no longer are connected or even appear to be related.

These relationships are not rare. As we can identify how they develop and the roles that members play in developing these trained relationships, we can see how in need of help families are and where change is needed. We can also break through our denial to later assist in our own recovery, the recovery of another or an entire harmful faith system.

The following material details each role of a harmful faith system to assist in identifying the unhealthy roles that all of us slip in and out of through our lives. In the religious addict, each role is a prison that locks away the real person behind the bars of obsession and compulsion.

The Role of the Persecutor

The first, most dominant role in a harmful faith system is that of persecutor. Persecutors don't start out to victimize their followers or families. They start out as unhealthy individuals who were often deprived or smothered by their parents as children. Rather than move beyond those issues, they compensate for them in ways that are victimizing. These people need to defend against their sense of brokenness and fallibility. This defensive plan leads to outrageous behavior that hurts many, especially those who possess a true faith and sin-

---

Persecutors don't start out to deceive and victimize their followers or families.

cerely seek God's will for their lives. Though the behavior may be outrageous, behind it is a very sad existence, a person who feels forced to carry on a role, forced to be something he or she does not want to be and was not meant to be.

Lee Whitcomb, like many other abusive fathers, was a persecutor. He found an answer he thought to be right and pure. He believed his practice of faith was focused on God. Since it was not, God became the afterthought of religion. Without a growing faith in God—just more rules and restrictions—Lee could not help victimizing his children. He loved them and wanted to help them, but he lost them to the practice of his religion. He didn't start out to do destructive things to his children, but his victimization produced some very destructive results. What made him perverse made his children wander. His failure to finally tap into a real God kept his children away from him and, all but one, away from God.

Evils of the Soul

Although his parenting was out of balance, Lee Whitcomb really did want the best for his children. He tried to protect them from evil by implementing rules that made him look good. He really did believe the protection would help the kids. Often people who are full of problems project them onto others, especially their children. Lee attributed his weaknesses to his kids and almost injected those weaknesses in them by placing so much emphasis on them. A daughter was attracted to "sleaze" because her father did everything he could to insulate her from it. It only made the "sleaze" more attractive and the perfect source of punishment to inflict on her father. If there had been balance in his parenting, most of Lee's children would not have deserted him and the faith for a lifestyle of sin and rebellion.

Childhood Problems

Lee Whitcomb began to serve the small church because he felt God wanted him to do so. He wanted to use the few gifts he had for God's glory. In the beginning all he wanted to do was serve God. I believe God was initially quite pleased with his dedication. As he progressed to power and prestige in that little church, his motives changed, and he gradually went from one of God's humble servants to an egomaniac demanding to be served by his family. If he had been raised in a balanced, healthy home, there is a good chance he would not have turned his practice of faith into a harmful system to save himself from a ruined past.

What led him to God led him away from God. That is why those in the church must not seek simple solutions to everyone's problems. Sometimes a relationship with God needs a cleansing of the past that will not occur without professional help. Those who are most against this type of help are often the ones who are in need of it most. Not everyone is suffering today because of childhood problems, but those who are often need help in resolving the sins of the past.

Self-Reliance versus Godly Dependency

God can take the worst possible background and use it to draw people to Him. When the world and parents and the system have all failed, God waits there ready to assist. Too often, rather than turn to God or persevere through God's help, people turn to their own devices, as corrupt as they may be, to resolve conflict and ease the discomforts that come with living.

The Lee Whitcombs of our day have found in their faith and religion a place where they can obtain what they always wanted and needed: acceptance, a way to be valued and esteemed. They find security and hope in a growing trust in God. However, when they no longer focus on God, their faith becomes harmful. Then everything is done for self in the name of God rather than every possible sacrifice of self being made in the name of God. This happens because the focus on God shifts to self and also to the fruit of the relationship with God.

It is like falling in love with the gift, not the giver. What was the fruit of being in a healthy relationship becomes the purpose of the relationship. The individual worships or idolizes the by-products of the relationship rather than God. It is idolatry of the altered moods or emotional change in oneself. The sinful self-obsession leads to idolatry and worship of those feelings that are developed through faith. Searching for the feelings, not God, becomes an addictive obsession. The feelings were not bad, but they soured when they became the sole motivation for the relationship with God.

The Lee Whitcombs of our day have found in their faith and religion a place where they can obtain what they always wanted and needed: acceptance, a way to be valued and esteemed.

Living in a False Reality

All Lee Whitcombs create a false reality, which is the purpose of any addiction. They invest their skills and talents in creating and feeding the false reality that drives an addiction. They use the power given to them by those who buy into their false identity with them to gain prestige and control of the environment and the people around them. This self-constructed creation mirrors back to them a sense of security and significance separate from a true faith and relationship with God.

Persecutors like Lee Whitcomb are usually very talented and capable of leadership in the church. Feeling that they are called of God, they feel invincible because they believe they are backed by God and His Word. They support their rules and regulations as they preach against anyone not willing to follow those rules. Any challenge or attempt to confront is disqualified and dismissed with a tirade that appears to be an accurate interpretation of God's Word.

It is actually just a distortion of the truth to support the harmful system established to meet the needs of the persecutor's ego. Using a tainted interpretation of Scripture in this way makes the persecutor tough to reach and his unreal world almost impenetrable. He takes his own tenets and turns them into teachings believed to be of God. Sadly, for those who believe them, they are not.

The Value of Performance

Persecutors are usually great performers and place a lot of emphasis on performance. Because they have often been rejected when they were younger, they don't want to risk rejection when they're older. Rather than trust God and risk being rejected or betrayed by God, they focus on what they do in the name of God and what they perceive are the instant rewards sent from God. In this way they lose all faith in God and totally rely on their abilities to find God's favor. Their performance becomes everything, and they surround themselves with people willing to say that the performance is outstanding.

Lee's wife played this role. Aside from the persecutor's performance and the applause of men and women for a job well done, he or

This self-constructed creation mirrors back to them a sense of security and significance separate from a true faith and relationship with God.

Aside from the persecutor's performance and the applause of men and women for a job well done, he or she feels worthless. Performance validates the persecutor's worth and being.

she feels worthless. Performance validates the persecutor's worth and being. Every day becomes a new battle to regain self-worth.

Although able to perform, the persecutor rarely feels good about the performance and must have adulation to compensate for a sagging ego. There is a constant fear that whatever the persecutor does, it won't be enough, and he or she won't be able to pick up the pieces this time. If things are going well, there is a constant fear that the other shoe will drop. This fear leads to harder work and more effort. Guilt burdens the persecutor if he or she is not doing everything possible to push the ministry closer to the vision he or she created.

The persecutor feels acceptance only when followers express pride and compliment the performance. Each new crisis becomes an opportunity to reestablish self-worth by being commended for the performance under pressure. The persecutor takes great pride in rising to the occasion, handling the new challenge, and proving to the family or followers of a church they are following a capable leader.

The performing persecutor appears to the world to be satisfied with the role of being driven to achieve, obsessed with success, and compulsive about everything. However, deep inside, the persecutor is not happy with the performing role, resents it greatly, and is very angry about having to do so much and feel so little for all the effort. The only time that anger is seen is in a rare loss of temper or in a regular outburst of intolerance from the pulpit. The persecutor lives with the anger, unable to express it to anyone because there are no intimate relationships to share with. The fear is that if anyone knew the persecutor was angry, it would dispel the myth that God's will was being done and the persecutor was happy in his or her role. So the only place the anger can be released is from the pulpit. When a persecutor preaches, most rational people stop and ask, "What is that guy so

The persecutor takes great pride in rising to the occasion, handling the new challenge, and proving to the followers they are following a capable leader.

However, deep inside, the persecutor is not happy with the performing role, resents it greatly, and is very angry about having to do so much and feel so little for all the effort.

---

angry about?'' What the persecutor would pass off as righteous indignation is in reality pure unresolved anger poisoning the faith of the minister and the followers.

Developing an Addiction

Because of the lack of self-worth and the need to feel good about self, addictions develop. Addictions are about finding safety and relief from feelings of worthlessness and pain. Some find safety in alcohol, some in drugs, and some in sex. Religious persecutors find it in the utilization of religion. A god, not the true God, is found to serve the need to hide pain and insecurity. A god, not the true God, is developed to hide feelings of rejection and abandonment. Religious persecutors need shelter, and they find it in religion rather than God. They become addicted to the feelings they can contrive out of manipulating people and the religious system they construct from their rules.

Everyone needs a source of protection in time of need. Without it a person becomes overwhelmed with the pressures of life. God is that shelter, and faith is the way a person finds that shelter. Putting religion in place of faith in God is evidence of no faith at all. The persecutors are afraid to trust God and find shelter in Him. In fact, they don't trust anyone. They trust their addictive relationship with the system and will do anything to protect that system. They are at war with themselves, and everyone becomes the enemy. Until they finally learn to trust God, they live a life full of fear and anxiety, wondering where the next attack will come from. They actually become addicted to the perception, believing that they are being attacked by those who have less faith in God.

When addiction sets in, the addict learns to trust the source of addiction for everything. The addiction, be it religion or alcohol, be-

---

Addictions are about finding safety and relief from feelings of worthlessness and pain.

Putting religion in place of faith in God is evidence of no faith at all.

comes the god of the addict. The persecutor finds religion to be an addiction that produces good feelings, prestige, and the ability to feel in control. This god of ungodly religion is the persecutor's entire world where every new day brings a new victim to come under the destructive power, control, and manipulation of the persecutor.

Persecutors manipulate their victims with guilt, shame, and remorse. They project their guilt and shame onto others. Feeling they have disappointed God, their parents, and everyone else, they bring people to their level by allowing them to feel what it is like to disappoint someone important and powerful.

An unreasonable father says to his children, "If it wasn't for you, I could make it. After all that I've done for you, don't you feel bad about being a hindrance to me? You need to pull your own weight, or I can't make it. It will be all your fault." An unreasonable father persecutes his children by making them feel responsible for the persecutor's image and future.

Disappointment

Persecutors are full of disappointment. They are disappointed in God and what He has provided them. They are disappointed in themselves because they are not as great as the others they compare themselves to. They are also disappointed in the people around them because they believe if those persons had worked harder, they could have gotten further. Persecutors set out to fulfill their dreams, call them God's plans, and then are disappointed in everyone when they don't produce the expected result and feelings. Each new accomplishment becomes an addiction, producing less and less gratification. It takes larger doses of challenge, just like the heroin addict needs larger and larger doses of heroin. Each time the accomplishment does not produce the reward, the disappointment with everyone intensifies.

He or she will do anything to experience an emotional high and break through to that state of existence where false pride can override the disappointment.

A disappointed persecutor is always in search of relief from the source of disappointment. He or she will do anything to experience an emotional high and break through to that state of existence where false pride can override the disappointment. The persecutor appears to be self-sufficient and self-satisfied. Yet those close to the persecutor know differently. The persecutor looks for compliments, begs for attention, and is willing to reward anyone for some bit of good news. The efforts that go into countering the disappointment build up the sagging ego and ease the pain of insecurity. Those who work with a persecutor know that the way to his or her heart is through compliments, flattery, and praise. Anything that supports the delusion that "I'm okay" provides relief.

Materialism

Although it was not true of Lee Whitcomb, persecutors often believe that people should be rewarded for their labors. They also think that no one labors like they do and no one should be rewarded like them. A $2 million salary, a second home, and a jet are all considered honest fruit of honest labor. They rationalize owning so much stuff and living so luxuriously by saying, "Isn't a workman worthy of his hire? Doesn't the Word of God promise abundant blessings? After all, I've worked hard for God. I did good. Can't you see how pleased God is with me?"

Having many material goods and using the interpretation that God always blesses with material goods are persecutors' attempts to convince themselves that they are pleasing God. Perhaps Satan sends these material things so they can continue on their binge of self-obsession, thinking God is doing the blessing. However, instead of considering that material things could be distractions, material excesses are viewed as proof that someone, God Himself, is pleased with their work. Each new toy of wealth becomes another excuse to find more signs of God's approval. When all the material things in the world provide less and less relief, persecutors must go for things outside the material realm. It may mean more power through politics. It

---

Persecutors believe that people should be rewarded for their labors. They also think that no one labors like they do and no one should be rewarded like them.

could mean an affair. There are numerous alternatives when wealth no longer produces the feeling of supposedly pleasing God.

Hidden and Observable Compulsions

Persecutors are very compulsive people. Their religion becomes an obsession, motivated by compulsion rather than conviction. Most people who are compulsive in one area are usually compulsive in other areas. That is why so much caution should be used when working with or supporting someone who appears to be driven to achieve for God. Being "called" is entirely different from being driven. The driven exhibit blatant compulsive behaviors that should make one wonder what is being hidden.

It is very difficult for religious compulsion to stand alone. Usually, a secondary compulsion reinforces the primary one and vice versa. One compulsion stands out for the world to observe. It is an "admirable" compulsion, such as work or a hobby or religion. The other compulsion is usually a hidden one that few people (if any) would consider admirable. The covert compulsion could involve sex, theft, or something else illegal or unethical. Until the persecutor allows faith in God to resolve issues of pain, insecurity, and abuse, a new compulsion will form to replace the last one the persecutor gave up.

A common cross-compulsion that comes with religious addiction is eating. Many people in our churches are overweight and cannot stop eating excessively. Rather than eat to live, they live to eat. Their compulsive religious addiction produces no lasting meaning, and they try to compensate with food.

One case of cross-compulsion did not involve food. Instead it was compulsive hand washing. The man came to the New Life Treatment Centers with many problems, but the most obvious one was that each time he shook someone's hand he would become anxious and irritated until he could find a place to wash his hands. He also showered several times a day and kept his room immaculate.

As he revealed his hidden sins, it became obvious why the pattern existed. He had had an affair with a woman of his church. It occurred early in his ministry, and it never happened again. His marriage

---

Being "called" is entirely different from being driven. The driven exhibit blatant compulsive behaviors that should make one wonder what is being hidden.

stayed intact but his behavior grew more and more bizarre over the years.

It turned out that the woman he had an affair with met him after church one day. While others greeted the pastor as they departed, she found her place in line. When she extended her hand, he reached to shake it, her eyes fastened on his, and she held his hand and would not release it. He was obsessed by the seemingly insignificant meeting. Eventually, his obsession led to infidelity.

He couldn't stop thinking about that original hand shake. He believed his life would have been entirely different if that hand shake hadn't taken place. His obsession led to his compulsive hand washing and other behaviors to free him from filth.

The man's obsession persecuted him and others around him. He was a tyrant who needed to have everything perfect. His life was a mess from the obsession of his mind that drove the compulsions of his body.

Manipulating with Contrition

Persecutors need forgiveness, and when in a bind, they ask for it. While they are asking, they appear quite sincere. But they are not. They ask for forgiveness only when they cannot talk their way out of something. When someone finally comes up with evidence of imperfection, there is a great shift in the emphasis of the persecutor. There is talk of the need to be involved in a forgiving faith instead of holding a grudge for wrongdoing. Tearful confessions usually do the trick to win back the doubting Thomases whose faith in the persecutor started to wane at the revelation of wrongdoing. With the persecutor's admission of guilt and request for forgiveness, most victims find themselves more than happy to continue with their support. Family members are willing to accept the act of contrition as evidence that change will occur. They do not hold the person to a new level of accountability, and eventually, the problems surface as they were before.

When persecutors are in charge of ministries, their acts of contrition should be followed up with a plan to implement change. They should also consider their position and future. If they don't, those in the church should force them to. Persecutors are forgiven. However, that does not mean they should continue in a place of leadership. In the role of persecutor, they are caught up in a most deadly and sinful condition called self-obsession. They are also in need of help from wise and godly people. If they are allowed to continue in their ministries, they will go on victimizing people until they run out of locations.

IMPORTANCE OF RELIGION

How important would you say religion is in your own life?

- 53% Very important
- 31% Fairly important
- 15% Not very important
- 1% No opinion

> —*George Gallup, Jr., and Sarah Jones,* 100 Questions and Answers: Religion in America *(Princeton, N.J.: Princeton Religion Research Center, 1989), p. 176.*

Then they will change professions and victimize people in other ways.

The greatest thing anyone can do for a persecutor is to force that person to seek help. The visible behavior that is deplorable is only a reflection of a deplorable and broken heart in critical need of repair. The behavior must change, but more important, there needs to be a change of heart. Allowing the persecutor to continue without change sentences that person to a lifetime of misery and pain. Hold him or her accountable to make those changes. Although it is painful, it will save many future heartaches.

Hope for the Persecutor

The hope for the persecutors lies in their identifying their sense of persecution. Deliverance from this torment comes from a willingness to feel the pain of being treated unjustly. The way out is through the pain and grief of being treated unjustly by people the persecutors cared for the most. Just as Christ bore the pain and grief of being unjustly crucified, persecutors and all of us must resolve our unjust persecutions with forgiveness as we share in the fellowship of Christ's sufferings.

The pain of resolving these issues and giving up old reliable behaviors is not easy to bear. It won't happen unless the persecutor is forced

---

The greatest thing anyone can do for a persecutor is to force that person to seek help. The visible behavior that is deplorable is only a reflection of a deplorable and broken heart in critical need of repair.

to make it happen. The evil behind many persecutors is that though the way out is through all the pain and confusion, that way is safely hidden by harmful convictions poisoning faith. These foundations of harmful faith are supported by those who share the hurtful faith system and depend on its continuance. Those equally confused people are called coconspirators.

CHARACTERISTICS OF THE PERSECUTOR

- Frequently defends own problems
- Feels a need to embellish the truth and make things appear more grand than they really are
- Feels the need to be in control
- Seeks power and control
- Speaks boldly about sinful behavior, even when involved in that same behavior
- Projects own wrongs onto other people
- Sees things in terms of very black or very white
- Believes people are extremely wonderful or bad, usually depending on the amount of support offered to the persecutor
- Has an attitude of superiority
- Appears very angry with those involved in sin
- Often is motivated by greed
- Fears sexual inadequacy
- Was probably born into an abusive or neglectful home that appeared wonderful to those outside the family
- Feels owed something
- Feels persecuted
- Is extremely self-centered
- Lives in a false world where person is convinced he or she is right
- Usually possesses special talents
- Contorts God's Word to fit own beliefs
- Surrounds self with people who are insecure and easily swayed
- Manipulates others using guilt, shame, and remorse

- Blames others for own failures
- Attempts to make others accept responsibility for own mistakes
- Feels disappointment in God, self, and others
- Usually is impressed with material goods and those who own them
- Is very angry
- Has compulsions in several areas
- Possesses an observable compulsion such as hard work that appears admirable to the world
- Possesses a hidden compulsion that would disgust most people if it were known
- Places great value on performance
- Deeply resents having to perform
- Is not involved in any accountable relationships
- Has no intimate relationships
- When in a bind will ask for forgiveness and appear sincere when doing so
- Fears not measuring up or losing image
- Fears that if no longer able to perform for the masses will be useless to God
- Needs professional help

The Role of the Coconspirator

The Ultimate Team Player

For every persecutor, there is at least one coconspirator who manipulates, plots, and plans to keep the persecutor in power and position. The persecutor and the coconspirator work as a unit; they operate as one. Both are addicted to religion as the means by which they experience feelings of acceptance and significance. In a family, if the husband is the persecutor, the wife is most likely the coconspirator.

In large organizations, there is usually more than one coconspirator. Several coconspirators work together to form a team of yes-men and yes-women that will do anything to protect and defend the persecutor. They feed into the persecutor's ego and further blind him or her from

*Several coconspirators work together to form a team of
yes-men and yes-women that will do anything to protect
and defend the persecutor. They feed into the persecutor's
ego and further blind him or her from reality.*

reality. When there is a conflict, they usually find a way to agree with
the persecutor and support his or her position. They are loyal and
supportive of the persecutor in every way. If it was not for them, the
persecutor's empire would fall quickly.

In a harmful faith system, these are the most dangerous followers.
They are as driven and misguided as the persecutor, and because they
are close to power, people trust them. Their faith in the persecutor is
the reason so many will continue to support that person when trouble,
rumor or admission of wrong surfaces.

In a family, the coconspirator is different from the enabler. As will
be presented in the next section, the enabler is passive in allowing the
persecutor to continue to victimize others. The coconspirator has an
active role. It occurs when both husband and wife are religious addicts
and victimize the family with the infliction of their trained practice of
faith.

The primary role of a coconspirator is to make the persecutor look
good. The coconspirator is the caretaker of the entire system and also
has the especially important task of being the caretaker of the persecutor's image. If the persecutor lacks compassion, the coconspirator will
supply it and make sure that the persecutor is identified by the family
or ministry followers as compassionate. When the coconspirator receives adulation from the persecutor, it is usually related to making the
persecutor look good by covering up or compensating for some major
flaw in the persecutor's character or image.

In a typical crisis, the coconspirator comes to the rescue of the persecutor, thus gaining special favor in the eyes of the persecutor. The
dynamics are the same in a family or in a ministry. The role has been
played out many times over the past few years as ministry scandals
have surfaced. What is seen publicly often goes on privately in the
family of the persecutor, also.

First, the minister confesses to the coconspirator that a great wrong
has been done. He or she admits that sin has occurred and that "now,
more than ever, I need your love, support, and forgiveness." The coconspirator is told that the persecuting minister has been under relentless persecution. There are admissions of working too hard and

becoming burned out. Perhaps there is the slight hint that if those around the persecutor had been more helpful, the disaster would have never happened. In a family, the coconspirator is made to feel guilty for the persecutor's act while at the same time being told of worth and value. With the persecutor's dramatic and tearful confession, the coconspirator is hooked, becomes addicted to the emotion, and with the intensity of the crisis rallies to save the persecutor, the victim of this "dreadful" situation.

Developing the Delusion

The coconspirators believe their actions are genuine. They say, "Yes, I know God's hand when I see it, and His hand is on this person." They see everything from the point of view that the persecutor has been called of God to head the family or run the ministry and that everything must make sense in light of that positioning by God. The coconspirators delude themselves and others and further enhance the delusions of the persecutor.

Each coconspirator sees the evil plot out to get the persecutor and takes it as a personal mission to protect the persecutor at all costs. When the persecutor heads a ministry, if it means that lies and distortions must be propagated to retain the minister in that ministry, lies and distortions will be devised. In a family, it could mean lying to authorities to prevent children from being taken out of the home. The ultimate act of loyalty to the persecutor is the willingness to lie. For lying to create the delusion of sincerity and purity, the coconspirator is rewarded with gifts, power, money, and prestige.

The Search for a Loving Father

Coconspirators are often adults who have felt inferior all their lives. Because they have never felt the love of a father, they search for significance from the love of someone else. They seek God's love, but during the search, they discover that the love of a human is more tangible. Their sincere desire to seek God is derailed into a desire for the favor of man. When they find that favor from a powerful leader or dominant spouse, they will die to protect their source of self-worth. They defend

The ultimate act of loyalty to the persecutor is the willingness to lie.

the persecutor and protect the empire or family because they know when it crashes, their own feelings of self-worth will die. The desire for right and wrong is replaced with the desire to feel good because they are part of something big. Having wanted security and significance all their lives, they finally have found someone or an entire organization that gives them that value. There is no way they will allow that value to deteriorate.

Family Coconspiracy

A coconspirator must be treated much differently from a person caught up in enabling behaviors. The coconspirator is in a different state of denial and often with greater barriers to reality. One case brought the severities of coconspiracy to the surface. A female was admitted to the unit who was in terrible shape. She had collapsed emotionally and spent hours crying, isolated from anyone else. Although she was suicidal, she was too weak to commit the act. She survived long enough for us to help her.

It was one of the most bizarre cases we have dealt with. She was raised in a rather repressive home where her father ruled with an iron fist. She and her three sisters obeyed him without questioning. He was demanding and rigid. Never did he reveal his emotions. He was always angry and never had time for the girls. This woman spent her life looking for a place to belong and someone to belong to. She felt like an outcast most of her life.

When she met the man who would become her husband, he had a strong personality just like her father's. Rather than be repulsed by it, she was attracted to it. From the beginning of the relationship, he was controlling and domineering. His spell of manipulation charmed her and she fell in love with him. They married and had two children. Both of them had similar conservative views in their practice of faith. Both believed that the husband should be head of the home and that the wife should submit to his authority. In practice, this belief became very distorted and gave the husband a license to exploit his wife.

The desire for right and wrong is replaced with the desire to feel good because they are part of something big. Having wanted security and significance all their lives, they finally have found someone or an entire organization that gives them that value.

He told her what to do and when to do it. She loved the control. She loved not having to make a decision. She went along with his autocratic rule. She told her daughters they must do the same. She demanded that they never question their father's actions, just do what he said must be done. They complied.

Our female patient was addicted to a lifestyle where she didn't have to accept responsibility for anything. Everything she did was at the instruction of her minister or her husband. She never made an important decision; she just followed orders. When her minister yelled at her and the rest of the congregation, she felt cleansed. It was so similar to her childhood that she was comfortable there. Everything was fixed with an order, a prayer, or a miracle. That existence allowed her to deny the reality of her broken childhood and her problems of inadequacy.

Her coconspiracy began when her husband started to control every aspect of their daughters' lives. His control became very destructive to both girls. Because of his uneasiness with himself, he refused to let other men be with his daughters. He convinced his wife that in our society, dating was evil, and all boys wanted only to abuse girls. While others were allowed to date, the girls were forced to stay home. When one was a senior in high school and the other a junior, they still were not allowed to date. Each day the mother took the girls to school and picked them up and prevented any outside social interaction. The girls were miserable, and their misery turned to despair and depression.

The coconspiring mother played an active role in the persecution initiated by the father. He made the rules, and she enforced them. She tried to convince the girls it was for their own good and pleaded with them to honor their father's demands. She helped her husband trap the girls, and she kept the trap fastened tightly. Without her help, her husband would not have been able to victimize the girls as he did. The more withdrawn they became, the greater her resolve to force them to comply with his demands.

The crisis occurred when a school counselor intervened. The younger daughter went to the counselor and told her how she and her sister were being raised. The girl explained that the dating prohibition was just a social symptom of a larger problem of control, manipulation, and victimization. The counselor had been worried about the depression of both girls and involved both in counseling while at school. Each session led closer to the confrontation that would collapse our patient.

The counselor called the mother to the school to talk about her daughters. She laid out the facts the girls had presented. She said that this type of parenting was as abusive as physical abuse. She explained that the girls had no social skills and were completely dependent on their parents while other kids were learning to separate themselves from their parents. The counselor told the mother that the girls were withdrawn and severely depressed. They had no friends, and many other students laughed at them. She went on to say that if something was not done, she would intervene and attempt to have the girls placed in a home where love was more important than rules.

The meeting broke through the delusions that the mother had carried for years. She realized she had been part of hurting the girls. She realized she had made excuses for her husband. She knew his problems were reinforced by her own. But she did not know how to fix it. She felt as if she was facing a wall of fire that she knew she had to climb. She collapsed into tears. She could not stop crying. Her sobs grew deeper, and she became hysterical. She was trapped, not her daughters. She felt the pressure of her self-inflicted trauma and could not continue with reality before her. The counselor brought her to us for fear that she would commit suicide after her strength returned.

The story doesn't have a completely happy ending. In this case, the husband was unwilling to work on his problems, and he divorced his wife. She did fairly well in treatment and through ongoing therapy regained control of her life. Her daughters also entered therapy, but it will take years to rebuild what was destroyed by the victimizing father. The key to the mother's recovery is her ability to forgive herself for helping her persecuting husband create a family where he did as he pleased while the rest of the family ceased to exist as individuals.

Hope for the Coconspirator

Coconspirators are addicted to religion, the religious system that gives them importance, and the embodiment of that religion, the persecutor. Coconspirators invest a lifetime of effort supporting the persecutor, so it is not easy to turn away from the system or the person that created it. Buying into the strong existence and lying to cover problems make it more difficult for coconspirators to turn away from the persecutor and the addictive relationship with religion. But it can be done.

The coconspirator can remove the obstacle that hinders the relationship with God. The coconspirator can have a clean slate by confessing the need to feel secure and the willingness to deny, distort, and lie to protect that place of security. The coconspirator must be willing to face himself or herself, see what is really there, and stand alone without being propped up by a devious and controlling persecutor who, along with everyone else, has victimized the coconspirator.

The coconspirator can be used greatly by God to bring people to Him. First, the coconspirator must be willing to pay the price of giving up or changing the relationship with the persecutor and confessing wrongs to those who have been victimized. Then the coconspirator must be able to forgive himself or herself and start over. When this occurs, there is tremendous hope for a new life free of control and the need to control.

The coconspirator can have a clean slate by confessing the need to feel secure and the willingness to deny, distort, and lie to protect that place of security.

CHARACTERISTICS OF THE COCONSPIRATOR

- Assumes the role of the ultimate team player
- Shows total dedication to the persecutor
- Always finds a way to support the position of the persecutor
- Feeds the persecutor's ego
- Is addicted to the power granted by the persecutor
- Keeps things going within the harmful faith system
- Ensures that everything is taken care of responsibly
- Typically is a small person who feels big when in on the action
- Willingly deceives to maintain the persecutor's power
- Is good at lying
- Enjoys being rewarded for willingness to distort the truth
- Usually felt inferior as a child
- Ties personal feelings of value to another person rather than to God
- Protects sense of self-worth by protecting the persecutor
- Appears unassuming and grateful to be number two in the organization

- Enjoys material things
- Is sincerely deluded
- Feels weak
- Lacks the strong charisma and leadership abilities of the persecutor
- Feels extremely inadequate
- May have had a large ministry that was lost due to the revelations of own immorality
- Works as a single unit with the persecutor
- Lives to be appreciated and recognized by the persecutor
- Needs to feel safe in work and relationships
- Is viewed by outsiders as trustworthy, conscientious, competent, mature, and reliable
- Needs professional help

The Role of the Enabler

The role of the enabler varies from that of the coconspirator. The coconspirator is actively involved in delusion and connives to keep the persecutor in power. The enabler is not as active in the deception; it is a passive role that allows, rather than promotes, victimization. The enabler is the spouse of the persecutor, and usually it is the wife.

Enablers are also found within the organization of the harmful faith ministry. They have lesser positions than those of the coconspirators. They are not active in the decision making of the organization but willingly support those decisions made at the top of the organization. They are ready to rescue the persecutor and placate whenever possible.

Addicted Caretakers

The enablers are the primary caretakers of the persecutor. They are often asked to do the behind-the-scenes dirty work of the persecutor and coconspirators. They resent being placed in these roles with these functions, but they rarely complain. They are religious addicts, addicted to a persecutor, the hurtful system, and their role. They are

The enabler is not as active in the deception; it is a passive role that allows, rather than promotes, victimization.

addicted to the feelings of worth they obtain when they are called on to fix the problems or cover up the wrongs of the persecutor.

They lose themselves in the life of the persecutor. The more they have invested in the persecutor, the more they resent themselves. Rather than break free of the system, they cling more tightly as they lose more and more of their self worth. They cannot view themselves outside the role of enabler. They become so dependent on the persecutor and the system that they will believe any lie or rationalization if it will maintain peace and the status quo of the relationship.

The addiction to the persecutor takes precedence over everything else. The addiction poisons them and robs them of their faith. They leave their faith in God and place it in the persecutor. They rationalize supporting evil and a victimizing system out of the need to be submissive. The addiction to the person is the single most important factor in allowing the wrongs of a hurtful faith system to continue.

Enabling Thoughts and Behaviors

Throughout a harmful faith system—whether it is a ministry or a family—there are many who exhibit enabling behaviors. There is always one who has a primary role of enabling, and this person exhibits more of these behaviors than anyone else. The enabling behaviors form the very identity of the person, who is insecure and unable to think for himself or herself. The primary function of the enabler is to allow the persecutor to continue and the harmful faith system to survive. Each behavior makes sense only in light of the drive to support the dysfunctional system.

One of the most enabling behaviors is going along with the group consensus. When this occurs in a misled ministry, damage can be

They are often asked to do the behind-the-scenes dirty work of the persecutor and coconspirators. They resent being placed in these roles with these functions, but they rarely complain.

done to thousands of people. Especially when the leaders of the organization are in agreement, the enabler will go along and comply with the desire to continue as if there was no problem. Thoughts such as these come to the enabler's mind:

Others are more knowledgeable about the situation than I am. I must go along with their decisions.

It is my place to be supportive, not to confront. My faith demands that I be obedient and loyal.

These people are so nice, especially to me. Their motives must be pure.

Perhaps I don't really know the pastor well enough to discern whether he is right or wrong.

Since they are closer to the situation, I will go along with them.

He must be "special" with special needs. Who am I to rock the boat?

I must be a faithful follower and not allow others to hurt the ministry.

These thoughts of inaction paralyze the enabler and prevent that person from doing what might be the most helpful. Helping would be seeing the reality of the problem and confronting it. Instead, the fearful enabler allows the problem to grow until someone else intervenes.

For example, in the family of the alcoholic, the husband and the wife may take on the roles of the addict and the enabler. Other family members will also act out roles. The enabler could cause the drinking to change course by seeking help or conducting an intervention. The enabler could be the catalyst for change since the addict depends on the enabler. But the enabler becomes comfortable in the role and allows the drinking to continue. The drinking is no more addictive than the enabling role. Instead of being able to intervene upon the alcoholic, the enabler must be intervened upon.

The same is true for the enabler of a persecuting religious addict who gets trapped in the role. Until a friend risks rejection and intervenes, the enabler will go on assisting the persecutor in staying in the victimizing role. As long as the enabler remains convinced there is no hope to change, the harmful system will continue in denial and hypocrisy.

The behaviors of the enabler serve as insulators from reality for the harmful system and especially the persecutor. When criticism is

---

As long as the enabler remains convinced there is no hope to change, the harmful system will continue in denial and hypocrisy.

The behaviors of the enabler serve as insulators from reality for the harmful system and especially the persecutor.

aimed at the persecutor, it is denied and covered up. Similarly, anyone inside the alcoholic family who would be so bold as to suggest that something is wrong is silenced by the enabler. The children in the alcoholic family or fellow workers in the organization soon learn that it is not safe to talk or express feelings, especially when those feelings doubt or question the persecutor's behavior. As long as the enabler pushes criticism aside or silences those who want to speak from within, the persecutor is free to continue unabated in the quest for power, insulated from the reality that might hamper his or her efforts.

Survival Mode

Unlike the persecutors and the coconspirators acting out addiction to conquer, the enablers act out their behaviors to survive. To them, the world is cruel, and the persecutor is a victim. They believe that if someone as strong as the persecutor can get in trouble, they would be destroyed quickly. They will do anything not to have to face the world alone. They rationalize that they are acting in their children's best interest. They state that their decisions are made in accordance with their faith. They are actually holding on for dear life, doing anything that will prevent them from having to endure the painful process of change and facing the world alone.

Because they are so determined to keep things as they are, they feel responsible for everything. They take the entire burden of the family on themselves. They work harder and harder to keep the family going and the persecutor in power. They neglect their needs for the sake of meeting the needs of the persecutor. They consider every new development a threat to their existence and protection the only means to survive. When the persecuting head of the family falls, the enabler believes if a little more effort had been given, everyone would have been happy.

Unlike the persecutors and the coconspirators acting out addiction to conquer, the enablers act out their behaviors to survive.

*The enablers carry the weight of the world, especially
the weight of the delusional world of the persecutor, and
everyone around the enablers seems to imply that more
must be done to help the persecutor and the ministry.*

It is very similar in a ministry. When ministries fail and ministers
fall, the enablers believe that a few more sacrifices would have saved
the day. The coconspirators fuel this thinking with manipulative comments in time of trouble. If the minister has an affair, the coconspirators confront the enablers about doing a better job of meeting the
needs of the minister. Others will ask for greater sacrifice and understanding from the enablers. These unrealistic expectations trap the
enablers into believing more work and more effort must be extended.
They break sometimes under the pressure. When this occurs, people
rally behind the persecutor pointing out what a burden a sick wife
must have been for all those years. The enablers carry the weight of
the world, especially the weight of the delusional world of the persecutor, and everyone around the enablers seems to imply that more must
be done to help the persecutor and the ministry. They fear they may
not survive if they do not comply.

Hoping for Change

Enablers know that what is happening is wrong. They want it to
change but are too afraid or don't know how to facilitate change. Enablers feel so powerless outside the world of the persecutor and are so
dependent on the persecutor that they believe they are unable to face
the consequences of change. They are different from the coconspirators who know things are not right but fight to keep them that way.
The enablers are so burdened by guilt that they want things to change.
They never stop hoping that somehow the persecutor will decide to
live differently, the ministry will go back to serving God, and everything will be wonderful.

They increase their efforts to support and love the persecutor, hop-

*Enablers know that what is happening is wrong. They
want it to change but are too afraid or don't know how to
facilitate change.*

The system, especially to the coconspirators, blackmails the enablers to stay in the supportive role—whatever the price.

---

ing this will result in the needed change. Their increased efforts of love and support only feed the ego of the persecutor and allow the persecution to go unabated. They feel sorry for all of the deceived victims but not enough to risk forcing change on the system. They hope and pray for something to make a difference while refusing to do what they can to change it. Enabling continues when confrontation would help the most.

Responding to the Harmful System

Enablers are responders. They respond to each new crisis and all of the subtle hints of the hurtful system to do what is needed to protect that system. The system, especially to the coconspirators, blackmails the enablers to stay in the supportive role—whatever the price. Each enabler acts for different reasons, but most are prone to respond to the twelve "poor me" appeals of the persecutor. An enabler who has been in the role for a long time will quickly move to feel sorry for just about anyone requesting pity. The persecutor presents a "poor me" facade and requests being rescued. Trained enablers quickly respond to the rescue call and move in to support and save the persecutor. Rather than take care of their own needs, they assist the persecutor in his or her helplessness.

The key response of the enablers is to support. When they doubt the persecutor and the mission of the ministry, they continue to offer support. They know few responses other than to defend and support the person in the midst of criticism. The persecutor's world may become more unpredictable, but at least there is the constant force of the enablers' support. This support allows the persecutor to believe he or she is right. It is fuel to continue the delusionary existence that exploits many victims. Only when the enablers withdraw support does the persecutor see any need to change or at least to consider change.

Only when the enablers withdraw support does the persecutor see any need to change or at least to consider change.

Hope for the Enabler

The only hope for enablers is reality. They must face the reality that the system continues in large part due to the enabling support offered the system and the persecutor. Enablers must come to grips with the reality that they are playing out an unhealthy role that has trapped them in a system that will eventually fail. The hope comes from ending the charade before more people are hurt and victimized.

A huge codependency movement has helped many destructive relationships change into productive ones where accountability for both partners is a priority. When enablers stop enabling, they can enter a new type of relationship where needs are met rather than ignored. The price is the loss of an enabling identity that is hard to sacrifice. Thousands of enablers have made the difficult move out of the role, and the world, especially their world, is a better place for it. When enablers do the courageous thing, victims are spared further victimization.

Enablers must come to grips with the reality that they are playing out an unhealthy role that has trapped them in a system that will eventually fail.

CHARACTERISTICS OF THE ENABLER

- Allows victimization rather than promotes it
- Supports victimization with silence
- Is dedicated to not rocking the boat
- Does not trust God enough to allow family turmoil or destruction of a ministry
- Appears powerless
- Receives praise for sainthood in being able to survive under severe persecution
- Can be perceived by coconspirators as the enemy or a threat to the coconspirators' position
- Allows the persecutor to live in denial
- Covers up the harm done to the family or the organization
- Eases the persecutor's pain

- Outwardly appears loving and supportive of the persecutor
- Inwardly is angry at living an unfulfilled life
- As persecutor begins to lose credibility, will start to develop other skills, such as obtain a degree in counseling, knowing the system and the family may fall apart
- Feels very little self-worth
- Becomes a caretaker of the persecutor
- Is addicted to the persecutor and the system
- Has the primary goal of maintaining peace and the status quo
- Has great difficulty thinking for oneself
- Goes along with group consensus
- Acts to survive
- Feels extremely responsible
- If the ministry fails, blames self
- Neglects personal needs for the sake of the ministry and the persecutor
- Never stops hoping things will change
- Never stops fearing what will happen if things do change
- Needs someone to intervene

The Role of the Victim

The most unfortunate of all the roles in a harmful faith system is that of the victim. Victims don't know what they're doing when they blindly support a hurtful faith system and its persecuting, victimizing leader or parent. They do everything out of a desire to know God and worship God, but their actions are misguided. They trust their parents and leaders to be people of integrity and will shun any mention that it is not so.

Victims sacrifice their time and money and faith to support the system.

Their blind allegiance is taken for granted because victims lose themselves in the family or the organization. They never make a fuss and never rock the boat. They just wait to carry out the next duty that is assigned.

Victims sacrifice their time and money and faith to support the system. The persecutor, coconspirators, and enablers manipulate these people to keep the family or harmful faith system going and the persecutor in power. When the harmful faith system is finally exposed for what it is, the victims must bear the feelings of being used to meet the needs of those in authority they perceived as having integrity.

Victims are compliant people. They cause no problems because they believe everything that is passed down from the top. From their positions in the background, they make everything appear okay with the blind support they offer. Each victim who stays inside a sick family will sacrifice individuality, just like an enabler. Their blind allegiance is taken for granted because victims lose themselves in the family or the organization. They never make a fuss and never rock the boat. They just wait to carry out the next duty that is assigned. Victims sacrifice personal needs and desires so that they can be part of the system.

The silent and invisible victims sacrifice their need to be significant in order to be valued by the system. They fear rejection and abandonment so much that they would rather be exploited members of something than be on their own and part of nothing. The leaders and parents in the hurtful system know this and exploit it regularly. Any sadness and pain from feeling insignificant is hidden from the other victims. Everyone acts as if it is a great privilege to be taken for granted and lost in such a worthwhile mission.

Spiritual Molestation

Victims place their complete trust in the parents or leaders of the harmful faith system, counting on their parents and leaders to take care of them and nurture their spiritual well-being. At the time when

The silent and invisible victims sacrifice their need to be significant in order to be valued by the system.

Spiritual molestation rapes the victims' minds of reason and strips them of their direct access to God. It takes away their self-respect and leaves them feeling broken.

the loyalty of these spiritually needy people is the strongest, the persecutors of the faith spiritually molest them. Spiritual molestation rapes the victims' minds of reason and strips them of their direct access to God. It takes away their self-respect and leaves them feeling broken.

Some turn completely away from God after they realize they have been so badly abused by the persecutor and coconspirators. If they are without support after the victimization, they are often robbed of their desire to know and draw closer to God. Left with their feelings of betrayal and lack of confidence in their ability to identify someone they can trust, they abandon their spiritual journey.

Once victims have been spiritually molested, the persecutors and coconspirators attempt to manipulate them into keeping the secret. Hell, fire and brimstone, and other tools of God's wrath are used as threats to not rock the boat or reveal the problems within the family or harmful ministry. The victims who succumb to the threats bear the pain of existing in a world of lies. When they are perceived as willing to go along with the lies and deceptions, they are repeatedly abused by being asked to adhere more closely to the rules of the family or ministry. Tragically, these victims feel they deserve the abuse. They feel as though they don't measure up, are bad, and should be satisfied to go along and be accepted. Rather than stand up for what they sense is right, they continue to work hard to measure up and meet the needs of the system that molested them.

Examples of Victimization

Victimization can occur in a family or in a ministry. The results are the same—lack of identity and loss of faith—but the form is quite different. In a family, a child can be victimized by believing that following rules will result in a relationship with God. The less these rules are

Once victims have been spiritually molested, the persecutors and coconspirators attempt to manipulate them into keeping the secret.

TRAGEDY STRIKES
THREE-YEAR-OLD GIRL

Michael Pacewitz, a man with a history of mental problems from a troubled home, killed a three-year-old girl. He was baby-sitting the girl and her baby brother, both children of a woman Pacewitz knew from the church they both attended. Pacewitz joined the church in an attempt to kick a drug habit and became very involved in running errands and cleaning for the church. "Joining the church made a positive difference in Pacewitz's life." No longer taking the medication prescribed to him upon discharge from a mental hospital where he was diagnosed as a schizophrenic, "Pacewitz said the church encouraged him to stop using the medication, saying God would heal him. 'We believe God is a healer,' the pastor said. 'But if you're sick, and we've prayed for you, go to your doctor and if you don't need (the drugs) anymore, your doctor will tell you.'" After killing the girl, Pacewitz told reporters that Satan had guided his hand: "I was just there, taking care of them . . . and I felt like a devil. That's what I thought when I killed the little girl. I was the devil."

—Carroll Lachnit and Donna Wares, "Search for Salvation,
Unanswered Pleas Led Up to Girl's Death," Orange County
Register, *March 11, 1990.*

rooted in the Bible, the more likely they will block the child's faith and rob the child of identity. Each time a parent tells a teenager what God wants, so that the parent can obtain what he or she wants, the teen suffers. Some parents use God as an excuse to guide a child into a career they want for the child rather than a career the child would love. Others victimize to feel some degree of power since they experience none in other areas of life. The victimization can even become sexual, using God as an excuse to molest children, telling them this is a way to protect them from the outside world.

One man did exactly that. When his daughter reached age fifteen, he began to fondle her, and he eventually had sexual intercourse with her. He told her of an evil world, full of disease and abuse. He told her that it was his job to protect her from it, that she should remain with him instead of seeking a husband who could be violent. He even told her if she did marry, God would punish her. This depraved man continued this way for three years until the girl finally had the courage to tell her mother. Though it was not easy, the mother believed it was true and took action to stop the abuse. The girl's view of God was

The victim's addiction to religion is most evident in the hours of sacrifice that are worked to develop the ministry.

---

incredibly distorted, and it took many hours of deprogramming to help her see that God is not a victimizing God.

When victimization occurs outside the family or in a harmful faith system, it can result in giving too much time in a fit of churchaholism. The victim's addiction to religion is most evident in the hours of sacrifice that are worked to develop the ministry. When trouble arises, even more time is spent attempting to fix the ministry. Just like the alcoholic who spends many hours at the bar and away from the family, the workaholic victim wastes time in countless meetings to cover the wrongs of the persecutor. The time should have been spent and could have been spent with his or her family.

The victims sacrifice time almost as if they are Christian martyrs who must go down with the persecutor out of faithful duty. While they attempt to make a name for themselves as sacrificial believers, family members wonder why God would take up so much of parents' time. When the ministry goes down and the victims realize all the work was for nothing, it is difficult to remain faithful and continue to draw close to God. Most would do well to obtain counseling once they discover they have been abused so badly.

When victimization becomes sexual, it can be very damaging. A faithful secretary, dedicated to meeting the needs of a minister may become trapped in a sexual affair that was never her intent. She may be manipulated and seduced and then convinced that for some reason it was okay to meet the "special" needs of the minister in this way. It is so sad to see several families destroyed by the uncontrolled lust of a persecuting minister who cares about nothing more than his own personal gratification. Anyone caught up in an affair of this nature needs to confess the involvement to another person of leadership and get out of the relationship immediately. The minister will meet his needs and then leave her for another as soon as he is through with the exploitation. No matter how the relationship evolved, it must be seen for what it is and stopped.

They sacrifice their happiness and self-respect in order to feel important and gain acceptance.

Victims make great sacrifices. They sacrifice their happiness and self-respect to feel important and gain acceptance. They unknowingly sacrifice their needs so that persons they esteem can be saved from experiencing the consequences of their own behaviors. Although they are unaware of it, their attitude of sacrifice has more to do with a lack of self-worth than anything else. In the name of God, they sacrifice far beyond what God would demand. The ways in which they give of their time, money, and themselves perpetrate the exploitation by a ministry that is not dedicated to serving God. The more the victims sacrifice, the more victims are created by the ministry.

Hope for the Victim

The result of spiritual victimization is often a hardened heart and many unresolved feelings of anger and resentment. The victim has bought into a false system of conditional love of God and tried to meet those conditions of sacrifice. When the harmful aspects of faith are revealed, the victim feels that an unloving God cannot be reached. The hope for the victim comes in seeing the unconditional love of God, love that does not depend on performance. When this is understood, the feelings of resentment and anger can be resolved. God's unconditional love is always available to radically change the victim's heart. There comes a point in a victim's recovery that the risky dimension of faith must be accepted. That dimension requires forsaking the comforts of trusting in a person or an organization and trusting in God alone. When this occurs, many victims find a true and pure faith for the first time without the distortions of persecutors.

The victim's hope must come through exercising the gift of free choice given to human beings by God. Free choice is never made in the midst of emotional blackmail or pressure to conform. The free choice of faith is made out of love for God and the desire to serve Him.

WHERE DOES ALL THE MONEY GO?

Jim and Tammy Bakker "lived on a lakeside spread not far from their 2,300-acre theme park. . . . She wore mink; he carried a Louis Vuitton briefcase; they had a Rolls-Royce and houses in Charlotte, N.C., and Palm Desert, Calif."

—"God's Green Acres, at Home with the Televangelists," Life, June 1987, pp. 58–62.

The hope for the victim comes in seeing the unconditional love of God, love that does not depend on performance.

Through this service and unconditional love, the victim can gain significance and security. The victim is freed to meet the needs of others out of love and service to God rather than manipulation and coercion.

CHARACTERISTICS OF THE VICTIM

- Makes tremendous sacrifices out of a combination of a desire to serve God and very low self-esteem
- Wants to feel a valuable part of something important
- Was often victimized as a child
- Looks for someone to make salvation easy
- Often experiences loneliness
- Actually believes money and effort will buy favor with God
- Willingly sacrifices time, money, and self for a cause considered to be of God
- It easily manipulated by persecutors and coconspirators
- Is spiritually molested by leaders or parents
- Feels victimized when the truth about distorted faith ministry is revealed
- Often abandons spiritual journey upon discovery of abuse by an exploitative leader or parent
- Is often threatened by coconspirators and persecutors to keep the victimization a secret
- Bears the pain of existing in a world of lies and deception
- Sometimes leaves one harmful faith system and moves to another
- Frequently is very emotional in the practice of faith
- Becomes isolated and lonely once disillusioned about a ministry or family

- Though astute in business and other affairs, naively practices a blind faith
- Refuses to doubt questionable activities; instead rationalizes why exploitative things would be necessary for the ministry's survival
- The more money given to a ministry, the greater the resolve to protect and defend it
- Gives untold hours to develop the ministry and then sacrifices further in attempts to fix it
- Sacrifices a wonderful family for the sake of a hurtful leader
- Often has a martyr complex
- May be seduced into a sexual relationship to meet "special" needs of the minister
- Is reluctant to stop the victimization for fear of looking foolish
- Often is involved with the harmful ministry out of a desire to be or look important
- Willingly pays a high price for acceptance
- Frequently needs counseling after discovering exploitation

The Role of the Outcast

Of the five roles in the toxic faith system, only one is not a religious addict or a possessor of harmful faith. In any dysfunctional system, there is usually someone who can see the problem and confront it. Unwilling to play the games of the persecutors and coconspirators, the person becomes an outcast.

These people who stand up for what is right and challenge the system and what is wrong with it lose their jobs, friends, and church. They become lone voices in the wilderness crying out for change that will not come as long as the persecutor dictates power, the coconspirators manipulate the system, the enablers allow it to continue, and the victims fall in line with blind faith. When outcasts surface, they are identified as troublemakers and pushed out of the system as soon as possible.

These people who stand up for what is right and challenge the system and what is wrong with it lose their jobs, friends, and church.

Forced to Rebel

In a healthy system, individuals serving in that organization have respect for the person and position of leadership. For it to remain healthy, there must also be respect for the workers. When there is no respect, the "hired hands" are not allowed to disagree. If they don't like something, they are labeled complainers, negative thinkers, and not team players. The harmful faith system has no place for anyone who challenges the integrity or disagrees with the methods of the leader. In the hurtful faith system, loyalty is equated with blind faith and complete agreement with the leader.

Allegiance that requires overlooking the truth must be pledged daily. When that allegiance is no longer there, the confrontational workers or church members are labeled outcasts and rejected by the organization. And so, they are forced to rebel since there is no room for disagreement within the organization.

As outcasts challenge the delusion of the system, they are discredited immediately. They express resentment for the autocratic system and the manipulation that stems from it. The harmful faith system creates a lose-lose situation where the outcasts must give up perceptions of reality or be willing to face complete rejection. Abandonment becomes the reward for trying to correct the ministry so it can succeed rather than be destroyed by scandal.

Outcasts can interpret reality for themselves. Even when their perception of reality goes against that of hundreds or thousands of followers, they can clearly see the problems and press for solutions to those problems. Outcasts are unimpressed by position or personhood. They love God and want to protect His people and His institutions from spiritual fraud.

The harmful faith system has no place for anyone who challenges the integrity or disagrees with the methods of the leader.

Outcasts can interpret reality for themselves. Even when their perception of reality goes against that of hundreds or thousands of followers, they can clearly see the problems and press for solutions to those problems.

For these people so dedicated to God, it is not hard to see others' dedication to egos and empires created by humans. They are forced to suffer for what they see because they refuse to watch people live a lie and abuse others. No harmful faith system can handle this keen insight and dedication to truth. They must place their jobs and the church they love on the altar of sacrifice as they are forced to move on to a place where hurtful faith is not practiced.

Hope for the Outcast

God honors those who are willing to sacrifice the comforts of going along with abuse for rejection and abandonment when the sacrifice is made in the name of what is right. There is a special place in God's heart for the heroes of a harmful faith system. Those who stand up for God and tell the world the emperor has no clothes will receive their reward sooner or later.

Having talked with some of these courageous outcasts, I know of the pain and suffering endured when they rejected the harmful faith system. But all is not terrible for the outcasts. They feel good about finally making a stand they knew needed to be made. They also feel the respect of others who value their courageous acts of rebellion. The hope for these outcasts is that there are many great men and women of God and many great churches where God can be found. Rejected in one place, they will be welcomed in another where pure faith is upheld and God is honored through the integrity of the leadership of the organization.

God honors those who are willing to sacrifice the comforts of going along with abuse for rejection and abandonment when the sacrifice is made in the name of what is right.

CHARACTERISTICS OF THE OUTCAST

- Is not a religious addict
- Does not possess a harmful faith
- Willingly stands alone
- Stands up for what is right
- Is willing to be rejected by others in the harmful faith system
- Can discern right from wrong
- Commits to leaders having integrity
- Refuses to be victimized by false teaching and lack of integrity
- Speaks out for truth
- Usually loses a job within a dysfunctional organization over concern for it
- Suffers rejection by friends after challenging the leadership of those with hurtful faith
- Often is treated as a leper
- Is begged by others in the harmful faith system to support the persecutor
- Endures shame for actions
- Refuses to respect or be manipulated by those in the dysfunctional system
- Sees the truth and acts on it even if it produces great personal pain
- Interprets reality for self
- Is motivated to protect people from spiritual fraud
- Is very dedicated to God and the people who seek a relationship with Him
- Commands respect of others for courage

Harmful faith lives within an unhealthy family or system of people trapped in roles that addict them and destroy their relationships with God. The persecutor starts the delusion and invites others to live within a false reality and play out roles to increase the ministry and his or her prestige. Coconspirators reinforce the false reality and are re-

*When misled faith exists within a harmful system,
everyone is affected; everyone is hurt by the damage of
the counterfeiting of faith in an all-powerful, loving God.*

warded for their assistance in manipulating others to follow the harmful faith. The enablers fail to question the false reality and cushion the blow of consequences when the immorality of the persecutor and the entire organization is revealed. Victims who fail to question reality succumb to the deception and sacrifice their time, talents, family, sexuality, money, and self-respect to support the hurtful faith system. Only the outcasts dare to be different and question the false reality they found themselves in. They suffer rejection and abandonment for the sake of what is right and their true faith in God. When misled faith exists within a harmful system, everyone is affected; everyone is hurt by the damage of the counterfeiting of faith in an all-powerful, loving God.

Harmful faith is all about addiction and victimization. Each person in his or her role becomes addicted to the type of power or security offered by that role. The longer the person is in the role, the more difficult it becomes to stop the addictive behavior unique to that role. The tragedy of the hurtful faith system is that everyone is a victim. Most people are victimized for profit and gain. They are asked for their money and their lives to support the leader and his or her lavish lifestyle. They sacrifice out of a belief that bigger is better, and they become bigger victims as the organization becomes bigger.

Each person in the system views the persecutor and the mission as more important than himself or herself. The persecutor is viewed as so important in the kingdom of God that nothing is too great a sacrifice for that person and his or her vision. Grandmothers like mine will send in their pension checks. Husbands and wives will send in their vacation and grocery money. People will lie and steal and give up their self-worth for the sake of the misguided leader. Children will fall in line after a parent's demands for conformity destroy identity.

The promises of God and God's special blessings will be used to

*Deliverance from earthly sorrow and oppression is the
hook, and the price is nothing short of prostituting the
faith.*

manipulate the masses much like Hitler's promise to restore the former glory of Germany. Deliverance from earthly sorrow and oppression is the hook, and the price is nothing short of prostituting the faith.

Every harmful system must have willing followers who will play their assigned roles without question. They become the caretakers of the system as it grows and the scapegoats as it falls apart. They are held in bondage due to their harmful convictions and misguided beliefs. They martyr themselves not for a loving God but for a harmful religious system that demands sacrifice as payment for services rendered.

The cause of all growth of a harmful system is desire for profit, power, pleasure, and prestige. These desires fuel the addictive nature of the system that hooks each member. Followers become addicted to the instant rewards of hurtful faith and a sense of belonging to something. They become compulsive in their practice of faith that is supposed to quickly bring the rewards of earthly gain. The compulsion for gain and the greed behind it allow the system to grow. Rationalization, justification, minimization, denial, and projection are all used to distort the real causes and motivations of misguided believers' behavior. This distortion is necessary to avoid the reality of conscience, inner fear, and an overwhelming sense of shame.

Regardless of the roles one plays, the misuse and abuse of religion constitute the primary addiction in this compulsive system. The system and the players within the system take precedence over a relationship with God. In the name of God, one person, a manipulative persecutor, can create a religion where he or she serves as the god. This self-made religion is used as an idol to avoid the reality of life, not as a means to a healthy relationship with God. The religion that drives a wedge between the believers and God becomes the most eternally deadly factor of all.

BORN AGAIN?

Would you describe yourself as a "born-again" or evangelical Christian, or not?

☐ Yes   33%

☐ No   63%

—*George Gallup, Jr., and Sarah Jones,* 100 Questions and Answers: Religion in America *(Princeton, N.J.: Princeton Religion Research Center, 1989), p. 140.*

The religion that drives a wedge between the believers and God becomes the most eternally deadly factor of all.

HARMFUL FAITH PECKING ORDER

- The harmful system has its own pecking order and uses certain dysfunctional roles for keeping that pecking order in place.
- The religious persecutor is bound by the fear of giving up the power-and-prestige position, lest he or she has to face failure and insignificance.
- The religious coconspirator is bound to the system to have a purpose in life and to avoid the fear of letting the persecutor down.
- The religious enabler is bound by the fear of ridicule and shame.
- The victim of religious abuse is bound to follow and blindly believe.
- The outcast is bound by the desire to let the truth be known and to be free from the hurtful system.
- The roles, except for that of the outcast, are driven by the fear of not belonging to the harmful faith family. The only thing more fearful than not belonging to the misguided family of faith is the fear of not belonging to anything at all.

CHAPTER 8

Ten Rules of a Harmful Faith System

Whether it is a family or ministry, any system must have certain rules to maintain it and keep its members in line. The rules form the distinct character or culture of the organization or family. Harmful faith is no different. Its rules are not written down, but they exist. Sometimes they exist only in the minds of the religious addicts who thrive on the system. Everyone within the system understands the rules and abides by them. As the system grows, new challenges arise, and the rules are periodically changed at the whim of the religiously addicted parents or leaders. Those who do best quickly figure out the rules that have been eliminated and the new ones put in their place. The following are some common rules of harmful faith systems.

Control

Rule #1: *The leader must be in control at all times.*

When a person becomes addicted to something, he or she is completely controlled by it. Deluded by the addiction, the addict is unaware of this loss of control and believes that he or she is in control. Control is a primary issue for most people who suffer from an addiction. Harmful faith, or religious addiction, is no exception.

When a harmful faith leader struggles with control on a personal

The more the person seeks to control the details, the less likely that person will be able to maintain a clear vision of the larger issues of balance and focus in the ministry.

level, he or she attempts to be in the center of control within the system in an effort to affect all the outcomes. The leader desires to have the final say in every decision, whether minimal or monumental. When a religious addict is a parent, the children grow up with little ability to think independently because adherence to the system is so strong. Anyone not adhering to the leader's tough standards is immediately dismissed so that total control, or at least the illusion of total control, can be maintained by the leader who is addicted to the organization and the control it provides.

Control is really an illusion. No parent has complete control in any family. No leader can predict all the circumstances and stress that the ministry will confront. The more the person seeks to control the details, the less likely that person will be able to maintain a clear vision of the larger issues of balance and focus in the ministry or family. The more control is sought, the less there is to be had in any circumstance.

Persons addicted to alcohol and drugs are keenly aware of how this paradox works. The Alcoholics Anonymous program has several sayings that illustrate the paradox of control: "Let Go and Let God," "Easy Does It," "One Day at a Time," and the Serenity Prayer. Each saying is a reminder that to stay in control, a person must give up control to God on a daily basis. Seeking to maintain control serves only to sink the person deeper into addiction.

If faith is harmful, it exists outside God. It creates a god much different from God the Creator. The control rule exemplifies how God has been re-created in the minds of the misguided leader and the religious addicts who follow that leader. There is little or no trust in the almighty God. Faith in self and the ability to keep things under control replaces a true trust that God is in control. Persecutors are very controlling people, and their coconspirators are just as controlling. In the entire system people fight for control while attributing complete control to the leader.

In the entire system people fight for control while attributing complete control to the leader.

"God, give us grace to accept with serenity the things that cannot be changed, courage to change the things which should be changed, and the wisdom to distinguish one from the other."

It is no wonder that so many leaders functioning under the false belief that they are in control, or making an attempt to gain control, break under the pressure. Some probably act unconsciously in a self-destructive manner to relieve themselves of the overwhelming position. They lose the power they fought for by attempting to maintain more power than they can handle.

The Serenity Prayer is a powerful tool for learning to relinquish control. This prayer of faith directly contradicts the persecutor's attitude toward problems and God's relationship to them. With a rule that the leader must be in control of all things at all times, the persecutor tries to change everything and control everything. The bigger the ego, the bigger the belief in the ability to change everything. Until the leader relinquishes control, the ministry continues to teach through example the philosophy, "I must take things into my own hands." That is exactly what religiously addicted followers do.

Blame

Rule #2: *When problems arise, find a guilty party to blame immediately.*

Almost every scandal that has been publicized has relied on this rule to explain or minimize the scandal. Two religious addicts were caught participating in sexual acts outside marriage. In the end they both confessed and accepted responsibility for their behavior. They did that only after they had tried every other option. One blamed Satan. His claim was that if his ministry was not so important, and Satan had not worked so hard to trap him, the affair would have never occurred. It was as if he had no choice but to succumb to the evil influence of the devil. The faithful followers were willing to blame Satan. They didn't force the minister to step down or obtain special help. He was determined more than ever to fight Satan, and they were willing to let him.

In another case the blame was placed squarely on the woman. She

OUT TO MAKE A BUCK

It is frightening how many well-meaning Christians exploit the gospel to make money. Consider the "Lord Moos Me Erasers" shaped like a cow's head, the cross donut (with filling), and the set of twelve thimbles with pictures of the twelve disciples (how did they get their pictures anyway?). Walk into just about any Christian bookstore and you will find a plethora of gimmicky items from jewelry to bumper stickers and bookmarks. Granted, some are in good taste, but then others border on the absurd. I wonder what Jesus would have thought about all these things. I fear He would have had visions of His temple-cleansing days.

was labeled a seductress who no man could resist. Her sensual powers, combined with the minister's burnout, led to the fall into sin. The confession was a bit clouded with blame of the woman and blame of the congregation who were so needy they took everything the pastor had. With no reserves left, he was unable to resist. The faithful followers rallied around him and prayed that he would find relief from the pressure. They also removed the temptress from the congregation to protect the minister. Blaming saved his position and the harmful ministry he developed.

From the example of addicted leaders, addicted followers learn to blame others, circumstances, and situations for the problems and conflicts that arise in their lives. There is no problem that cannot be discounted by the words, "Satan took hold of me and would not let go until I had sinned greatly." By denying and dodging personal responsibility, whenever possible, the religious addict can avoid the reality of needed inner changes. Also, the object of blame is shamed and made a reject of the harmful faith system.

Families are more powerful than ministries in affixing blame. When dad is a persecutor, all problems will be pushed off on the wife and kids. It's amazing that the wife or children can exist in a system where any mistake could be a reason to punish everyone. This was the case in one family. If a light was left on and no one claimed responsibility, all the children were beaten. The father believed those acts of

By denying and dodging personal responsibility, whenever possible, the religious addict can avoid the reality of needed inner changes.

irresponsibility were why he could not get ahead financially. He believed he would have financial success if his family would be more cooperative. The reality was that he was so irresponsible that he lost more money than his family would ever save him. Not seeing this, he placed the blame wherever he could, usually with his innocent children.

Perfectionism

Rule #3: *Don't make mistakes.*

A harmful faith system traps all its religious addicts into the tyranny of perfectionism. Because they are taught that they are in an elite system, the followers believe they can attain perfection, believe they need to attain it, and feel terrible shame when they do not attain it. They all strive for perfection and make themselves sick in the process. The priority is shifted away from believing in God to avoiding failure, ridicule, and criticism. The irrational belief is that if they can attain perfection, others will not be able to find fault with them or their actions. Then, once they have measured up, they will obtain acceptance, love, and the feeling of belonging.

The underlying communication of "don't make mistakes" warns against failing or not measuring up to perfection. It increases shame and fear and motivates the members of the hurtful system to deny and repress their humanness. A mistake is considered a reason to fear that faith is not strong enough. It becomes the motivation to work harder to compensate for a lack of faith that has produced the mistake. Perfectionists are driven by the desire to measure up to a standard that can never be obtained. Having failed to reach that standard, religious addicts look to the system and increased involvement in it as a means to measure up.

Embracing sin, not denying it, allows people to learn and grow from it. Acceptance of the inevitability of sin is the acceptance of full humanity. It also leads to the realization of the need for a divine Savior to make up for what we cannot do on our own. In accepting Christ, the Christian acknowledges that personal perfection can never be obtained. The person who does not acknowledge that lives in constant

---

It increases shame and fear and motivates the members of the hurtful system to deny and repress their humanness.

They lose if they stay in the system and don't measure up, and they lose if they are thrown out and rejected.

fear of not measuring up. The fear of making a mistake, the fear of sinning, keeps the victim of perfectionism from experiencing the grace of God and maintains the performance orientation in the harmful religious system.

The dysfunctional system has no room for error and no room for the people who make mistakes. People in need, people who mess up, people who reveal their humanness, glaringly point out the weaknesses of the harmful system if they are allowed to continue in the system. To maintain the delusion, religious addicts must remove those people from the system.

This expulsion process also motivates others to measure up to the perfect standards of the organization. They try harder, lest they be thrown out, too. But the system expects something that cannot be delivered. As long as the leader knows how to manipulate, the erring perfectionists will stay locked in their positions within the organization. They will be locked in until they commit one of the unpardonable sins and then they will be thrown out. They lose if they stay in the system and don't measure up, and they lose if they are thrown out and rejected.

The rule of perfectionism denies the follower the right to embrace the limitedness of the human condition. If the person has never dealt with feelings of inadequacy and inferiority, never accepted individual limits, each mistake will be devastating. The victim will be driven to perform, measure up, and do things "right" to avoid feelings of inadequacy and insecurity. The practice of faith becomes obsessed with the faithful's performance.

The perfectionist practice of faith becomes product oriented; the relationship with God is less important than the product of acceptable behavior. Anything short of perfection elicits the shame of not being quite good enough. Shame is the religious addict's reward for endeavoring to be Christlike and perfect. The misled believer, never having experienced the acceptance of having one's struggle valued, endeavors

The relationship with God is less important than the product of acceptable behavior.

Pure faith is not product oriented; it is process oriented.
It is the endeavor to become all we can be.

---

endlessly in the avoidance of the shame and pain of not measuring up and the hope that this time "I'll do it right."

Pure faith is not product oriented; it is process oriented. It is the endeavor to become all we can be. For Christians, the struggle to become Christlike is important. Although we can never be perfect, we endeavor because we feel acceptable to God, self, and others. Not measuring up does not bring shame; it brings about a change or repentance from sin. It validates the inability to be perfect and the need for a saving God.

Perfectionism is the denial of our humanity with shame as its reward. Pure faith is the acceptance of our humanity with peace and serenity as its rewards. In a healthy system where failure and mistakes are accepted as parts of the human condition, the endeavor to grow closer to God and stronger in faith is valued. Fulfillment and satisfaction replace shame and remorse. There is the expectation that mistakes will be made and they will be corrected with the help of God.

Works—how much one gives, knows, worships, prays, meditates, and so on—become the measuring stick of one's spirituality in a system of religious addiction. The relationship is based on the fear of disappointing God. In a healthy system, acceptance is based on love. Our Father, who is love, accepts us because of who He is and not because of what we do. The believers in a healthy system accept persons because of who they are and not because of what they do or don't do. This acceptance frees people from the bonds of perfectionism and shame.

Delusion

Rule #4: *Never point out the reality of a situation.*

Religious addicts aren't interested in reality. They don't want to know how things are. They are interested in how things should be and

---

Perfectionism is the denial of our humanity with shame as its reward. Pure faith is the acceptance of our humanity with peace and serenity as its rewards.

Religious addicts aren't interested in reality. They don't want to know how things are. They are interested in how things should be and how everyone can work together to create the illusion that everything is the way it should be.

how everyone can work together to create the illusion that everything is the way it should be. Anyone not creating that illusion will be discounted or removed from the organization or family. To talk of reality is to commit organizational suicide. If more faithful followers were willing to commit organizational suicide and become outcasts of the harmful system, all of the other religious addicts would be forced to face reality and change to meet the needs of the ministry and the people it is supposed to serve.

No one wins, and everyone is a potential victim when this kind of rule exists. No one is willing to speak up. Everyone becomes a submissive servant. A family is no longer a family, it is a military unit of commands, orders, and the following of dictates. If an issue is so important that someone must break the bad news to the group, tremendous effort is exerted and pain is experienced as everyone tries to figure out how to best present the facts. An entire organization can be destroyed when the energy goes into protecting the religious addicts instead of ministering to the people.

One organization had many locations where ministry was conducted. The leader counted on the offerings of the ones in each satellite organization to cover the costs of that ministry and provide additional funds to support the headquarters. The leader had told the board of directors that the plan would work and expansion would be no problem. The organization's accountant knew that each month the ministry got deeper and deeper in debt. Vendors were paid later and

---

GOLDEN CALF FOUND

"The first golden calf ever found was unearthed in Israel just a month ago." It is a rare and precious 4$^1/_2$ by 4$^1/_2$ inch figurine and brings with it remembrances of the Old Testament command to not worship anything other than the Lord God Almighty.

—*"Anthropology: Golden Calves of the Week,"* U.S. New & World Report, *August 6, 1990, p. 11.*

later to continue the illusion that enough cash was available. No one wanted to break the news to the leader because he became such a tyrant when things were not going well. A messenger with bad news was often identified as the source of the problem; it was no wonder it took so long to muster the courage to deliver the bad news.

When the accountant finally told him about the problems, the leader was furious. He couldn't believe that things were in such bad shape and he had been left out of the information loop. He fired the accountant for not keeping him informed. He refused to acknowledge that it was almost impossible to inform him without being punished for it. The accountant broke the rule of never being the person to deliver the bad news. He lost.

Perpetual Cheerfulness

Rule #5: *Never express your feelings unless they are positive.*

Religious addicts don't care about people. They don't care how people feel or what their needs are. They care about their own feelings and their own needs. Addicts who know the rules will never reveal a thought, feeling, or doubt that would make the harmful leader feel uncomfortable. The leader wants to be reinforced only with positive feelings and statements of affirmation. There is no room for those who are negative, depressed, or worried about a problem. In a hurtful faith system, followers must attend with pasted-on smiles as if all is well. People exhibiting problems are considered outcasts and are ostracized accordingly.

A harmful system denies people the chance to feel what they feel. "You can't be angry with God" is the communication in a dysfunctional system. If individuals feel sad, there is something wrong with them: they don't have enough faith; they aren't being prayerful enough; sin is in their lives. Whatever the communication, the message is that they can't feel what they feel without being shamed or being made to feel inadequate. Be it the church of the "frozen chosen" or the church of the "eternal smile," certain feelings aren't al-

Real feelings are abandoned for the "good" ones supporting the myth that the truly faithful are free of problems.

Harmful faith leaders don't want to face the reality of human needs, their own and others'. They want to live in a world where everything can be fixed with a great sermon or a quick prayer.

lowed if they want to be part of the community. Feelings must be hidden if adequate support of the hurtful system is to be rendered.

Many churches today are not places of openness. They are places where fakes attend who look good, talk well, and support the image of perfectionism. Every problem must be wiped away with a quick "Praise the Lord!" Real feelings are abandoned for the "good" ones supporting the myth that the truly faithful are free of problems. Revelation of problems would indicate lack of faith and weakness.

Religiously addicted parents have a low frustration tolerance. They don't want to be bothered by problems that interrupt their all-important busy schedules. They get involved only when it will make them look good or at least make them look as if they are interested in people. Parents often have a Messiah complex that leads them to believe they can and must fix everything. Someone who is in pain repeatedly is evidence that some problems are not solvable by the parent or that faith isn't working. That hurts too badly, so the person who has the unsolvable problem or unresolved needs must be removed.

Harmful faith parents and leaders of organizations don't want to face the reality of human needs, their own and others'. They want to live in a world where everything can be fixed with a great sermon or a quick prayer. The illusion that allows the organization to grow, the family to look good, and the leader to continue to be out of touch from people and their needs takes precedence over real needs and real feelings.

Blind Loyalty

Rule #6: *Don't ask questions, especially if they are tough ones.*

Religious addicts must be blindly loyal. Questions, especially the tough ones, reveal that a follower has some doubts and lacks faith. Any questioning is considered resistance to the organization, or the leader of the family. Questions are met with responses that indicate certain issues are not to be shared. For example, expenditures of the organization are said to be beyond the understanding of the followers.

Religious addicts learn to either follow blindly or get out quickly.

A father who spends unaccounted for hours away from home is not to be bothered with "why" from anyone in the family. Actions can be understood only if people know the big picture, which is portrayed as too complex for the "common" members of the group or children in the family. Religious addicts learn to either follow blindly or be punished.

Questions are difficult for persecutors to handle. Each one is viewed as a personal affront and a threat to the ministry or family. A person who is intent on getting accurate answers to questions will not be a part of a harmful system. If a person struggles to find the truth, it will be nearly impossible to locate. If a person wants to move up in the dysfunctional system, that person must not ask questions when things do not add up or make sense.

There was a time when everything in the solar system was said to revolve around the earth. Those who questioned this belief were outcasts, and some were even punished. It was too much of a threat to believe that the universe functioned with something other than the earth in the center. In a system of religious addiction, the misguided leader believes that the ministry or the family should revolve around him or her. Anyone questioning that approach or suggesting that the ministry revolve around people's needs has no place in the system.

Conformity

Rule #7: *Don't do anything outside your role.*

Harmful faith systems don't permit personal growth. Those who remain in the system must learn their roles and not deviate from them. Otherwise they will be perceived as rebellious and unstable. A harmful faith leader doesn't want individualism; he or she wants predictability and conformity. If a person can't adhere to the rules of the

---

Harmful faith systems don't permit personal growth. Those who remain in the system must learn their roles and not deviate from them.

assigned role, that person must be ejected from the system. Either learn to play it safe within a role, or don't play at all. Either play the role assigned, or leave and don't look back.

The harmful system is intent on maintaining the homeostasis of the system, that is, keeping the boat from rocking. "Don't do it differently"; "We know what is best for you"; "Just play it safe and do what we tell you"—all are guidelines for acceptance. To risk, to dare, to imagine being something other than what the system wants one to be, to behave in a manner that is not the "norm" for the system—these actions elicit the judgment of the system.

Adherence to a role is often accomplished through shaming the victim. Those at the top encourage followers to shame the rebel to intimidate him or her back into submission. To someone who dares to be different, the hurtful system responds, "You're selfish"; "You're stupid"; "You're crazy"; "You're in rebellion"; "You're a sower of discord"; "You're not committed"; "You're not in God's will"; "You're not fulfilling God's call for your life"; "You need to learn to be obedient"; and "You need to learn submission to authority." The shaming can be so effective that no one would dare continue in the system after being humiliated publicly and privately.

A tough role is that of coconspirator. Coconspirators are in place to meet the needs of harmful faith persecutors. When their contacts or resources are depleted, the persecutor will replace them with other religious addicts with more money or influence or people more willing to believe in the persecutor or manipulate for the persecutor. They are also removed if they appear to be a threat to the persecutor in any way.

WHO IS GOD?

When asked: Do you believe in God or a universal spirit?

- 94% said yes

Here's what people think about God:

- 84% think He is a heavenly Father reached by prayer
- 5% think He is an idea not a being
- 2% think He is an impersonal Creator
- 4% don't know
- 5% don't believe in God or a universal spirit

—George Gallup, Jr., and Sarah Jones, 100 Questions and Answers: Religion in America (Princeton, N.J.: Princeton Religion Research Center, 1989), p. 4.

The only people who can exist over time in the harmful system are those who stay within the bounds of their roles and continue to find new ways to serve the leader within those roles.

This is especially true of others who serve alongside the persecutor. They can begin to threaten the leader's authority. If they are perceived as more talented or more respected, they will be discredited and replaced.

The only people who can exist over time in the harmful system are those who stay within the bounds of their roles and continue to find new ways to serve the leader within those roles. The more a person can accomplish for the hurtful faith leader, the longer the person will stay and the more respected the person will become within the operation.

Dysfunctional families have little difficulty keeping their members locked in their roles. Most do not want out of their roles because they are so dependent on them for survival. They feel insecure outside the roles they have created for themselves. A hero will only look good and will so chastise him or herself for looking bad that no one else need do it. A scapegoat will look bad and enter in repeated negative behaviors to continue to look bad. Self-defeating behavior is all the person knows so it is instantly repeated. A lost child will quietly exist alongside the other family members without rocking the boat. The harmful faith family leader has little problem with compliance because the members have staked out their roles and refuse to give them up.

Mistrust

Rule #8: *Don't trust anyone.*

This rule encourages isolation and alienation from human emotions and intimacy in interpersonal relationships. It seeks to block risking, vulnerability, and self-disclosure by discouraging trust between family members or a harmful system and anyone outside the system. Trust is discouraged among the members so that the system maintains allegiance and power to the leader. The one to be trusted must be the leader of the family or organization. Each member is disconnected from other members, and everyone depends on the leader. Family members will be less likely to bind together to thwart the system. And

Where one must sacrifice the reality of what one thinks, feels, hears, and sees, trust is impossible. In the absence of trust are manipulation and fear.

members will be less likely to get together and discover the truth by putting the whole picture together.

Trust cannot exist where reality is created as you go. Just when a person starts to become comfortable with the way things are, the leader changes the rules or perceptions to meet his or her needs. The follower's or family member's immediate response is the awareness that no one but the leader or parent should be trusted to interpret or direct what is going on. Everyone else is unaware of the changes until the leader explains them. Only the head of the system can be trusted to prepare the family for the future.

Religious addicts exist inside a system based on false reality. The rules are made up, and the people living within those rules are unreal. No one can trust in a system where no one is being real. When people do not say what they think or express what they feel, no one can be trusted. Where one must sacrifice the reality of what one thinks, feels, hears, and sees, trust is impossible. In the absence of trust are manipulation and fear. Victims allow themselves to be manipulated as long as they are in the system. Unable to rely on anyone but the leader, they permit that leader to reign over them.

Avarice

Rule #9: *Nothing is more important than giving money to the organization.*

Giving is an important part of anyone's faith. You don't really experience the depths of faith until you are able to give a portion of your money to God rather than spend it all on yourself. Christ often talked about money because it is such a clear indicator of what is within a person's heart. A person's canceled checks and credit card expenditures point to what that person is like. When a portion is freely given to God, it indicates that the believer's heart and mind are committed. Someone who does not yet understand the role of giving in the practice of faith has missed many blessings that come from trusting God with financial resources.

You don't really experience the depths of faith until you are able to give a portion of your money to God rather than spend it all on yourself.

Harmful faith organizations do not keep giving in perspective; they do not view it as an act of worship. It is a means of funding for them. Religious addicts believe that nothing is more essential than the organization's continuation, which is funded by the gifts of the followers. The more hurtful the organization, the more manipulative it will become in obtaining money from the followers. Desperate cries for money are sure signs that the organization depends on the manipulations of people, not on faith in God.

At one point, I was somehow placed on the mailing list of a very unwholesome religious organization. Its leader was a master at raising money. His concern was for his organization. He could have cared less how much someone had to sacrifice to keep his group going.

I pay my taxes and have never been sued personally, but when a yellow slip is left in the mailbox telling me to pick up a registered letter the next day, I worry. I wonder if it will inform me about a tax audit or something equally official. This misguided organization sent me a registered letter.

The next day when I opened it, I was furious to discover that it was a fund-raising letter. It started with, "No one likes to receive a registered letter." I can't imagine how much money was spent on that clever manipulation to raise funds. I can't imagine how many people fell in the trap of thinking that since the organization had to resort to registered mail, it must be in the biggest need ever, so they wrote out a check immediately.

When ministries meet our needs, we must support them. But we must do that out of love and worship of God, not the manipulation of

---

CHARISMATIC LEADERS

An article discussing charismatic leaders, the type who lead with a great deal of charisma, states that they are people who offer "certainty and conviction to those who lack the inner strength to develop their own. The charismatic leader's strength, then, develops upon our weakness."

—Michael Scott Cain, "The Charismatic Leader," The Humanist, November/December 1988, p. 36.

MEANING AND PURPOSE IN LIFE

Which of these most helps you find meaning and purpose in life?

AGE	13–15	16–18	20–29	30–39	40–49	50–59	60–69	70 or older
Religious TV/ radio programs	1%	0%	1%	1%	2%	1%	1%	1%
My own private religious experiences	22	33	50	40	28	26	22	22
My church	60	48	44	53	57	66	72	75
Religious groups outside my church	17	18	5	7	13	7	5	1

—Peter L. Benson and Carolyn H. Eklin, Effective Christian Education: A National Study of Protestant Congregations (Minneapolis: a research project of Search Institute, March 1990), p. 29.

people. The gift of money must not stand in the way of widows having enough food to eat, children having clothes to wear, or money being available to pay for heat in the winter. Yet, thousands of horror stories tell of people who have given so much money under pressure that their health and well-being have been jeopardized. Harmful ministers don't care about those people. They care about their empires and their egos. People are seen as sources of funds to keep the organization going rather than individuals worthy of service from the organization.

Many ministries do a commendable job of communicating their needs and requesting support appropriately. The church I attend does not take up an offering. Those who give either send it in by mail or put it in a box at the back of the church. The church has never had a problem with money. God has blessed it without people being manipulated to give. There is another reason it has not had a money problem. One board member is a financial manager who holds the pastor, the staff, and the other leaders of the church accountable to a budget. His efforts have freed the church from manipulating others. It has not

The more hurtful the organization, the more manipulative it will become in obtaining money from the followers.

If the organization you support begs for your money and seems to place greater importance on your money than on you, stop supporting that organization.

---

been easy for the pastors to stay within the budget, but because they have stuck with it, the church experiences the blessings of financial freedom. That is an example of doing it right.

A ministry of great service to many people is Focus on the Family, led by Dr. James Dobson. This organization raises money without manipulation. Very little of its radio air time is devoted to asking for financial support. Each month a four-page letter comes from Dr. Dobson, communicating the realistic goals of the organization, personal insights into problems, and a gentle request. The ministry has not gotten overextended and has not needed to resort to desperate means of fund raising. If it does get in a pinch, additional help is requested and the ministry's budget is cut rather than desperately manipulate supporters. But people are encouraged to give to their church first and to Focus on the Family second. It is all done with balance and a godly perspective. No promises of instant relief or wealth are ever offered.

A harmful system is off balance, desperate for your money. Those in the organization will do anything to get your money. They waste money, overextend the resources of the ministry, and then expect you to make up the difference. Nothing is more significant than raising money and manipulating you into giving more than you rationally should. If the organization you support begs for your money and

BOY SCOUTS ATTACKED FOR TEST AFFIRMING BELIEF IN GOD

"The head of the Unitarian Church has attacked the Boy Scouts of America for denying promotion to a scout who refused to affirm belief in God as a 'Supreme Being.' Paul Trout, 15, of Shepherdstown, WV, was refused promotion to the rank of Life Scout. William F. Schultz, president of the Unitarian Universalist Association, accused the Boy Scout organization of seeking to establish a 'religious test for membership.'"

—Evangelical Newsletter, *vol. 12, no. 18, September 27, 1985, p. 1.*

Protecting the image of the leader protects the image of the organization, and it becomes a major priority.

seems to place greater importance on your money than on you, stop supporting that organization.

Spotless Image

Rule #10: *At all costs, keep up the image of the organization or the family.*

The harmful organization or the harmful faith family exists in a world of denial. It denies everyone's humanity, including that of its leader. One foundation for the growth of a hurtful organization is the image of a godlike leader. The leader must be presented as having a level of perfection that others cannot obtain. A father of a sick family will not admit to problems or ask for forgiveness. Protecting the image of the leader protects the image of the organization and the family, and it becomes a major priority. No one must know of marital problems, unless somehow the secret leaks. Then everyone must work to ensure that the leader is perceived as the ultimate mate, able to resolve the crisis of marriage with godly wisdom that no one else could have had. The coconspirators and enablers around the leader work together to create awe in the minds of the followers. Every problem must have a solution that makes the leader appear sacrificial, loving, and serving beyond what most people are capable.

The flaws of a harmful organization must be covered at all costs. Anyone who rebels against the system must be personally attacked so people will think the problem is the person, not the system. People are not allowed to discuss negative aspects of the organization among themselves, so they certainly must not be allowed to discuss the flaws outside the organization. If a financial crisis arises, the coconspirators must work closely and quickly to figure out a way to communicate the problem without destroying the image of the organization or the leader. Using deception and lies may be the only way to uphold the image.

Deception and lies are utilized and accepted if that is the only way the image can be upheld.

Eventually, enough cracks can destroy the facade completely, and people recognize the organization for what it is.

When an organization exists in a false reality, image is integral to its success. Without an image of perfection, reality sets in, and people stop supporting the harmful faith system. Everyone must work hard to ensure that the image and the false reality are upheld. Perception becomes reality and image the key to continued support from followers. The leader's job is to fool as many people as possible into believing that the image is reality.

However, this rule is never observed 100 percent. There are always some in the organization or a family who come to see it for what it is and challenge the false perceptions. They become outcasts, but as they go out, they place a crack in the delusive image of the leader, the family or the organization. Eventually, enough cracks can destroy the facade completely, and people recognize the organization for what it is.

In a healthy system, the system provides for the needs of those who are a part of it. They feel confident that the system is there for them. In a harmful system, members are there to keep it going. If they are willing to stick to the rules, the system can expand. If they sense a problem with the system and begin to break rules, the hurtful system will fall apart. The misled faith leader ensures that all of the other

PSYCHICS

"According to writer and sociologist Andrew Greeley and colleagues at the University of Chicago, a growing number of Americans are reporting paranormal or mystical experiences. National surveys by the Gallup Organization support Greeley's findings. More 'ordinary' Americans are having psychic experiences or are less reluctant to talk about experiences they've been having all along. . . . Some feel the failure of organized religion to meet the spiritual needs of many is partially responsible." Others feel it "is the inability of traditional psychotherapists to significantly help their patients that has prompted more and more Americans to seek psychic counsel."

—*Jane Mersky Leder, "Psychics at Work," McCall's, October 1987, p. 159.*

God is replaced with self-obsession and the huge egos of those who believe they are doing the will of God.

addicts—coconspirators, enablers, and victims—know the rules and abide by them. Anyone who hints at not following the rules is dealt with quickly so the organization or family will not be damaged.

All rules have something to do with maintaining religious addiction within the system. They are designed to fuel the addict's ego, protect the addict's position, and perpetuate status quo. This is the central poison in the family or organization and in the faith of the addicted followers. God is replaced with self-obsession and the huge egos of those who believe they are doing the will of God. Addicts believe their motives are pure because they are not willing to admit they have a part in a system that holds them up with their harmful beliefs rather than points them toward God.

The healthy system is a safe place for persons to explore what they think, feel, hear, want, and act or imagine without fear of retribution and rejection. Those in the system are not judged and measured but guided and supported. The individual who felt in bondage over a problem of the past, a hurt or a disappointment, comes to the healthy organization and feels a new freedom. The struggler opens up to other strugglers and, from the support offered there, is helped with the problem. People are also led to a stronger faith by the love that is freely shared.

Likewise, the hurtful system starts out good. Everything looks wonderful. As involvement increases, the rules emerge, and the struggler starts to comply, becoming a victim of the system. The initial freedom that came with getting into the system is removed by the restrictive rules that must be followed.

A harmful system convinces each member that the way to a

GIVING TIME AND MONEY

"In 1989, Americans donated more than $50 billion to churches, with the vast majority of that money going to Protestant churches. In addition, more than $10 billion worth of time was donated by church volunteers for the work of local churches."

—*George Barna*, The Frog in the Kettle *(Ventura: Regal Books, 1990), p. 135.*

stronger faith in God is through the organization or the head of the family. The rules are there so that a person can make it through with little difficulty, as long as there is strict compliance with the rules. In a healthy system, each person goes by the rules of God, not the dictates of people; each person is freed to develop a relationship with the Creator, not with an organization; each person is responsible for individual growth in faith; and each person has the capacity to reach for God and find Him reaching back. The only rule is perseverance in seeking Him.

TEN RULES OF A
HARMFUL FAITH SYSTEM

1. The leader must be in control of every aspect at all times.
2. When problems arise, find a guilty party to blame immediately.
3. Don't make mistakes.
4. Never point out the reality of a situation.
5. Never express your feelings unless they are positive.
6. Don't ask questions, especially if they are tough ones.
7. Don't do anything outside of your role.
8. Don't trust anyone.
9. Nothing is more important than giving money to the organization.
10. At all costs, keep up the image of the organization or the family.

CHAPTER 9

Treatment and Recovery

Since the beginning of New Life Treatment Centers, we have treated many people afflicted with a religious addiction and a harmful faith. However, they have never come to us saying they are religious addicts. They are depressed, alcoholic, overweight, anorexic, suicidal, and in numerous other forms of despair. They don't know what they have; they just know they're miserable. It has been a most fulfilling experience to watch these people discover that at the roots of their other problems lie hurtful beliefs and a harmful faith. "The lights come on" as they discover they have been chasing an illusion, a dream, rather than seeking God. While they are with us, they grow by leaps and bounds. Their focus is renewed, and they understand who God really is for the first time. When they change their core harmful beliefs, many of their other problems subside immediately. As they turn their lives and will over to God, they find the serenity that has eluded them.

All persons get involved in a recovery program. They work out the harmful beliefs in God and their distorted views about themselves. In addition to recovery groups similar to Alcoholics Anonymous, they enter into group therapy with other patients, which is led by therapists. As they share their problems and hear others share, they identify their character defects and gain insight into how to correct them.

"The lights come on" as they discover they have been chasing an illusion, a dream, rather than seeking God.

KARL MARX

"Religion . . . is the opium of the people." Maybe Karl knew something when he communicated his famous statement. Religion with all its rituals and trappings can indeed be hypnotic. When all you do is jump through hoops to try to get to God, it is easy to either give up or get weird trying to earn God's favor.

If religion is a drug of the people, a relationship with an all-loving God can keep each person truly full of life. Only when a relationship with God transcends all religious trappings does true fulfillment come. Religion and striving will not fulfill the empty places in our hearts. They will only dull the emptiness like a drug. It is only in a pure relationship with God that forgiveness is experienced, and it is then no longer necessary to continue to run from pain. God loves us wholly and forgives us completely. No drug can offer that.

Each therapist that works with a patient has certain objectives in mind for that person. As each objective is accomplished, the patient moves closer to being able to function normally, free of conflict and depression. Specific areas must be addressed for these objectives to be achieved. The following material covers some areas vital to regaining a pure faith.

Breaking Through Denial: Beginning Recovery

The number one objective in the recovery of the religious addict is to break through the denial that addiction exists. We must help the addict identify that the relationship with religion has become of primary importance. The addict must accept that the religion is harmful and has hurt relationships with family and friends.

This process of breaking through denial begins with the first confrontation or intervention. When those close to the addict finally express how they feel and how they see the harmful faith, denial begins to fade in the addict with a good chance for recovery, and acceptance

The number one objective in the recovery of the religious addict is to break through the denial that addiction exists.

Although they know they need help, most addicts are re-luctant to let go of the addiction that has become a very reliable friend.

---

begins to grow to take its place. If the addict will not admit that a problem exists—and many fight to the end to deny that there is one—there is little hope for recovery. Once the addict can identify how the religious addiction is abusive and destructive to relationships with God, self, and others, the number one objective is achieved.

Then treatment can begin. Although they know they need help, most addicts are reluctant to let go of the addiction that has become a very reliable friend. When others rejected the addict, the addict could turn to the practice of harmful faith and those within the hurtful faith system who were always accepting. When the world became too painful, the religious addict could count on the addiction and other addicts to create a delusional reality that felt a lot better for the moment. It always made life tolerable, and though it never completely satiated the addict's neediness, it was always there to provide comfort, a sense of belonging, power, and a feeling of being right or righteous. It is impossible to give up all of those benefits in an instant. The process takes time, effort, and a willingness to be vulnerable.

Bill came to us severely depressed. His marriage was in the midst of divorce; his plans to be a minister were shattered. Feeling that his friends, family, and God had abandoned him, he was on the brink of suicide.

During the course of treatment, it was disclosed that Bill spent most of his time involved in the church. He was heavily involved in missionary work, Bible studies, and all church functions. Bill was a religious addict. He was driven by his need to please God. He had, for the most part, abandoned his wife long before she filed for divorce.

OCCULT GROWTH

"The factors that seem to lead to the occult growth are on the increase; a breakdown in the traditional family, resistance toward traditional religious beliefs and an increasing number of youths who feel both alienated and powerless over their lives."

— *"Psychiatric Hospital Weans Youths Away From Satanism,"*
Lake Charles American Press, *March 24, 1990.*

CURIOUS ABOUT THE OCCULT

Connie Elliot, a twenty-three-year-old, attractive woman, has learned a lot about spiritual things for her young years. Growing up, she was always curious about the occult. Experiencing quite a bit of pain in her family life, Connie battled depression and was on a quest to find a way to overcome her problems: "She said her deepening involvement with the occult coincided with a serious bout of depression." Although she got more and more involved in the occult, "she said the occult failed to give her the satisfaction in life she craved." Through the confrontation and perseverance of her aunt, Connie finally came to see how deceived she had been: "Elliot said her aunt was able to demonstrate to her the Bible had all the answers she had been searching for. 'Four days later, an overwhelming peace came over me like peace I had never had in my life,' she said. 'The void was gone when I became a Christian.'"

—Paul R. Huard, "Former Witch Finds Bible Provides
Answers for Life," Yucaipa & Calimesa News-Mirror, March
7, 1990.

Religion for Bill was a way to escape his fears of intimacy and vulnerability. If his family or friends needed support or emotional intimacy, he simply didn't have the time to give them. He felt that it was his wife's job to raise the family while he served the Lord. He used religion to remain distant from those who loved him most.

Bill's harmful faith deluded him into believing that he was being persecuted because of his faith. The more his family complained about his absence, the more he quoted the Scriptures on submission and the great commission. He believed that God would make his wife and family understand. After all, his absence was biblically justified, at least in his mind. Whenever Bill was confronted he would simply defend himself with Scripture and retreat into prayer. His prayers became the way he could avoid the conflict in the family and delude himself into believing that God would make everything okay and make things work out.

Bill had quit his job in a "step of faith" believing that God would provide. He had invested the family's savings "in the kingdom of God" and the missionary work he was so consumed with. The more the bills piled up, the more time he spent in prayer and worship.

Finally the bill collectors foreclosed, his wife left him, and he was emotionally incapacitated. He no longer found the relief in prayers; he felt unworthy to have God answer his prayers.

Bill had hit rock bottom. He no longer had the answers, and he sought help. In treatment, we put Bill into a support group. Though he still maintained that God was all he needed, the group was able to lovingly confront his delusion that if he continued to hang onto the same hurtful perceptions of God things would be different. Group members told how harmful faith had nearly destroyed them and how they had finally challenged their destructive beliefs. They all knew what Bill was going through; they accepted him where he was and valued him. Any time Bill reverted to the old pattern of biblically justifying his position, they understood. They knew eventually he would see how his justification of his position was self-defeating. It was an exercise in "godliness" rather than in self-defense.

Bill began to feel understood; at the same time he was able to see the need for change. He began to identify the harmful thinking that surrounded his addiction. He was able to see how he used his addiction to avoid feeling and being intimate with his family, friends, and even God. He saw how his religious dogma separated him from the people he loved the most.

The people around him saw the change in Bill. He no longer tried to use Scripture to defend himself and shame others for "not understanding." Bill was able to move in humility. And as Bill continued his treatment, the family also entered into therapy. The wounds of addiction began to heal, and Bill's anxiety lifted. He was able to develop friendships with those who did not share his religious beliefs. He was able to share without cramming things down their throats. In doing so, he began to identify the characteristics of pure faith and incorporated them into his belief system. He made great progress because he was able to start at the beginning by finally surrendering to God.

Surrendering to God: Spiritual Recovery

Often the initial motivation to change is not to find something better but to eliminate something that feels worse. The religious addict may be motivated by a desire not to find God or grow toward God but to eliminate the guilt that goes unresolved in religious addiction. The addict may have recognized how he or she was using religion or what it was doing to others. These thoughts may leave the addict feeling so depressed, worthless, powerless, and guilty that any alternative is considered better than continuing without change. The feelings of guilt and failure may be the pain needed to get that person to surrender to God.

The religious addict may be motivated by a desire not to find God or grow toward God but to eliminate the guilt that goes unresolved in religious addiction.

Surrendering to God is a process. The length and the difficulty of that process depend on how long the addict was involved with the addiction and how far it progressed. The more hidden the addiction has become, the more difficult the surrender process will be. Before something can be surrendered to God, it must be uncovered, revealed in all its terror, and acknowledged as real. Those private repressed sins are very difficult for the egocentric to admit. It is even more difficult to admit to not knowing what to do about them or how to fix them. This is the point of surrender where an addict is finally able to say that life has become unmanageable. Without a relationship with God, there is no power available to change. Surrendering is the process of letting go and trusting that God can and will handle the problems that have been acknowledged.

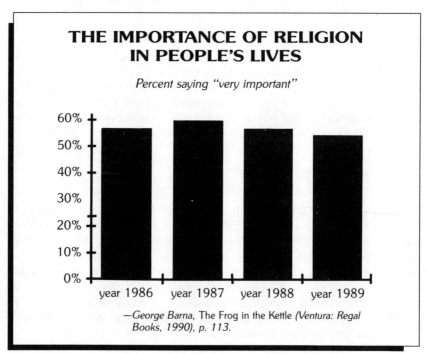

THE IMPORTANCE OF RELIGION IN PEOPLE'S LIVES

Percent saying "very important"

—George Barna, The Frog in the Kettle *(Ventura: Regal Books, 1990), p. 113.*

This is the point of surrender where an addict is finally able to say that life has become unmanageable. Without a relationship with God, there is no power available to change.

This was an extremely difficult step for me at a traumatic period of my life. I had paid for an abortion for a woman who was pregnant by me. The guilt was incapacitating because I felt solely responsible. Guilt crushed me until I was able to accept God's forgiveness for the problem. Even with that acceptance I did not fully surrender the problem to God. I implemented a system of hard work that led me to hours of Bible study, prayer sessions, and church attendance. If anyone asked a question I had a spiritual answer. I felt great about me because I worked hard to feel that way. Others did not feel so great about me. I was worthless to them. I was so pseudospiritual that I did not communicate with them. Someone had to spell out what I was doing before the situation sank in. Only then was I able to surrender to God completely.

Working on Hurtful Thinking: Mental Recovery

Hurtful thinking is one key way the addict maintains a delusional reality. Quite frankly, the religious addict's thinking is disordered. Treatment involves confronting harmful thoughts and replacing them with thoughts based in reality. The following are some common thoughts and thinking patterns that we confront in treatment.

Thinking in Extremes

Misled thinkers believe that people and issues can be viewed totally in terms of white or black, all good or all bad, completely right or completely wrong. This thinking drives the religious addict and fuels the crusades against the corrupt. Everything is extreme to the addict. One mistake and the religious addict feels like a failure, so all errors are denied. This leads to the denial of even small problems in an effort to defend against feelings of total failure. People will comment, "I cannot understand why that man cannot admit even one mistake." If one mistake is admitted, that person will feel like a complete failure as a human being. The act is so internalized that making the mistake

Misled thinkers believe that people and issues can be viewed totally in terms of white or black, all good or all bad, completely right or completely wrong.

---

moves the addict to believe he or she is capable only of making mistakes. Since no one can exist this way, denial becomes the defense. The addict denies the one extreme of bad and creates the illusion of living at the opposite extreme of perfection.

Treatment involves confronting thinking in opposite extremes. Religious addicts, though members of churches for years, must be reprogrammed. They must be told over and over that making a mistake does not make them mistakes, or produce failure. Additionally, a person who makes one mistake or disappoints them in one way is not all bad. There are still some very wonderful things about that person.

Sin is an act; it is not a description of every facet of your character. You do not have to be perfect to be good. You do not have to be perfect to be accepted. God does not accept you based on your perfect performance, and it is futile to attempt to gain further acceptance from Him. God is interested in a relationship, not hard work and trying harder. God cares about you. You, with all of your imperfections, are the focus of God's love. These thoughts must replace the extremes of hurtful thinking.

The religious addict needs to change from being product oriented to being process oriented. The addict needs to recognize that life is a learning process and the product of who you are is ever-changing. Sin must be perceived as a part of humanity that can be overcome through

---

MIRACLES

Here's what people said in response to this statement:
   Even today miracles are performed by the power of God.

- 51% completely agree
- 29% mostly agree
- 9% mostly disagree
- 6% completely disagree
- 5% don't know

—George Gallup, Jr., and Sarah Jones, 100 Questions and Answers: Religion in America *(Princeton, N.J.: Princeton Religion Research Center, 1989), p. 10.*

The addict needs to recognize that life is a learning pro-cess and the product of who you are is ever-changing.

the power of God. People can recover from failure. People can change. Accepting these truths reduces the fear of making mistakes or falling short. After the mistake, there is a process that can restore the person to a relationship with God and others.

Religious addicts are very hard on themselves and everyone else. They are driven by their all-or-nothing thinking. They must have mercy on themselves and on others. They must relax their perfection-ism and allow it to be replaced with an acceptance of their humanity. Christ spoke of this ability to not see things in terms of extremes. When He was confronted about breaking a law on the Sabbath he told His critics that He desired mercy rather than sacrifice.

Pure faith is a faith of mercy. We have the benefit of a merciful God. The addict must be helped to incorporate that mercy into views of other people and self. This can bring great relief to the addict and begin the process of reestablishing relationships that had been rejected due to thinking in extreme opposites.

Religious addicts are very hard on themselves and everyone else. They are driven by their all-or-nothing thinking.

Drawing Invalid Conclusions

Religious addicts have the ability to turn anything into a negative. From their feelings of inadequacy, they can contort any set of circum-stances into a doomsday scenario. If they sin, they think they have

---

SEARCH FOR MEANING

"For growing numbers of people an individual search for meaning has become the central religious experience, replacing unquestioning obedi-ence to religious authority."

—Kenneth A. Briggs, "Religious Feeling Seen Strong in U.S.," New York Times, December 9, 1984.

RELIGIOUS QUESTIONS

Which of these gives you the most help with religious questions?

AGE	13–15	16–18	20–29	30–39	40–49	50–59	60–69	70 or older
Religious TV/ radio programs	2%	0%	1%	2%	1%	1%	4%	1%
My own private religious experiences	22	33	45	28	32	24	30	37
My church	59	44	43	61	57	70	59	59
Religious groups outside my church	17	23	11	9	11	5	7	3

—*Peter L. Benson and Carolyn H. Eklin*, Effective Christian Education: A National Study of Protestant Congregations *(Minneapolis: a research project of Search Institute, March 1990), p. 32.*

knocked themselves out of any chance of going to heaven. If the boss has a negative opinion of some work, it must mean that being fired is imminent. If something happens one time, it must mean it will happen every time. If a father deserts me when I am young, every male will desert me. If I fail at one job then I will fail at every job. They make all-inclusive statements: "God never answers my prayers," and "God never listens to me." *Never* and *always* are integral to their statements about themselves and their expectations of others. Things are *never* right; they are *always* bad and becoming worse. The conclusions of religious addicts are not based in reality.

Not all of the conclusions are negative. A religious addict can use the same technique to avoid reality. Instead of saying, "God never takes care of me," an addict might say, "God takes care of every area of my life." Although the statement is true to the degree that God cares about every area of our lives, He will not magically make a car payment or always heal a baby who could be easily healed by a doctor.

When people focus on the irrelevant and the negative, they focus on only one part of reality and thus distort the whole of reality.

Drawing the wrong conclusion—if I do nothing, things will work out anyway—can be just as destructive as drawing a negative conclusion.

Treatment becomes a process of confronting these thoughts of unreality. Group time is spent in identifying unreasonable and irrational conclusions. The sources of those conclusions are rooted out. The addict comes to see life as it really is. Every event is not considered an indictment on the future. Each day is handled one day at a time, without projecting hardship on tomorrow.

Faulty Filtering

When people focus on the irrelevant and the negative, they focus on only one part of reality and thus distort the whole of reality. They become so selective in what they will respond to that much of what is good is discarded. One negative detail disqualifies the rest, even when that negative detail is less relevant than the more positive whole.

Here is an example of how a person can select a small part from the whole. You can take a blank piece of white paper and draw a dot in the middle of it. Nine out of ten people would tell you that they see the black dot you drew on the paper. They have effectively selected the dot and abstracted it from the context in which it was seen. In actuality however, they saw the dot on the paper and most probably the person holding it and all the peripheral visual content surrounding the person holding the paper.

That is the way many religious addicts live. But their filtering does not involve a harmless piece of paper and a dot. Their faulty filtering evolves around their faults and character defects. They see only personal sin or the sin in the world and refuse to look at all of the good and positive things. Addicts focus on the negative of the world, and the world becomes too depressing and uncomfortable to live in. Ad-

---

KNOWLEDGE OF THE BIBLE

- 31% knew that the expression "God helps those who help themselves" is *not* in the Bible.
- 52% correctly stated that the book of Thomas is *not* part of the Bible.
- Only 45% knew that the book of Jonah is in the Bible.
- 58% did not know who preached the Sermon on the Mount.

—*George Barna*, The Frog in the Kettle *(Ventura: Regal Books, 1990), p. 118.*

dicts must then escape into the addiction of religion for mood alteration.

Religious addicts who do not properly filter information are easy to spot. They are hypercritical and negative about everything, including themselves. When they come into treatment nothing is right. The bed tilts, the walls are the wrong color and the food is terrible. Although the food *is* usually terrible, they are focusing on all the wrong things.

Staff members must bring them back to reality. They are told that the one overriding problem that has been filtered out is that they called us for help; we didn't call them. There was a reason for the phone call. They are confronted with the need to work on themselves. Eventually, they begin to filter back in some of the important issues that relate to them and treatment. They are asked to look at the lives that have been affected by the treatment and talk to grateful patients who survived the food so they could break through their denial. When the filter starts to let reality sink back in, religious addicts become ready to concentrate on personal issues of change.

Invalidating the Positive

Invalidation does not ignore information; it just disqualifies the facts or distorts them. This is usually done toward the negative. The conversation of a religious addict is full of "yes, but's" that must be confronted throughout the treatment process. Someone will say to a religious addict that he looks wonderful today. The dedicated addict will retort, "Yes, but I feel terrible. And I know if I feel this bad, I am going to look much worse tomorrow."

Every positive can be contorted into something negative and wrong. If they cannot think of a proof that the compliment is false, they will rationalize the motives behind the statement: "They're just being nice to me," or "That person is out to get me or wants something I have."

The most dedicated religious addicts have a technique that is refined to look good while it degrades themselves. If a woman makes a wonderful flower arrangement and someone comments on it, she retorts, "It wasn't me, Christ did it." Let's face it. Christ didn't buy those flowers, put them in a vase, and arrange them in such a way to

Invalidation does not ignore information; it just disqualifies the facts or distorts them.

As the addicts invalidate the information, they invalidate themselves.

have beauty and symmetry. The addict has such a hard time acknowledging what might be a special talent that she feels the need to invalidate any statement that compliments the talent.

When people show appreciation, religious addicts will say, "Don't thank me; thank God," or "It was God's will." This is not humility; this is something very terrible for religious addicts. As the addicts invalidate the information, they invalidate themselves. They support their self-defeating conclusions about themselves by discarding anything counter to that negative image.

Treatment confronts the self-defeating statements and actions. First, the person must see the pattern. Then the person discovers why there is a need to do this. The next step is to replace the disqualifying statements with accepting statements. In this way an addict may learn to accept a compliment for the first time. Cracks in the negative facade let through some good feelings about self based on the reality of God's love and sacrifice. The recovering addict recognizes the good that has been created within and appreciates it. The person accepts being created in the image of God and feels God's love for the first time. As these positive thoughts take root, the person's misery is reduced along with the need to resort to the addiction for relief.

Discarding the Negative

The flip side of invalidating the positive is the religious addict's discarding negative behavior to maintain a hurtful sense of self-worth. An example would be the promiscuous follower who filters out his negative behavior by seeing only his positive actions, thus allowing himself to do immoral things that he would condemn as immoral if he saw others doing them. This is done through the rationalization of having special needs or being the exception. Some say they have the freedom to experience things that are clearly immoral. The religious

For these people, treatment includes facing up to their wrongs, who they have hurt, and the restitution that must be made for the wrongs.

GOD'S PRESENCE

I am sometimes very conscious of the presence of God.

- 46% completely agree
- 35% mostly agree
- 11% mostly disagree
- 5% completely disagree
- 3% no opinion

—George Gallup, Jr., and Sarah Jones, 100 Questions and Answers: Religion in America *(Princeton, N.J.: Princeton Religion Research Center, 1989), p. 162.*

addict is able to "yes, but" into continuing the most destructive and negative behavior.

For these people, treatment includes facing up to their wrongs, who they have hurt, and the restitution that must be made for the wrongs. At times these people are the most resistant to treatment because when they face who they are and what they have done, their world really crashes around them. Sometimes they become so depressed they are difficult to motivate. These cases require more time than most.

Thinking with the Heart

Thinking with the heart is the condition where feelings, not facts, are the basis of reality: "I feel bad; therefore, I must be bad"; "I feel hopeless and powerless; therefore, I must be hopeless and powerless. If I am hopeless and powerless, there is no reason for me to go on"; "I feel like a disappointment to God; therefore, I must be a disappointment to God. There is no sense in trying to have a relationship with Him. He won't like me anyway." These are common thoughts of addicts so caught up in their emotions that they interpret the world only by the way they feel. In this self-obsessed existence the only thing that matters is how they feel, not what is real.

This emotional reasoning reflects the misled believer's basic belief system. A core belief for an addict is "I'm basically a bad, unworthy person." An addict feeling this negatively about himself or herself is

In this self-obsessed existence the only thing that matters is how they feel, not what is real.

not going to have many positive thoughts about anything. Treatment involves separating the evidence of reality from feelings. The recovering addict is able to identify a thought or perception based on emotion versus one based on the evidence at hand. This separation allows reality to sift into the person's thinking and eventually erodes some of the negative thoughts.

A woman dated a very wealthy man for over five years. Every year she went to Europe with him and his family, and she loved mingling with the upper class. One day she suggested they marry. His rejection was immediate. He demeaned her and said he could never marry her because she was too large and unattractive.

She felt like a failure. Because she felt so negative about herself, she was negative about everything else. She felt God was down on her personally. She did not know what she had done to offend God, but she believed she must have done something very bad because He had yanked away her future. From that time on, all her decisions revolved around those terrible feelings about herself and God. Her thinking had to be changed before she could find peace with her emotions.

Surrounding Oneself with Shoulds

An addict will self-induce pressure with internal "should" statements. This is a predominant reason for the need to find mood alteration. *I should have done better* and *I should have done more*—these stressful thoughts drive the addict deeper into the addiction. The addict never measures up to the expectations of old thought patterns that play a recurring theme of "never good enough." The statements are unrealistic measuring sticks that become more and more demanding.

Addicts actually believe that these unrealistic demands must be met. They drive themselves to meet the demands in an effort to avoid disappointment or the indictment of failure. Disappointment and depression are the only rewards of this tyrannical existence.

Some addicts have the harmful belief that Christians should be happy all the time. If the Christian addict experiences sadness, there must be something wrong personally. This destructive thought process drives the addict into more and more religious compulsive behavior in search of happiness. The addict reasons that since there should

The statements are unrealistic measuring sticks that become more and more demanding.

THE SPIRITUAL ITCH

"Obviously, these counterfeit spiritualities do not work. But their persistent growth and appeal should teach us two important lessons. First, human beings created for fellowship with God abhor a spiritual vacuum. And second, only the real thing will effectively scratch the spiritual itch."
—Terry C. Muck, "Salt Substitutes—Grassroots gullibility for
spiritual counterfeits demonstrates a great hunger for things
of the spirit," Christianity Today, February 3, 1989, p. 14.

be constant happiness but there is not, there should be greater, more intense efforts to find the elusive happy goal.

Other religious addicts focus on the belief that others should be more Christlike. Frustration and anger mount when those persons fail to meet the unrealistic expectations. These negative emotions drive addicts further into the addiction to alter their mood of destructive anger. They will act out compulsively.

Long hours of supposed intercessory prayer or intense witnessing (which many times is Bible bullying for the most part) take precedence over everything else. The addicts work to push others to live up to the expectations of what the addicts think they "should" live up to. The need for others to live up to these expectations is based not on spiritual concern for them but on the addicts' need to avoid feelings of frustration and anger.

"Should" statements are not reality based. They leave no room for being human, and their purpose in the addictive process is to build up feelings of guilt, disappointment, and inadequacy. They must be replaced with thoughts based more in reality. "It would be nice if Christians were more Christlike"; "I wish the pastor understood"; and "I wish I were (or it would be nice if I could be) more obedient"—such statements are taught as replacements for the tyrannical "should" statements.

Treatment helps addicts remove the "should" statements from the thought processes. Repeated confrontation provides the impetus for them to rethink the demands placed on others and themselves. Each

You can almost see the relief come over them when they finally accept that their standards were too tough and they can relax in their attempts to measure up.

Feeling responsibility for everyone else allows the addict to lose touch with his or her problems.

addict learns a whole new way of thinking about performance. You can almost see the relief come over them when they finally accept that their standards were too tough and they can relax in their attempts to measure up.

Maintaining Hyperresponsibility

Religious addicts will take responsibility for anything. Pastors will feel responsible for the problems and sins of the whole congregation, believing something can be done to control their behavior. Parents will feel responsible for their adult children, even though they have been out of the home for years. Every terrible thing that someone else does is an invitation to personalize the act, take responsibility for it, and experience shame over it. This compounds the low self-worth that plagues the addict.

At the heart of this hyperresponsibility is the addict's desire to be in control. Treatment focuses on the person's giving up the desire to be in control and giving up the egocentric feeling of being responsible for so many things. The addict also needs to refocus. Feeling responsibility for everyone else allows the addict to lose touch with his or her problems. Treatment takes the eye off everyone else and brings it back to rest on the religious addiction. Some have labeled this hyperresponsibility as codependency. Others call it a self-defeating personality disorder. It can be changed with repeated confrontation and the addict's turning over control each day to God.

The initial therapeutic endeavor, after the religious addict has accepted that there is a problem, is to identify hurtful thought processes reinforcing a harmful belief system and delusional reality. Treatment becomes a training ground for teaching the religious addict how to think. Mental circuits that have been shut down are turned back on.

The initial therapeutic endeavor, after the religious addict has accepted that there is a problem, is to identify hurtful thought processes reinforcing a harmful belief system and delusional reality.

The information fed to the patient needs to be in accordance with solid biblical principles.

The religious addict's hurtful thinking has become a way of life and an irrational way to interpret life. Treatment helps the religious addict identify what is real and how to act on that reality by thinking in a different way. If the religious addict does not choose to think differently, there is little hope for change or effective treatment.

Working on New Information

Religious addicts are often victims of a lifetime of propaganda. They don't know what to believe about God, the Bible, faith, or Christ. They are usually ignorant about addiction and other dependencies. In treatment books, tapes, and lectures are used to reeducate religious addicts. Many books on the market explain the dynamics of addiction, codependency, counseling, and recovery. Carefully selected materials, including the Bible, provide each addict with a new foundation of information that can lead the retreat of addiction.

While religious addicts are learning to process and resolve their emotions, they are being saturated with new information each day. For this reason a treatment center must be carefully chosen. When the religious addict starts over, a whole new value system is evolved. If that person is in a center where the values are destructive, irreparable damage will be done. The information fed to the patient needs to be in accordance with solid biblical principles. If it contradicts the principles of the Bible, it is going to hurt the process of coming to know God. Hours of treatment are spent acquiring new information to alter the addict's harmful beliefs and eventually the compulsive behavior. The religious addict must learn to question rather than disqualify.

One purpose of information in treatment is to change a naive believer into a questioning seeker. Most religious addicts have sought easy solutions and what appeared to be the quick fix. Anyone with what sounded like a good idea was believed wholeheartedly. Treatment attempts to change this. The process of evaluation must accom-

One purpose of information in treatment is to change a naive believer into a questioning seeker.

Addiction is not just something the addict does. Addiction is a part of the character and nature of the person.

---

pany all of the material that is presented. Otherwise we put a person back out into the world as susceptible to manipulation as before.

A basic skill taught by case managers in treatment is to ask, "What do *you* think?" The religious addict has often been victimized by controlling persecutors who do not like the questioning of what they say. The religious addict is trained to believe without doubt. The support group, both in treatment and after the patient is discharged, is important for the evaluation of information. The group becomes a safe place to check out the validity of new information. The transformation from a convinced knower to a questioning seeker provides the recovering addict with a safety shield against hurtful information that could damage treatment.

Addiction is not just something the addict does. Addiction is a part of the character and nature of the person. A bond forms between the person and the addiction that makes them inseparable. The bonding is strong because it has become a form of survival for the addict. The addiction becomes the person, and the person becomes the addiction.

The bond to the addiction must be transferred to other people. If it isn't, the recovering addict will merely intellectualize the problem, and the new addiction will easily become knowledge. That is why a person cannot just read a good book and have a radical life change (that is, without divine intervention). The group provides accountability and a new bond to replace the old one. Acquisition of new information needs to occur within and alongside a support group so that the assimilation of the information into the new recovering person is a balanced and healthy process.

HEALING

"The simplistic solutions of the extremists on both sides are attractive precisely because they are simple. But it is as wrong to say that the church has no part at all in the ministry of healing as it is to say that the only thing that prevents people from being healed today is their lack of faith in miracles."

—Colin Brown, "The Other Half of the Gospel?" Christianity Today, April 21, 1989, p. 29.

If a person is to recover from religious addiction, it will be done with the assistance of a group of caring individuals. It cannot be done alone.

Working in a Support Group

I can't overemphasize the importance of support groups. If a person is to recover from religious addiction, it will be done with the assistance of a group of caring individuals. *It cannot be done alone.* Millions have attempted to recover from addiction without the assistance of a group. Although they may stop the addictive behavior, they will not develop a balanced recovery. Sooner or later they will trip up and either fall back into the addiction or find another one to replace the original one.

At New Life Treatment Centers, all patients are introduced to a support group. Those groups that work with the twelve steps seem to be the most helpful. Some groups develop their own steps. They have ten or eight, and they are quite helpful, also. The number and the type of steps are much less significant than what happens in the group. The group must provide a combination of support and accountability. It must supplement the entire recovery program, not become its single focus. If it becomes the single focus of recovery, it can become a substitute addiction and be just as unhealthy as involvement in a harmful faith system.

In the recovery community, people are quick to find points of division and superiority. Sometimes this centers on whether or not the twelve steps, originating from Alcoholics Anonymous, are helpful or harmful. Some believe they are wonderful steps back to a full relationship with God and a restored relationship with others. Others believe they detour people from a relationship with Christ and replace the church and pastor's leadership role.

Both sides are right in some cases. The twelve steps can be a wonderful guide to spiritual growth and maturity. They can also become an obsession that prevents people from achieving complete spiritual

The group must provide a combination of support and accountability.

Whether a group has eight, ten, or twelve steps, it is important that the group be a healthy one that can serve the dual roles of encouragement and confrontation.

recovery. Some recovering addicts use their twelve-step theology to replace involvement in a church. This is just as destructive as having no recovery program at all. The church is a special place where spiritual gifts can be used to serve and worship God. There is no good excuse to avoid church involvement. Since religious addicts are susceptible to latching on to systems, they need to be extremely careful that the steps are used in a balanced manner.

Some people believe that the twelve steps are the only route to recovery. They are down on the church, treatment centers, counselors, and everything else not related to the twelve steps. Sometimes these rigid recovering addicts are so fragile in their recovery that the suggestion of another source of recovery is too big a threat to accept. They can become harmful members of the group and hurt others in that group. Whether a group has eight, ten, or twelve steps, it is important that the group be a healthy one that can serve the dual roles of encouragement and confrontation.

I was speaking at a recovery conference where many Christians get together each year to rally for the cause of recovery in churches. It was obvious after talking to just two people that there was a major rift between two factions. One believed that the twelve-steps were terrible and the other believed that they represented biblical principles. The two sides were angry with each other. Each felt the other was out of line and wanted to convince the other of their error. It struck me as ironic that all those people were supposed to be recovering. Recovery never focuses on someone else's problem, it always focuses on the self.

BELIEF IN GOD

"In recent years, researchers have consistently found that . . . about 40 percent of Americans attend religious services weekly, three-quarters of them pray at least once a day, and more than 90 percent profess belief in God."

—Kenneth A. Briggs, "Religious Feeling Seen Strong in
U.S.," New York Times, *December 9, 1984.*

Recovery is never "working someone else's program," it is always working your own. These people were judging each other rather than appreciating the thousands that each group was helping each year.

Often people in need of a support group will use some philosophical basis for a reason not to join—they attended a bad group or heard bad things about another group. These excuses are used to avoid doing the work needed to get well. If the people would focus on their problems and their need to recover rather than on the group's problems, they would find most groups helpful and healthy.

Characteristics of a Healthy Support Group

Certain characteristics of a support group need to be evident if it is to provide a healthy environment for growth.

Acceptance

A healthy support group is made up of loving and accepting people. It will welcome a struggling addict into the group and assist as the addict develops a new identity free of addiction. The group will lovingly assist the person in cultivating a new relationship with God and His Son. If it is a mature group, it will not reject the person because of differing beliefs, but it will patiently work with the person as the search for truth is conducted. If the addict feels rejection due to beliefs, looks, or any other peculiarity, he or she may leave the group and never return to another support group. In a healthy group, a person is allowed to be different and make mistakes without being shamed.

Unconditional Positive Regard

True love values persons for who they are rather than for what they are able to do. True love, the experience of unconditional positive regard, is an extremely healing force. The experience of true love from the group enables addicts to love themselves, God, and others. Addicts in a group where true love exists are free to love others in that

A healthy support group is made up of loving and accepting people.

True love, the experience of unconditional positive regard, is an extremely healing force.

same freeing manner. It becomes an emotional and spiritual bond without equal.

Love is the central theme of Christianity, yet it is sometimes difficult to find around Christians. Christ demonstrated His love when He gave His life. He gave His life not because of what people did, not because of what people deserved, but because He was able to love us as we are. As we participate in recovery groups, we need to stick to the model set by Christ and provide the same unconditional love to other recovering strugglers. If we are not able to provide that for a recovering addict, we are doing much more harm than good and have formed our own harmful faith system.

Freedom of Expression

Addicts need a place to express emotions without having to worry about living up to someone's expectations. They need a place where they are free to explore perceptions, thoughts, and feelings. They need a forum where new ideas and new forms of communication can be practiced with the support of the group. Within the group, members should feel freedom to be who they want to be without fear of retribution. In the group, addicts practice for the real world where rejection is standard. Just like a loving family, the group needs to be a safe place where addicts find relief by saying the tough things rather than holding them in.

Nonautocratic/Noncontrolling

The addict needs to experience a "new family" or group where he or she has equal power and rights. This will be a new experience for the religious addict who was indoctrinated in a misled system that related from the "one-down" or "one-up" position. The addict, having learned how to control or be controlled, needs to learn how to

Just like a loving family, the group needs to be a safe place where addicts find relief by saying the tough things rather than holding them in.

When the addict begins recovery, the hurt and broken family must begin recovery, also.

accept responsibility for his or her behavior only. The addict needs a group where no one gives the orders and no one person is in control.

When all of these elements are found in a recovery support group, the addicts attending grow and mature. They grow in their recovery, and they grow in their faith. When they stop growing, the group lovingly confronts them and moves them back into the recovery mode. All groups are not wonderful like this. No group is like another, and an addict should attend at least five different groups, if possible, to determine which one would be most beneficial and comfortable for spiritual growth.

I have a friend who is a recovering alcoholic. More accurately stated, she is an alcoholic who no longer drinks. This person does not attend A.A. or any other type of support group. She is a miserable person who always has another reason to be upset about some other imperfection in her life. She is an extremely sad case and hard to be around. She loved the camaraderie of the bars she drank in, but she won't gather with those who have shunned the bar for a time to grow. She loved to tell her drinking friends of her problems, but she refuses to share her problems with those who could help. She spent hours drinking and taking drugs with friends, but now she has no time to spend on her own recovery. She had a lot of excuses for not joining a support group. None of these excuses is a good one. Anyone who needs recovery can never find an excuse good enough to justify not being part of something that has helped thousands of people restore their relationship with God. Addicts, whether drug or religious, can benefit from the support of a group whose purpose is to help people find a way back to a loving, caring God.

Working on the Family

Like all other addictions, religious addiction hurts families and destroys many. Frequently an addict will move away from the rest of the family, feeling justified in doing so in the guise of finding a deeper faith. Many family members give up on ever having a normal relationship with the addict.

When the addict begins recovery, the hurt and broken family must

Families of religious addicts tend to be very angry. They are angry with the addict and angry with themselves for not being able to change the addict.

begin recovery, also. Any effective treatment must involve the family. If it cannot be facilitated at the time of intensive treatment, it can occur later. However, if it does not occur, the family will surely disintegrate. While the addiction developed, everyone in the family took on a particular role. The family became dysfunctional, just like the addict's original family where the seeds of religious addiction were planted. Family members need help out of those roles. If they do not obtain it, they will move on to their own addiction and dependency problems. While they remain with their own problems, there will be little support for the recovering religious addict.

Families of religious addicts tend to be very angry. They are angry with the addict and angry with themselves for not being able to change the addict. Treatment must be a time of expressing those negative feelings and moving beyond them. If they are not resolved, they will lead to alienation and the rejection of the recovering addict. The healing of this anger and other emotions is a slow process, and everyone needs patience as each member finds a way to express and resolve negative emotions. Once this occurs, the family has the opportunity to re-form and bond into a unified unit of support and love. If treatment does not make every attempt possible to achieve this family recovery, it is not doing what is required to counter the power of addiction.

One young girl on our adolescent unit had been involved in a group that worshiped Satan. Part of her treatment was to help her see why she enjoyed being with such a destructive group and to help her find more positive ways to obtain the same things. The other part of her treatment was to help her family sort through their problems so the girl would have a supportive environment to come home to. One issue that became clear in the first session was the extreme anger of the father. He was furious at his family and himself. When the counselor mentioned that she saw an extreme amount of anger, he yelled at her and walked out, saying he did not need to be humiliated in front of his family. This reaction is common. The chances of recovery are greatly reduced when a child goes back into a family where the father is furious and everyone is a victim of that anger. The family treatment aspects of a program go a long way to provide support for the addict and the opportunity for recovery for the other family members.

When the harmful faith system is abandoned, many so-cial relationships go with it. If these are not replaced, a terrible void will hamper recovery.

Working on New Friends: Social Recovery

When the harmful faith system is abandoned, many social relation-ships go with it. If these are not replaced, a terrible void will hamper recovery. The recovery support group is for encouragement and ac-countability, but it cannot fill this void. New friends and social rela-tionships are needed for the same reasons as the support group, but they are also needed for fun. Recovery is serious business, and too often those involved with it stop having fun. They become so serious that sometimes people encourage them to go back to their addiction rather than continue to act so lifeless.

Recovering addicts must seek supportive people. They are rarely found in bars and night clubs. They are most likely found in choirs, at the gym, by a swimming pool, in a club, or in a college course. Mak-ing new friends and going new places with them are parts of a compre-hensive recovery program. Appropriate treatment helps persons plan how to develop new sources of social support.

Working on the Body: Physical Recovery

Religious addicts tend to have poor dietary habits, are often over-weight, and totally lack physical exercise. They spend so much time on their addiction that they don't have time to exercise. They are so compulsive that they eat everything in sight. They are drained of energy and feel bad about themselves because they look and feel bad. Treatment addresses these needs with the same level of importance as the other areas of recovery.

The recovering religious addict sees the body as the temple of God and takes care of it accordingly. Rest, exercise, and nutrition are not

The recovering religious addict sees the body as the tem-ple of God and takes care of it accordingly.

afterthoughts, but priorities in recovery. The moods stabilize as sugar and caffeine are minimized in the diet. Exercise provides a natural form of relaxation. Proper rest reduces stress and irritability. This one area is often the most neglected in a recovery program. As a result, many addicts return to their old compulsive behaviors. They look miserable and feel miserable, so they return to the source of mood alteration that lifts them out of their misery.

There is great hope for the recovering religious addict. The hope comes in developing a new faith, pure and free of the poison of addiction. Hope does not just spring forth on its own, however. It must be cultivated through a recovery program that encompasses every area of the addict's life and includes the addict's family. The recovering addict must learn to think differently, relate differently, and find different people and places for support and fun. When it all comes together, the recovering addict comes closer to God.

Treatment facilitates the recovery process. It brings the forces of recovery professionals to bear on the addict and the addiction. It is not a cure-all or a quick fix. If it works, it works because the addict decides to make it work with God's help. A person obtains nothing more from it than is put into it. One of its greatest values is the bringing together of fellow strugglers, some sick and some well, to help one another find a new life and new hope in a loving God. It is my hope and prayer that if you or someone you love is in need of treatment, you will seek it out and initiate the process of change.

There is great hope for the recovering religious addict. The hope comes in developing a new faith, pure and free of the poison of addiction.

CHAPTER 10

Seventeen Characteristics of Helpful Faith

Recovery from religious addiction is the detoxification of faith. Through Bible study, church attendance, prayer, communication with other believers, and time, harmful faith is purified into a helpful faith. For many different reasons, the religious addict comes to possess a hurtful faith. Instead of bringing a person closer to God, that faith has moved God away and replaced God with dependency on rules, religion, false hopes, and magical thinking. Through recovery, the addict attains a new knowledge of God and develops a strong, healthy faith. When faith is helpful, the dependency on God becomes a godly dependency. The following discussion provides seventeen key characteristics of a helpful faith.

Focused on God

Helpful faith is completely focused on God. It is not based on who we want God to be or what we want God to do. The caricatures of

---

Instead of bringing a person closer to God, that faith has moved God away and replaced God with dependency on rules, religion, false hopes, and magical thinking.

A BREATH OF FRESH AIR

"Day of Discovery" is a weekly half-hour Christian show that does not ask for money on the air. "'Day of Discovery' still operates under the original strict principles laid down by the founder: If the ministry can't pay for it, it won't do it. 'We speak as God provides,' the grandson says. And because the founding principles are still in place, 'it's a whole lot easier to make financial decisions. We just won't allow ourselves to become over-extended. If we don't have the funds, we'll cut back on the stations.' De-Hann doesn't see this as cause for embarrassment or a defeat for God's work. Instead it's simply good stewardship and a positive witness."

—Bob Chuvala, "Television Preachers Who Don't Ask for Money," Christian Herald, October 1987, p. 20.

God, created by our self-obsessed society, are replaced with the real God of the Bible. The Bible is our best link to knowing God. Men and women through the ages have always come up with new concepts of who God is and what He does. They become very confused in their "make it up as you go" theology; they have no standard or source of authority. But the Bible is the Word of God and can be trusted to reveal to us who God is. Through studying it, we can grow in knowledge of God and in faith.

Throughout the Bible, God is seeking after His people. He is persistent in His desire to have fellowship with His creation. God loves us and wants a relationship with us, even if we are guilty of many sins. Some of the great men and women of the Bible did many terrible things, and yet God loved those people and didn't turn His back on them. This fact should be reassuring. People may tell us that we have been rejected by God, but the God of the Bible is a loving God who has gone to a great deal of trouble for all of us.

If you believe the Bible to be the Word of God, you must believe that Christ is His Son. Helpful faith must encompass all of who God is, including the Holy Spirit and Jesus Christ. If people could put their faith in the fact that Jesus died for our sins, it would go a long way toward ridding the world of the shame and guilt felt from sin. God has

The caricatures of God, created by our self-obsessed society, are replaced with the real God of the Bible. The Bible is our best link to knowing God.

It is a tremendous relief when a person finds that performance can be replaced with the person of Christ.

taken care of us because He knew we could not be perfect. It is a tremendous relief when a person finds that performance can be replaced with the person of Christ.

The common denominator of many popular religions today is the focus on self rather than on God. One man became involved with a Christian cult because of the promises it held for the individual. These promises included a healthy body, a wonderful family, and enough money to obtain whatever was needed. He was in complete bliss as long as his focus was on what he could obtain to better himself. But he realized how absent God was from his life. He was aware of his constant focus on himself rather than on God. He discussed it with one of the leaders of the church. The leader explained it away as a God who wants everything for you and people who are unwilling to have it all. The man walked away from the church and his addiction to its promises. He never went back because his new search focused on God and he found Him.

Growing

Helpful faith grows and matures over time. Bible study and prayer assist in the process, but the difficulties of life are the great faith growers. It is our nature to find quick relief from pain. In our fear that we will live in pain forever or that the pain will overwhelm us, we run to the closest form of relief available. This does not allow for growth in faith. When we feel pain and stand firm, trusting that God will see us through, we are rewarded with a strengthening of our faith that will make the same crisis less traumatic.

I have watched hundreds of alcoholics go through the detoxification process. They have spent years trusting in a bottle for relief. Then because the pain of drinking becomes greater than the original pain they sought to squelch, they decide to stop. The first three days of

In our fear that we will live in pain forever or that the pain will overwhelm us, we run to the closest form of relief available.

ASKING GOD QUESTIONS

Suppose you could ask God any three questions on this list. What would they be?

Will there ever be lasting world peace?	37%
How can I be a better person?	33%
What does the future hold for me and my family?	31%
Will there ever be a cure for all diseases?	28%
Why is there suffering in the world?	28%
Is there life after death?	26%
What is heaven like?	22%
Will man ever love his fellow man?	21%
Why is there evil in the world?	16%
When will the world end?	16%
Why was man created?	10%
Don't know/don't believe in God	8%

—*George Gallup, Jr., and Sarah Jones,* 100 Questions and Answers: Religion in America *(Princeton, N.J.: Princeton Religion Research Center, 1989), p. 172.*

detoxification are the most vulnerable time in their lives. They are physically weak and mentally unstable. At any moment they want to tear away and return to a drink, but they persist and make it through the painful process.

Once they make it through this period and they regain their physical strength and their mental capacity, they feel clean and pure. Their faith is often all that brings them through. Their first step into sobriety is a big one because if it is the right step, it is a step toward letting God handle things one day at a time. If their focus is correct, they grow spiritually and emotionally. Sometimes they grow more in the first year than they have in the past twenty.

The misled faithful go through no less traumatic and painful times when they remove themselves from the addictive behaviors that have compulsively captured them. They are vulnerable, left without the old thoughts that could make everything instantly better. When they are determined to face the storms with only their faith in God and the

When they are determined to face the storms with only their faith in God and the support of other nontoxic believers, they set themselves up for growth.

When security depends on God, there is no longer a need to feel threatened.

---

support of other believers, they set themselves up for growth. God will take that little amount of pure faith and grow a deep and abiding faith from it. To start that process of growth, God does not need a lot of faith. He needs only a little seed of healthy faith to work with. Christ described this small faith as being the size of a mustard seed (Matt. 17:20). From that small speck of faith the impossible can be accomplished as long as the focus is on God.

Respectful

As faith grows, respect for others grows with it. Too often religious addicts attack others out of their own insecurities. When security depends on God, there is no longer a need to feel threatened. People can be appreciated for their strengths *and* their weaknesses. Their differing views can be seen as a result of different people at different places in the progression of growing faith. Those who are of different denominations or even from different factions within a denomination are no longer perceived as the enemy when a helpful faith exists.

Through the Bible, God instructs us to have respect for all people. He warns against showing favor to any one group such as the wealthy. We need to see each person as a wonderful creation of God with gifts and talents sent directly from God. Faith frees us from the fear of others and allows us to love them. If we have helpful faith, we can love them and trust God to work on their problems as we pray for God to do so. First Peter 2:17 tells us to show proper respect for everyone and love all believers alike. When faith grows to reach this level of respect and acceptance of others, it frees us to serve God.

Free to Serve

First Peter also addresses the need for God's faithful followers to live in freedom (see chap. 2). This freedom does not allow us to do everything we feel is right. It is a freedom that moves us to serve others. Rather than be locked into a confining role or serve to work our way to heaven, we can be free to serve others as an act of faith to

CHRISTIAN BELIEFS

Here is what Americans think on a variety of statements involving the Christian faith:

	completely agree	mostly agree	mostly disagree	completely disagree	no opinion
I believe in the divinity of Jesus Christ	69	19	3	5	4
I believe that God loves me even though I may not always please him	68	21	3	4	4
I wish my religious beliefs were stronger	51	27	11	8	3
I believe in the full authority of the Bible	51	26	9	9	5
I try hard to put my religious beliefs into practice in my relations with all people, including people of different races, religious attitudes and backgrounds	49	35	7	5	4
I receive a great deal of comfort and support from my religious beliefs	46	32	11	7	4
I constantly seek God's will through prayer	36	31	19	11	3
My religious faith is the most important influence in my life	34	38	17	8	3
I sometimes do things I want very much NOT to do because I believe it is the will of God.	23	26	19	23	9

—*George Gallup, Jr., and Sarah Jones,* 100 Questions and Answers: Religion in America *(Princeton, N.J.: Princeton Religion Research Center, 1989), p. 188.*

God. Galatians 5:13 instructs, "You, brethren, have been called to liberty; only do not use liberty as an opportunity for the flesh, but through love serve one another." When most people think of liberty or freedom, they think of having permission to do pleasing things. Some feel a liberty to drink; others feel free to drive expensive cars. Helpful faith is not focused on these things. It does not free us to participate in or flirt with evil. It frees us to love one another and to show that love by serving one another.

Where helpful faith exists, people are amazed at the service shown to others. Out of a deep faith in God, we are free, not bound, to serve others.

If our society has gone over the edge on any one point, it is the emphasis on our own needs, desires, and demands. For years, people lived in terribly oppressive relationships where their needs were not met. We have made great progress in identifying those unhealthy situations and motivating people to grow into healthier ones. We have shown individuals who were plagued with undeserved guilt how to rid themselves of those negative feelings. However, in the process we have gone too far and gotten people to focus on themselves, not on others. We have driven people into an obsession with their needs; they are reluctant to love their neighbors as themselves. Helpful faith reverses this trend and brings a healthy balance back to relationships. Where helpful faith exists, people are amazed at the service shown to others. Out of a deep faith in God, we are free, not bound, to serve others.

Self-Worthy

The healthier the faith, the more valuable we can feel. Too often we have based our self-worth on what the world views as valuable. The world thinks money is the barometer of value, and if we do not have it in great amounts, we feel bad about ourselves. Physical beauty has almost become a religion unto itself, and those without it feel no value in a society that judges the heart by the looks on the outside. In this age of technology, IQ is used as a determination of who is to be esteemed and who is to be relegated to a lesser position. It is hard for us

---

PRAYER

Do you ever pray to God?

☐ Yes   88%

☐ No   11%

—George Gallup, Jr., and Sarah Jones, 100 Questions and Answers: Religion in America *(Princeton, N.J.: Princeton Religion Research Center, 1989), p. 38.*

to measure up. The more we focus on the world's standards and values, the more negative we feel about ourselves.

God has a different system, and if our faith is in Him, we can feel tremendous relief. Christ talked about the worth of an individual. His words are good news to all of us who will never be fashion models, members of a society of geniuses, or holders of Swiss bank accounts. Christ told His followers not to be afraid of those who attack a person physically because they cannot touch the person's soul. He explained that even though sparrows were sold for about a half cent each, not one sparrow can fall to the ground without God knowing it. And the Savior of the world told us not to worry because we are more valuable than many sparrows. He also said that the hairs on our heads are numbered by God. (See Matt. 10:28–31.)

If God knows the actions of all the sparrows and cares about them, we can feel wonderful about ourselves, knowing He cares much more for us. If our sense of self-worth is wrapped up in God, we don't have to worry what the world will think of us or do to us. The fact that God sent His Son to die for us should be an overwhelming affirmation of the worth of each individual. The problem comes when we measure ourselves by the world's standards, take our faith away from God, and place it on our own powers and efforts to measure up. Helpful faith stays focused on God and the value He has given each of us. In this value system of the Creator, no one need feel disappointment over not measuring up to the world. The person with a helpful faith feels valuable to the Creator.

One of the groups I have published with has a leader who talks a lot about self-worth. He believes many people make terrible decisions due to low self-worth. I happen to agree. However, an acquaintance of mine kept bothering me about working with a group that focused on self-esteem. His belief was that worth should come from God rather than self. I agreed but explained that many people believe in neither self nor God for worth. Self-worth is an offensive term to some, but it should not be if it is founded on our worth as creations of God. Worth based on anything else is not true worth anyway. Every time we were together, I ended up arguing this point with this man. Finally I had to confront him. I told him I had never met anyone with lower self-esteem than him. If his perspective was so great, why did it result in

If our sense of self-worth is wrapped up in God, we don't have to worry what the world will think of us or do to us.

Being vulnerable means being real. It is the ability to risk rejection by laying before others all that we are and are not. If our faith is in God, we don't need to fear being real.

such a negative self-concept? It was as if I had hit him with a pipe. He began to cry and confess that he felt terrible about himself. Though married and a Christian, he was a compulsive masturbator. He felt terrible about himself and wanted help. His state is a common one. Often those who are most offended about the concept of self-worth are the ones who have the least amount of it.

Vulnerable

If we believe the words of Christ who tells us not to fear, we are free to be vulnerable. Being vulnerable means being real. It is the ability to risk rejection by laying before others all that we are and are not. If our faith is in God, we don't need to fear being real. The stronger our faith, the more we are driven to be real. Our acceptance by God is much more important than acceptance by others. Being accepted by God, we can face rejection by others.

So often a harmful faith system breeds the desire to hide and cover up as Adam and Eve were driven to do. Helpful faith frees us to come out of hiding and share our imperfect selves with others. Ephesians

---

JUDGEMENT DAY

Here's what people said in response to this statement:
   We will all be called before God at the judgement day to answer for our sins.

- 52% completely agree
- 28% mostly agree
- 8% mostly disagree
- 6% completely disagree
- 6% don't know

—George Gallup, Jr., and Sarah Jones, 100 Questions and Answers: Religion in America *(Princeton, N.J.: Princeton Religion Research Center, 1989), p. 18.*

CHURCH INVOLVEMENT IN THE FUTURE OF TODAY'S YOUTH

	Age 13–15	Age 16–18
WHEN YOU ARE 21, DO YOU THINK YOU WILL BE ACTIVE IN A CHURCH?		
No chance	2%	0%
Small chance	8	12
Fair chance	18	22
Good chance	48	40
Excellent chance	25	25
WHEN YOU ARE 40, DO YOU THINK YOU WILL BE ACTIVE IN A CHURCH?		
No chance	1%	0%
Small chance	6	5
Fair chance	17	18
Good chance	44	41
Excellent chance	32	36

—Peter L. Benson and Carolyn H. Eklin, Effective Christian Education: A National Study of Protestant Congregations (Minneapolis: a research project of Search Institute, March 1990), p. 29.

6:16 tells us that we can use our faith as a shield. We don't have to stand behind a facade of materialism or any other earthly creation. We can hold firm to our shield of faith and be vulnerable to others. A true test of faith is how much a person is willing to risk rejection by the world. The mark of the faithful is vulnerability with others due to a complete focus on God.

Trusting

Helpful faith grows trust in three areas. First, there is a trust in God that grows the more we give to Him. As we give our time, money, and hearts, He rewards us with comfort and peace, and then we trust Him with more of what we have and who we are. Every day the recovering religious addict must turn over more and more to God and trust Him with greater things. This relieves the addict from the burden of control. As the addict allows God to be in control and trusts His control, the addict is free to live without being driven.

As the addict allows God to be in control and trusts His control, the addict is free to live without being driven.

Some people have lived such terrible lives that they fear God and don't totally trust Him. Colossians 1:20–23 addresses this very issue; God speaks to us, telling us that through Christ, He has cleared a path to Him. The price that Christ paid on the cross has made peace with God for the one who trusts in Him. He says that many were far away from Him to the point of being His enemy. Many were separated from Him by their thoughts and actions, but God has brought them back as His friends. Through the death of Christ, we are able to be in the presence of God with nothing held against us. The only requirement is that we fully believe the truth that Christ died to save us, and so we can place our total trust in that marvelous event. If we believe these things, we have no reason not to trust God with all that we have.

The second area that trust affects is our trust of others. Although we have been deceived by many, as we heal we can learn from those who have tried to hurt us. Eventually, we will be able to trust others again. Placing our trust in God allows us to trust others because we know that we do not have to allow ourselves to be victimized by others again.

Third, growing faith helps our trust in ourselves. If we do not have a faith anchored in God, we trust in the most convenient object available. As each new object of faith fails, we lose faith in our ability to make good judgments. As our faith in God grows, as we trust Him more and rely on Him to help us, we find ourselves respecting our judgments because they are anchored in God. We do not trust ourselves more because we have become smarter but because we have our focus more securely on God.

The religious addict has been functioning by trusting in his or her efforts to win favor with God. This futile existence must be forsaken

---

HEAVEN

Percent of Americans who believe in heaven:

1980	71%
1952	71%

—From the Gallup Organization, as reported in "DemoMemo," American Demographics, July 1990, p. 8.

We no longer sway with the whims of the day or run from fear of others. Knowing God will not betray us allows us to trust Him, others, and ourselves.

for the life of faith. From Hebrews 4 we learn that all may enter the kingdom of heaven if faith in God is real. Effort and works must be replaced by complete trust.

As our faith matures, trust in God will grow with it. We no longer sway with the whims of the day or run from fear of others. Knowing God will not betray us allows us to trust Him, others, and ourselves.

For many, trust is not a difficult concept. For others it is almost impossible. One broken woman was a victim of her father's sexual abuse. After years of meeting his addictive sexual needs, she lost her ability to trust God or any other human being. People would ask her to trust in Christ, but she could not allow herself to trust any male figure. Finally she began counseling sessions with a gentle man of integrity who had her best interests at heart. He guided her through her fears. He not only showed her that not all men are untrustworthy, he showed her that some are capable of caring with no strings attached. He also led her to trust in God who loved her. Her faith had been poisoned by a man who abused her. It was restored and filled with trust by another man who could be trusted.

Individualized

Religious addiction takes away a person's identity. Conformity is the order of a harmful faith system where religious addiction abounds. Rules and roles are priorities over the worth and development of each individual. Recovery is the healing of self-identity as it relates to God. Helpful faith allows a person to express faith as an individual, not just as a conformist to a system.

God has created each person individually in His own image. He does not want to waste the uniqueness of any of us. He has given us many unique gifts that He wants us to develop in service to Him. The

Helpful faith allows a person to express faith as an individual, not just as a conformist to a system.

As helpful faith grows, shame diminishes, and we delight in finding that we do not have to live in the image of another person—only in the image of God.

church is one body of many members. We must continue to come together as a group so that God can use our individual gifts for the benefit of all who worship Him. As helpful faith grows, shame diminishes, and we delight in finding that we do not have to live in the image of another person—only in the image of God.

Ephesians 4:11 relates that some people have been given gifts of being able to preach. Others are better at serving and caring for other members of the church. God has made us uniquely for service to one another. When we abandon that uniqueness, we abandon God's will for our lives.

Relationship Oriented

In most harmful faith systems of religious addiction, the focus is on what people do and how well they conform to the rules of the group. In helpful faith, the focus shifts from rules to relationships. Frequently, the religious addict abandons relationships, believing that God is all that matters. God has shown us that the more we love Him, the more we will seek out others and manifest His love through relationships with others. Instead of being obedient to another's rules, the person of helpful faith strives to develop intimacy. Sharing the faith and loving another in faith build the relationship with God.

Too often people see faith as a hot line or pipeline to heaven without regard for other struggles on earth. Once I discussed harmful faith with a minister. He told me that three years previous, he had been a full-fledged religious addict. He said he was obsessed with himself and his own knowledge of God. The more his addiction grew, the more isolated he became from others. He had no time for people. He was short-spoken, and most people hated to be around him. One day a woman who had supported the church for some time came to see him.

Instead of being obedient to another's rules, the person of helpful faith strives to develop intimacy.

WHAT DO EVANGELICALS BELIEVE?

Evangelical is a bit nebulous to define. Philip Edgcumbe Hughes took a stab at a definition in the *New Oxford Review*:

- The centrality of the cross.
- The sovereignty of God.
- The authority of Holy Scripture.
- The priority of preaching.
- Ministry to the whole person.
- The Christian hope.

> —Evangelical Newsletter, *vol. 12, no. 18, September 27, 1985, p. 1.*

She said she wanted to say only two words, "Forget yourself." He asked her what she meant, but she didn't say any more. He thought and thought about it. He became obsessed with learning what she had meant. He called her and she told him she was coming for another visit the following week and would give him two more words. When she arrived the second time, she looked him in the eye and said two more words, "Serve others."

The minister said the woman's words revolutionized his faith. He realized that he had been serving himself and had forgotten how important relationships were. He began to rebuild what he had torn down and, in so doing, his faith became real.

Personal

Religious addicts become accustomed to what is taught as an impersonal faith. They are mere members of the group, not individuals loved and cherished by God. The entire harmful faith system is based on the absence of personal convictions and the acceptance of someone else's definition of faith.

Helpful faith is a personal experience generated internally through trust in God rather than externally from rules by other people. Each

Helpful faith is a personal experience generated internally through trust in God rather than externally from rules by other people.

Obedience to rules is balanced with freedom to serve others in ways of individual expression.

---

individual is personally led by the Holy Spirit. Each person can read God's Word and hear God speak through His Word. Christ died for each individual. The healthier the faith becomes, the more personal it becomes. A personal relationship forms between the believer and God. That relationship becomes so strong that no criticism or system can break the personal bonds formed between God and the believer.

Balanced

Helpful faith is balanced. It is not so preoccupied with work that family is destroyed. It is not so intent on witnessing to people that we fail to meet their needs. It does not become so involved with memorizing Scripture that the Author of Scripture is forgotten. Obedience to rules is balanced with freedom to serve others in ways of individual expression.

Harmful faith is based on "either/or," "black or white," "us versus them," and "all-or-nothing" mentalities. It is so extreme that there is no room for compromise, no middle ground for others outside the system. Helpful faith accepts the fact that life is not black or white and allows the believer to feel okay about the struggle with the gray areas of life. It rejects the "us-versus-them" mentality. The person with helpful faith sees himself or herself as a part of a greater community, all struggling with the relationships we have with ourselves, our God, and our fellow human beings.

Where helpful faith grows, every area of the believer's life is improved. In the balanced practice of faith, families grow closer, friends become stronger, and conflict is resolved more easily. The focus is on

---

18 YEARS OLD

"Research consistently shows that people are most likely to accept Christ as their Savior before they reach the age of 18. Currently, about two-thirds of all decisions for Christ happen by that age."

—*George Barna,* The Frog in the Kettle *(Ventura: Regal Books, 1990), p. 119.*

God, and the individual is seen as a valuable creation of God, worthy of God's attention. Rigidity is replaced with understanding. Those who grow in the faith find comfort there because their lives regain perspective. They find wholeness in their balanced faith.

Nondefensive

Helpful faith takes a nondefensive position against those who would challenge the beliefs and the exercise of faith. Helpful faith welcomes critical evaluation and tough questions as opportunities to learn and relate. Those in a healthy system refrain from defining the truth for others and welcome the chance to share what they believe the truth for them may be. Those who question their faith are not considered disobedient. They are merely encouraged as they explore their doubts.

Those in a harmful faith system are afraid of every threat to the system. They feel personally threatened because much of their faith was developed by their rules rather than the Word of God. When God is in charge, there is no reason to feel threatened. He is in control, and He will champion the faith. Helpful faith attracts people to it rather than repels them. Those who become defensive repel other people— they forget how attractive Christ was as He drew people to Him. What a relief to the healthy believer not to have to defend every criticism made by everyone outside the faith!

Nonjudgmental

In the beautiful Sermon on the Mount, Christ gives us specific instructions with regard to judging others. In Matthew 7:1 He instructs us not to judge others or we will be judged in the same way. All too often we are guilty of the very things we point out as wrong in others. Recovering religious addicts stop judging people and start listening to them. When this occurs, compassion and empathy develop in the hearts of believers. This overcomes a major flaw of a harmful faith

Helpful faith welcomes critical evaluation and tough questions as opportunities to learn and relate.

THE AVERAGE AMERICAN

The average American is a thirty-two-year-old woman, is married, and has a child: "Although she hasn't been to church in the past week, the average American was born Protestant (65% of all Americans). She believes in God (94% of all Americans) and life after death (69%)."

—*Source: The* Almanac of the American People *by Tom and Nancy Biracree, 1988, as reported in "Meet Jane Doe," American Demographics, June 1989, p. 27.*

---

system: it is so focused on the system that the needs of people are forgotten. Their behavior, not their needs, is the priority.

Healthy believers don't judge what people say; they listen to what others have to offer. They evaluate it; they do not judge it. In judging, people are placed in a system of conditional acceptance. Helpful faith removes the conditions and the need to judge. Healthy believers look for the similarities of experience to establish a relationship. Each person is seen as a fellow struggler in different stages of the struggle. Healthy believers are so busy developing a personal relationship with God, they have no time to judge where others are in developing their own relationship.

Reality Based

The misled believer denies reality. Faith is not based on a belief in the supernatural power of God; it is based on a desire to see magical solutions that stop pain.

The healthy believer embraces reality. Helpful faith acknowledges the supernatural power of God and does not need miraculous intervention to believe God is real. The healthy believer does not look for God to magically change the circumstances but looks to Him in the midst of trials.

Because faith grows strong, there is no need to deny reality. Believ-

---

Helpful faith removes the conditions and the need to judge. Healthy believers look for the similarities of experience to establish a relationship.

THE NATURE OF MATURE FAITH

A study researching faith came up with these eight core dimensions to determine maturity of faith:

1. Trusts in God's saving grace and believes firmly in the humanity and divinity of Jesus
2. Experiences a sense of personal well-being, security, and peace
3. Integrates faith and life, seeing work, family, social relationships, and political choices as part of one's religious life
4. Seeks spiritual growth through study, reflection, prayer, and discussion with others
5. Seeks to be part of a community of believers in which people give witness to their faith and support and nourish one another
6. Holds life-affirming values, including commitment to racial and gender equality, affirmation of cultural and religious diversity, and a personal sense of responsibility for the welfare of others
7. Advocates social and global change to bring about greater social justice
8. Serves humanity, consistently and passionately, through acts of love and justice

—Peter L. Benson and Carolyn H. Eklin, Effective Christian Education: A National Study of Protestant Congregations *(Minneapolis: a research project of Search Institute, March 1990), p. 10.*

ing God is faithful to help them through their trials and tribulations, healthy believers have no need to walk away from reality. They see the problems before them, do what they can to resolve them, and trust God to do the rest.

Able to Embrace Our Emotions

Helpful faith gives a person the ability to embrace his or her emotions. The Christian must recognize that Christ did not deny His emotions; He embraced them. As He walked the earth, He revealed His

The healthy believer does not look for God to magically change the circumstances but looks to Him in the midst of trials.

The Christian must recognize that Christ did not deny His emotions; He embraced them.

---

love, anger, sorrow, and many other emotions. His grief became so great that He said His soul was full of sorrow unto death (see Mark 14:34). This must confirm to all of us that He felt the depths of emotion.

In faith there is no need to hide our feelings. We should rejoice that God has given us emotions to experience the extremes of life. We must acknowledge them, confess them when they are self-centered, and express them as they develop. Too many religious addicts are filled with hidden anger and fear. As they find helpful faith, they feel freedom to release those emotions that were bonds to the religious addiction.

Able to Embrace Our Humanity

Helpful faith allows us to embrace humanity. It acknowledges the capacity to sin and make mistakes. There is no illusion of perfection, no need to drive to be perfect or hide when we are not. Helpful faith allows us to experience God's mercy and grace.

The misguided believer obeys God out of a fear of God's anger or a fear of rejection from the system. The mercy and grace of God are lost to a superficial existence of living up to another's standards. Performance for acceptance overpowers the knowledge that no one can act good enough to get to God.

Helpful faith knows that mercy and grace are gifts freely given. If they were to be earned, they would not be gifts. Healthy believers follow God out of gratitude for mercy and grace, accepting the fact that everyone will fail and that God's infinite wisdom has already

---

UFOs

According to the U.S. Government, UFOs don't exist. But the National Science Foundation reported in 1986 that 43% of the citizenry believes it "likely" that some of the UFOs reported "are really space vehicles from other civilizations."

—*Otto Friedrich, "New Age Harmonies," Time, December 7, 1987, p. 65.*

There is no illusion of perfection, no need to drive to be perfect or hide when we are not. Helpful faith allows us to experience God's mercy and grace.

made a provision for that failure. We do not need to deny who we are to be acceptable to God. He made us this way and loves us anyway.

Loving

Helpful faith and the healthy believer are characterized by the capacity to love and be loved. Helpful faith allows a person to love self, God, and others. The healthy believer is able to extend to God and others the characteristics outlined in 1 Corinthians 13. As mentioned in this Scripture, the exercise of helpful faith allows a person to be patient with God, to trust that God will not abandon or reject.

Healthy believers are patient with others and themselves as they allow God to correct their character defects. This patient characteristic of love is seen only in the hearts of the healthy faithful. If faith does not move persons to love more, it is not healthy.

Helpful faith produces kindness toward others as believers mature in love for them. Healthy believers are also kind to themselves and find no need to punish themselves when they miss the mark. This kindness is so attractive that others come into the faith because of it.

The love of helpful faith is also humble. There is no pride where the focus is totally on God. There is no rejection or rudeness on the part of the healthy believer. There is a blatant absence of self-seeking. Forgiveness is offered up freely. Grudges and helpful faith do not exist together. There is rejoicing in truth and sadness over evil done to God and others.

Healthy believers are full of love. Love is the most predominant characteristic of those who have a helpful faith. The love is healing and helps them bear up under every trial. It is the foundation for a future with God and growing relationships with others. If believers have all of the talents in the world but do not have a deep and abiding love, faith is worthless. But where love is present, faith grows, and

We do not need to deny who we are to be acceptable to God.

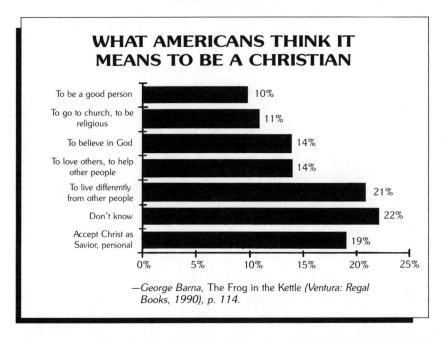

WHAT AMERICANS THINK IT MEANS TO BE A CHRISTIAN

- To be a good person — 10%
- To go to church, to be religious — 11%
- To believe in God — 14%
- To love others, to help other people — 14%
- To live differently from other people — 21%
- Don't know — 22%
- Accept Christ as Savior, personal — 19%

—George Barna, The Frog in the Kettle (Ventura: Regal Books, 1990), p. 114.

people are attracted to God by the loving service of those with helpful faith.

The development of a helpful faith in God is the greatest process and achievement of a lifetime. It is a never-ending process with seasons of tremendous growth and times of near stagnation. At times God seems to direct every step we take, and at other times He feels as distant as another solar system. He wants us to seek Him as He seeks us. As we trust Him more, we find Him more loving and accepting of who we are. He desires for us to grow and is tolerant of us as we stubbornly refuse to do so. He is always there for us, and those with a helpful faith return to Him quickly after each relapse into sins of self-obsession.

I pray that you will grow strong in your faith. I hope that your search for profit, power, pleasure, and/or prestige will end as you find God to be the source of fulfillment. The wounds of addiction do not

Healthy believers are full of love. Love is the most predominant characteristic of those who have a helpful faith.

He is always there for us, and those with a helpful faith return to Him quickly after each relapse into sins of self-obsession.

---

heal quickly. Be patient with yourself, and give yourself time to heal through God's love. As you heal, remember that you are still susceptible to falling back into your addiction. You are vulnerable to false teachers and false teachings. I encourage you to consider the words of Paul in 1 Thessalonians 5:21: "Test all things; hold fast what is good." As you grow in faith, test the faith and teachings of others so you will no longer be led astray. God loves you and wants you for His own. The more you give of yourself to Him, the more joy you will have.

God bless you on your journey of faith as you seek to find God as He is.

The wounds of addiction do not heal quickly. Be patient with yourself, and give yourself time to heal through God's love.

Are You a Religious Addict?

Yes	No	
☐	☐	1. Has your family complained that you are always going to a church meeting rather than spending time with them?
☐	☐	2. Do you feel extreme guilt for being out of church just one Sunday?
☐	☐	3. Do you sense that God is looking at what you do and if you don't do enough He might turn on you or not bless you?
☐	☐	4. Do you often tell your children what to do without explaining your reasons, because you know you are right?
☐	☐	5. Do you find yourself with little time for the pleasures of earlier years because you are so busy serving on committees and attending other church groups?
☐	☐	6. Have people complained that you use so much Scripture in your conversation that it is hard to communicate with you?
☐	☐	7. Are you giving money to a ministry because you believe God will make you wealthy if you give?

☐ ☐   8. Have you ever been involved with a minister sexually?

☐ ☐   9. Is it hard for you to make a decision without consulting your minister? Even over the small issues?

☐ ☐   10. Do you see your minister as more powerful than other humans?

☐ ☐   11. Has your faith led you to lead an isolated life, making it hard for you to relate to your family and friends?

☐ ☐   12. Have you found yourself looking to your minister for a quick fix to a life-long problem?

☐ ☐   13. Do you feel extreme guilt over the slightest mistakes or identified inadequacies?

☐ ☐   14. Is your most significant relationship deteriorating over your strong beliefs compared to those of a "weaker partner"?

☐ ☐   15. Do you ever have thoughts of God wanting you to destroy yourself or others in order to go and live with Him?

☐ ☐   16. Do you regularly believe God is communicating with you in an audible voice?

☐ ☐   17. Do you feel God is angry with you?

☐ ☐   18. Do you believe you are still being punished for something you did as a child?

☐ ☐   19. Do you feel if you work a little harder, God will finally forgive you?

☐ ☐   20. Has anyone ever told you a minister was manipulating your thoughts and feelings?

If you answered yes to at least three of the above questions, call:

1-800-NEW-LIFE

or

1-800-332-TEEN

Twelve Steps to Overcoming Religious Addiction

The twelve steps have provided a path to recovery for millions of people for over half a century. Here they have been adapted to apply to those recovering from religious addiction. Working these steps could be your means of escape from religious addiction and into a real faith in God.

1. We admitted that we were powerless over our compulsive religious behaviors and harmful faith—that our lives had become unmanageable.

2. We came to believe that a Power greater than ourselves could restore us to sanity.

3. We made a decision to turn our will and our lives over to the care of God.

4. We made a searching and fearless moral inventory of ourselves.

5. We admitted to God, to ourselves, and to another human being the exact nature of our wrongs.

6. We were entirely ready to have God remove all these defects of character.

7. We humbly asked Him to remove our shortcomings.

8. We made a list of all persons we had harmed, and became willing to make amends to them all.

9. We made direct amends to such people whenever possible, except when to do so would injure them or others.

10. We continued to take personal inventory, and when we were wrong, promptly admitted it.

11. We sought through meditation and prayer to improve our conscious contact with God praying only for knowledge of His will and the power to carry that out.

12. Having had a spiritual awakening as a result of these steps, we tried to carry this message to other religious addicts and to practice these principles in all our affairs.

Where Life Begins Again

Adult and Adolescent Programs

With many locations, New Life Treatment Centers regularly treats adults and adolescents from all parts of the United States.

If life's problems have created more pain than you can handle alone, there is a way to let go of the hurt.

New Life Treatment Centers has helped thousands of adults and adolescents begin a new life through our caring programs. We can help you or a loved one with thoughtful, experienced guidance from qualified professionals who care and understand.

The voluntary program at New Life Treatment Centers is designed to meet the needs of people in crisis. Our purpose is to assist those who are hurting in identifying, understanding and coping with life's problems that have resulted in dysfunctional and destructive feelings and behaviors.

We are firmly committed to a personal faith in Jesus Christ, and emphasize consistent use of God's word as the primary resource of strength and understanding. This belief is combined with the highest quality clinical care available and proven twelve-step principles of recovery.

Our professional team is composed of psychiatrists, psychologists, marriage, family and child counselors, case managers, a chaplain (or youth pastor on adolescent units), and occupational therapists.

All treatment is conducted in a licensed psychiatric unit as part of a fully-licensed and accredited community hospital.

New hope for a new life begins with your phone call. Let us help you, your child, or someone you care about start a new life today.

For help at the New Life Treatment Center closest to you, call:

1-800-NEW LIFE (for adult care)
1-800-332-TEEN (for adolescent care)

Please call today. Because you can let go of the hurt, and begin a new life.

New Life Treatment Centers helps people dealing with these problem areas:

General Psychological Disorders

There comes a time in many people's lives when everything seems to fall apart. You may be faced with one or more of the following:

Depression. Much of the joy you used to experience is gone.

Stress. You are overwhelmed by everyday problems.

Panic Attacks or Phobias. Uncontrollable reactions or fears have gripped you.

Codependency. The problem of someone you love has now become your problem.

Religious Addiction. Your focus has gotten off God.

Chemical Dependency

When drugs or alcohol control a life, that life is out of control. Addiction to drugs or alcohol means living life on the edge. On the edge of one more drinking binge, one more day of missed work, one more blow-up with someone you care about. You may try to keep your addiction under control, but almost daily you continue to justify it one more time.

If chemical dependency is controlling your decisions, your money, your time, your life, the time to get help is now. Not tomorrow or next week. Because putting off recovery only deepens addiction, guilt and pain.

Compulsive Sexual Behavior

When sexual behavior is out of control, creating guilt, shame and remorse, there is help for a new life through confidential treatment.

Statistics show that most likely, there are men and women who attend church with you, work alongside you, who perhaps even are close friends that are experiencing out-of-control sexual behavior.

New Life's treatment is available with total confidentiality and involves clinical methods of breaking through denial, changing false beliefs, and building broken relationships. God's forgiveness is further renewed through a new understanding of His true design of sex, love, and intimacy.

Compulsive Eating Disorders

How do I know if I, or someone I know, has an eating disorder? If you answer "yes" to any of these questions, you may have an eating disorder.

1. Do you eat large amounts of food in short periods of time?
2. Are you afraid that you can't control your eating?
3. Do you eat normally around others, but binge alone?
4. Is your greatest fear in life that of gaining weight or becoming fat?
5. Have you frequently tried to lose weight by fasting, self-induced vomiting, used diuretics, laxatives, diet pills, or excessive exercise?

On the surface, you may think food is the problem. But you may not realize that it is the "feelings" behind the eating disorder that are the problem. And all your anxiety about food only fuels a destructive cycle.

Now that cycle can be broken. Trained New Life Treatment Center professionals, in a totally confidential setting, are waiting to help.

Call New Life Treatment Centers Today

800-NEW LIFE
(for adult care)

800-332-TEEN
(for adolescent care)

You can let go of the hurt

Stephen Arterburn is the founder and chairman of New Life Treatment Centers, Inc. He has fifteen years' experience in psychiatric health care. Arterburn, who was awarded two honorary doctorate degrees during 1991, is a member of the Board of Directors for the National Association of Christian Recovery, Overcomers Outreach, and the National Council on Sexual Addiction. He is the author/coauthor of fourteen books. He and his wife, Sandy, and daughter, Madeline, live in Laguna Beach, California.

Jack Felton is an ordained minister and licensed therapist at New Hope Christian Counseling Center, Inc., and is Minister of Outreach and Staff Therapist at LifeCare Christian Therapy Centers. Felton is a frequent lecturer, television guest, and radio host in the Southern California area.